About This Book

Balancing humor and seriousness, David Anderson recounts stories of his medical career, his involvement in the Amanda Knox case, and his efforts fighting injustice and imbecility in medicine, geology, paleontology, and other areas that have attracted his polymathic attention. This is a delightful and utterly charming memoir, full of eccentric and amiable characters—and deeply imbued with a passion for life. Highly recommended! ..... **Douglas Preston, author, The Monster of Florence, and The Lost City of the Monkey God**

This is a feast of a book in the old sense, in which the reader can fully engage not least In his fight to clear the names of several individuals wrongly convicted of heinous crimes. I had the privilege to work on one of his earlier books, but that did not really prepare me for the breadth and scope of this spectacular work. And the poetry (in the Appendix) suggests that he might well have pursued a career on the stage or as a reciter of verse. Prepare to be entertained.' ..... **Bryan Gibson, author and Director of Waterside Press**

The narrative is fascinating and easily digested by a wide range of readers, and the richness of David Anderson's life denies the need for hype. An unexpected and pleasant reward is the sprinkling of informative passages that educates the reader into what otherwise would remain esoterica. This memoir is neither falsely hilarious nor dramatically gripping. It is real life as most of us may wish we could have lived .... **Professor B L Lasley, UC Davis, California**

His 'asides' contain a wealth of medicine, art, music and profiles of some famous and infamous people. His sense of humour lies somewhere between those of Mark Twain and Spike Milligan. This book illustrates well the adage: 'It's not the dog in the fight, It's the fight in the dog". The years as student, then qualified doctor from 1959 to the late '60s are a 'must read' for today's students and doctors, as he describes the dying days of hands on, eyes and ears wide open, experiential, non-disposable, low-tech medicine, practiced by worn out juniors dominated by autocratic consultants ...... **Professor A M Martin, Edinburgh**

Where Angels Fear to Tread is a journey through David's life, people, places and artists all punctuated with mischievous wit. It is illustrated with photographic archive images, and intimate graphic drawings and watercolours by David and his father. Further works are shown from the Author's private collection of mostly contemporary art, from the hands of artists he has known and met, altogether making this memoir a superb read and a visual feast ..... **Geoffrey Key (artist), Manchester**

WHERE ANGELS FEAR TO TREAD

My Life in Medicine and Minding Other People's Business

DAVID COUSSMAKER ANDERSON

authorHOUSE

AuthorHouse™ UK
1663 Liberty Drive
Bloomington, IN 47403 USA
www.authorhouse.co.uk
Phone: 0800 047 8203 (Domestic TFN)
       +44 1908 723714 (International)

© 2018 David Coussmaker Anderson. All rights reserved.

No part of this book may be reproduced, stored in a retrieval system, or transmitted by any means without the written permission of the author.

Published by AuthorHouse 08/15/2019

ISBN: 978-1-5462-9832-8 (sc)
ISBN: 978-1-5462-9833-5 (hc)
ISBN: 978-1-5462-9831-1 (e)

Print information available on the last page.

Any people depicted in stock imagery provided by Getty Images are models, and such images are being used for illustrative purposes only.
Certain stock imagery © Getty Images.

This book is printed on acid-free paper.

Because of the dynamic nature of the Internet, any web addresses or links contained in this book may have changed since publication and may no longer be valid. The views expressed in this work are solely those of the author and do not necessarily reflect the views of the publisher, and the publisher hereby disclaims any responsibility for them.

Contents

Acknowledgements ix
Foreword xi
Introduction xiii

Chapter 1: Origins 1
Chapter 2: Boarding School 22
Chapter 3: Medical School In Scotland 34
Chapter 4: At last a doctor 51
Chapter 5: Early married life 62
Chapter 6: California 87
Chapter 7: Medicine in Manchester 97
Chapter 8: Manchester, Music, Musicians and Artists 124
Chapter 9: Medicine in Hong Kong and a Second
            Chinese Nightmare 137
Chapter 10: Life in Hong Kong after The Chinese
            University 161
Chapter 11: Medical Teaching Films and Third World
            Health Problems 173
Chapter 12: Where Shall We Retire to? 192
Chapter 13: Discovering Hongshan Neolithic Jade 200
Chapter 14: Where Is China's Missing Meteorite-
            Impact Crater? 212
Chapter 15: On Impacts and Climate Change, Past
            and Present 227
Chapter 16: Behind the Scenes in Italy's and Other
            Injustice Systems 238

Chapter 17: Some Personal Life Health-Lessons 261
Chapter 18: Retirement in Umbria, Italy 270
Chapter 19: An Afterword of Concluding Thoughts 277

Illustrations 285
Appendix
    Recitations and poems 309

Acknowledgements

I know that some will see writing a memoir as an extreme self-indulgence, and that others may resent my rooting up old secrets about people long since buried. Where I was insensitive I am grateful to those who told me so directly. Occasionally I have deleted, but more often I have tried to re-write more sensitively, especially where completely omitting reference to some person or event would have left too large a hole in my life's story. I am also very grateful to family members, especially to my older brother Antony, for help with recollection and correction of memories of my early life and our antecedents. I thank many friends who have looked at one of my earlier drafts. I owe special thanks to Carol Easton, who nudged me into action; to Chris Redfern who was from the first imperfect page enthusiastic, and suggested things that needed to be strengthened; to Caroline Ziesler for her help with proof-reading; to Bryan Gibson of Waterside Press, for some useful expert professional advice and encouragement; to Geoffrey Key who encouraged me to include some of my drawings as illustrations, even though these have all to be in black and white; to my former boss Lord Turnberg of Cheadle for his kind Foreword; to Ross Slade and Chris Roberts for their help with the cover design; and to my sons, granddaughters, siblings and cousins for being part of the story and for their encouragement. Finally I thank my dear wife Jenny for sticking with me patiently through much of the journey I describe; for reading what I have written, and for giving her perspective on many of our shared experiences. Un abbraccio a tutti.

FOREWORD

by Lord Turnberg of Cheadle

By describing himself as never single-mindedly pursuing one line to the exclusion of others, David does himself a disservice. I first met him in the 1970s when I attracted him to come across to my Department at Hope Hospital from our rival, the Manchester Royal Infirmary, much to their concern. It was immediately obvious that here was a man who pursued whatever motivated him at the time, with a steely determination that brooked no opposition. He fought against anyone and anything that seemed to him to smell of illogicality or cant. And he fearlessly said it like it is in a way that was both stimulating and intimidating if you were not on the same wave length. Always entertaining, his boyish charm won most people over; but fools were left wondering where they had gone wrong.

He always then and ever after took up his enthusiasms with enormous gusto. As he says, he may not have followed any one line single-mindedly, but any line that he did take up was followed without the least hint of deviation. Any opposition stimulated rather than deterred him. And his highly tuned sense of justice meant that he took on many difficult causes without any fear, sometimes much to his own disadvantage. It was this idea, that right would always win in the end, that led him to tilt his windmill at one of the most powerful and politically astute men in Hong Kong whose ruthless manipulations of the system meant that David could not win. But that never deterred him and he describes well the battles and underhand tactics employed, to which he never yielded. His keen sense of justice later led him into battle across a much broader field when he pulled every stop he could to defend Amanda Knox and her then boy friend, Raffaele Sollecito, accused of the murder of Amanda's flatmate in Italy. He went to extraordinary lengths to expose the failures in the Italian judicial system and even wrote a book on this and other miscarriages of justice.

But this only gives a part of the picture of a man who picks up interests that may be a part time hobby for some, but for him are all consuming. China and its history fascinates him. This led him into the field of Chinese ceramics and jade. Unsurprisingly his studies of neolithic jade were pursued with an academic's forensic skill that has resulted in a learned and well regarded book. His studies of craters in China and what caused them, and the wider field of geology, have occupied his attention more recently. And all this while a Professor of Endocrinology and a practicing clinician who made important contributions in the treatment of Paget's disease, the management of diabetes, and in the understanding of the actions of sex hormones. Furthermore his enthusiasm for medical education led him into producing a highly regarded series of video based teaching aids, inevitably against opposition that brought out the best in him in the sport of uphill struggles.

Never still, he has moved around the world, from Scotland to London, America, Manchester, Hong Kong and now to Umbria to live with a variety of ex-pats in a place to which, he says, nobody comes because they are normal. Here is an exciting story described with great gusto. It is a highly entertaining account of a life lived to the full, in and out of Medicine. Where, one wonders, will it lead this restless man to next and what sort of nuisance will he bring to wherever that is? It is a great read especially for those who may think that a medical career is dull.

Leslie A Turnberg
June 2018

Introduction

A favourite quote from James Thurber, when I was a teenager was; 'Fools rush in where angels fear to tread, but the angels are all in heaven, while not all of the fools are dead'. I have never been an angel, but obviously I am still endowed with that greatest of human privileges; though at times foolish, I am still alive. I still love life, art, music, and most people; and the words and humour with which to characterise them. Such as, for instance, that almost lost art of recitation, which is built on the power of the impossible put into words somehow to encapsulate the possible ... 'Tha's 'eard of Sam Locket, the singer, as sings i't ol chapil choir, tha's noticed 'e's no bin there recent, I'll tell thee 'owt come to transpire'... or, 'As time went by declining health, transmogrified this man of wealth, 'tiil it was excellently clear that Uncle Bill's demise was near. At length his sole idea of fun was sitting snoozling in the sun...' I love these wonderful word-songs, that have been carefully crafted by one person to encapsulate something we can treasure, by repetition, forever.

A great friend of Jenny's and mine, Carol Easton, said recently when as usual I was talking too much, 'You know, David, you've had an interesting life, you should write those stories down'. So if you need to blame someone, you can blame her, because I needed a trigger for action, and that is why five months ago I started to write this memoir. I wanted at first to see whether I could at least entertain myself, with an account of what I have experienced over more than three-quarters of a century of living among interesting people and in interesting times. I feel honoured to still be in some sort of cerebral shape to record it. But in the process I also want to explore some more serious things I have learnt from minding my own business, Medicine, and sometimes also that of others.

Obviously a great deal of our individual characters is genetic; environment is also important, but essentially secondary. Identical twins aside, each individual is genetically unique. This applies to empathy, where I am concerned with original synapses rather than original sins. Some are born with a defect in the brain's central empathy circuit necessary for socialisation, developing a conscience, and inhibiting targeted aggression, and they can never feel another's distress as their own. Abuse, rather than help such a child, and you may finish with a monster who ruthlessly exploits the weaknesses of others. One sees obvious examples in Politics, both sides of the Law, Big Business and even Medicine.

When writing I realise there is a fine line to tread between humour and harm; but I also don't want to fall into the situation of my military Uncle Mark, who wrote four memoirs, the last of which included some important people from World War Two, and for the legal sanitation of which he paid more than the total sales of the book. I have tried also to be honest about at least some of the stupid things I myself have done over the years.

At first I hadn't thought too much about how I should write this memoir, except that it should be semi-chronological. I could see no harm in the odd side-track, if it was where a particular subject led. It seemed better than expecting the reader to divert into half-page footnotes that are too small to read, but too interesting to be missed. I want to apologise to many people who have been important in my life but who I have left out. And

I know I must have got some of it wrong, but even so I hope that the general drift is right. When writing of the past much of what happened does come back, as if in a vivid dream (and indeed sometimes during sleep). Such as things or people whose names you struggle to recall, but you know are locked up like waving quanta somewhere in the dark recesses of the subconscious. As soon as you look it up on Google, or worse your wife remembers for you, you are hit by immediate recognition. How could I have forgotten that? So, warts and all, here goes.

CHAPTER 1

ORIGINS

I owe my existence, in some indirect way to the late Führer Adolf Hitler (née Schickelgruber), because I was conceived in early 1940 towards the end of what was known as the phoney war. That was when (a bit like the phoney Brexit) not much was happening. If he had launched his offensive on the Low Countries and France a month or two earlier, my father, Major William Faithfull (Will) Anderson, would have been sent to France too early for my conception. My brother tells me there is in Mum's diary a pregnant pause between two exclamation marks on February 28th; it is well established that I was born on December 1st. Apparently Dad had been out on exercises the night before and my mother wrote that she went to bed for an hour around 9 am ...(pregnancy pause)... when he returned. So it seems I should thank a nice landlady for allowing a daylight extension of night exercises, as well as a nasty and pretentious psychopathic leader for not invading earlier. Who knows? This may in some obscure way help to explain my later obsession with psychopaths. But it may also be seen by my remaining friends as evidence that (as his mistress Eva Braun doubtless used to say) even Adolf had a good side. And how many people can pinpoint to the very hour, precisely when they were conceived?

David Coussmaker Anderson

Dad, who was a professional soldier and sapper, played a significant part in slowing the German advance in northern France, for which he received a bar to the Military Cross he had earned in a smaller war on the North-West Frontier of India. Stationed at Latte St Quentin, west of Arras, he spent a day in the town library examining maps of the shunting yards. Then he organised his men overnight to move by hand a massive amount of rolling stock from the marshaling yards onto the tracks, in such a way as to optimally block the potential path of the German panzers moving north. The German air force, seeing this blockage the following day, made this work even more effective by bombing the rolling stock so it could no longer be rolled. Half the sappers escaped to Dunkirk and home, while the rest, including Will, who was slowed up by having an injured man in his party, were captured on May 29th, and led off to prisoner of war camp. The wounded man, Sapper Norman Dixon, who later became sports editor of the Daily Express, kept in his wallet for the rest of his life the instructions he was left by Major Anderson, as they eventually had to abandon him to give any chance for the rest of the party to escape. Will spent the rest of the war as a POW first in Laufen, (Oflag VIIC), where he looked out onto the Alps where he had skied with his wife so recently. After a year, on suspicion of organising escapes, he was moved to the bad-boys camp, Oflag IVC, in Colditz Castle, Saxony.

Mum, meanwhile had no idea whether Will was alive or dead until she received a telegram from the War Office on July 17th, to say he was a prisoner of war. Of course I was ignorant of all this, but a medical footnote is that, probably from prenatal stress, I was born with hypertrophic pyloric stenosis. That means that the outlet from the stomach will not relax, and no milk gets through. It is characterised by projectile vomiting. My mother, who was a meticulous notekeeper, (see illustrations) nicely documented how my weight, ten pounds at birth and unchanged for three months, abruptly changed once she started to precede each meal with Eumydrin drops to relax the pyloric sphincter.

A brief history of my parents wartime, and my father's activities in Colditz, is to be the subject of another book by my older brother Antony and me. Mum was a resourceful woman, who organised a Prisoners of War Parcel-Packing Centre in Farnham to dispatch food and other items via the Red Cross to British prisoners in Germany. The latter included sketching paper and watercolours, many of the resulting paintings surviving the war because they were allowed out via the Red Cross. Dad was an accomplished watercolour artist. He also managed to purchase a German (Hüller) oboe with his officer's pay, and played it intermittently through the war, in musical groups of varying size and mixtures. Since the oboe can penetrate thick walls, especially if played badly, it had a bit-part to play as a safety signal in Pat Reid's escape, later immortalised in *The Colditz Story*. The orchestra was, incidentally, decimated when all four (and Dutch) violins escaped from Colditz at the same time, never to return. I later acquired the oboe when it was finally agreed all round that painting was Dad's artistic *forte*, while the cello was Mum's, and I came to hate playing the violin, and asked to play the oboe instead. The instrument was therefore generously released to me at the age of fourteen and I took it up with the same enthusiasm with which I had dropped the violin. The Hüller oboe is now on display in the Colditz museum, along with a lot of the materials Dad used to forge escape documents.

It has been said that the oboe is an ill wind that nobody blows any good, so I hope it was just a coincidence that my first oboe teacher died of a heart attack three weeks after I began to take lessons. He was replaced by a brass band enthusiast named Les Morley, who as far as I know never played the oboe. I had my first lesson from a genuine, and indeed famous oboist, Professor Tony Camden, in Hong Kong nearly fifty years later, when the Colditz oboe was gracefully pensioned off as being past its best, and I bought a new one. When violinist and pianist friends and I tried out before him Bach's wonderful oboe and violin double concerto we were to play at a charity concert, Tony was very kind. 'Well, on the positive side, at least it's recognisable', he said.

My mother and her two sons spent the war with her parents, in a large house, Cheniston, on the Tilford Road in Farnham, Surrey. We shared it with Mum's violinist sister, Elizabeth, who was my godmother, whose husband John Napier was also a sapper and had been Dad's best man; and with their two children Rob and Jane. Our grandfather, Edmund Henderson Hunt ('Father' to his children, and 'Arder' to us) was a retired surgeon who had spent most of his career in India. He was a keen collector of Celadon porcelain, an archaeologist, a pipe smoker, and an expert beekeeper, and he was Antony's and my surrogate father throughout the war. Granny Hunt was a keen gardener and likewise dedicated to her grandchildren. Many years later, in 2000, when I started to collect Hongshan jade on eBay, I wanted to use the Arder as my eBay name, but found it had already been appropriated. So instead I chose Grannyhunt, with considerable bidding success, possibly because no one surely was going to bid against a delightful old lady? I know my grandmother would have been both impressed and tickled pink at that. People were often tickled pink when I was a child.

PAEDIATRIC EXPERIENCE OF MILITARY DISCIPLINE

As the war was about to end and my father was liberated from Colditz, Antony and I came face-to-face with military paternal discipline as applied to uncomprehending small boys. During the summer of '45, we went on holiday to the Isle of Wight, where we experienced the pleasures of swimming while shivering in the Solent. We were enticed to pass that most painful of points whereby the toes and thighs have adapted to wet in the near-Arctic water, but the trunks and covered grommets are still warm, dry, and comfortable, by the offer of a penny. Now the old penny didn't buy very much even in post-wartime Britain, (there were twelve to a shilling twenty of which amounted to a pound sterling) but in its favour it was of disproportionately large size. After much anguish and when standing on tiptoes could no longer suffice, the seventh wave arrived to make grommet and crotchets give a loud quaver and shrink perceptibly. The small boys gave a scream, followed by anguished pleas not even a highly-decorated military father could resist. 'Daddy, have I earned my penny yet?' I doubt if such discipline would pass NSPCC inspection nowadays, but we went for it then, I suppose because we had no choice.

He obviously loved us and was always making us things. One was a family of wooden ducks designed to waddle down a gentle slope under gravity, which he gave me on my fifth birthday. Another was an impressive painted metal Isle of Wight car ferry we played with for years till it rusted away. That Christmas, he and Arder laid on an elaborate spoof by a supposedly distinguished visiting surgeon called Sir Pontefax Bulldozer. Daddy, we were told, had been called away, and at first I mistook Sir Pontefax for him, much to my five-year-old embarrassment. 'No, David. This is Sir Pontefax Bulldozer, Daddy's been called away to the War Office.' Arder had developed a swollen abdomen, and this necessitated an operation on an improvised operating table, that was back-projected as a shadow show onto a large sheet for us children to witness. Sir Pontefax removed various festive objects, and we watched gobsmacked from the other side. I suppose it was all just as likely as the Father Christmas chimney story. It gave a great deal of fun to the adults as well - and some presents to the children.

Obviously it must have been a disappointment to Dad to find that although we were clearly on the right road as human beings (or 'human beans' as I used to think), we were not very far along it. I never remember being kissed or cuddled by my father. Once on impulse. after Mum had died, when he was over 90 and had had a stroke I said, 'Dad, for the first time I'm going to give you a kiss'. To my surprise he seemed genuinely pleased. But when he returned from Colditz we were in every way still children, and therefore militarily incomprehensible. Such are the side-effects of war. In later childhood, the main activity he and I shared was to go sketching together. This was mainly in warmer climes, in places like India and Zanzibar, but also on the Isle of Sark. It impressed me when sketching with Dad that he was immensely tolerant of small boys, who routinely gathered around him in hordes, and were allowed to remain as long as they remained silent, which of course they seldom did. But they stayed anyway.

I was exposed in late 1946 to a life-changing and career-deciding event. I started to get colicky abdominal pains, and people who loved me were very worried. Mum had two medical brothers, Uncle John and Uncle Alan, and she would repeatedly pull rank over her GP, by invoking one or other. Alan was the chief surgeon at Barts (St Bartholomews Hospital in London), and notable for the *Hunt shunt* for portacaval obstruction. He was also not averse to operating on family members, something that seemed natural to the small boy that I then was. So one fateful day I was admitted fighting and screaming to Wrecclesham Grange, a small private hospital, where under anaesthetic - chloroform I suppose - the offending appendix was removed. I was declared cured, the pains stopped, and I returned home with the slightly swollen appendix in a lidded bottle full of methylated spirits. I was so impressed with this miracle that I immediately decided that I was going to be a doctor, and I never wavered from this paediatric career decision. I think I was judged to be too clumsy to become a surgeon, especially when I ran off up stairs to fetch my appendix to show some visitors, rushed down again, tripped up and spilled bottle, appendix, and meths across the living room carpet. Not a great start to a medical career, but never mind, the bottle didn't break; the appendix was scooped up, rinsed and replaced, the meths topped up, and it remained a family icon for the next twenty years, till my wife threw it away as being something distinctly disgusting.

A MUCH-LOVED GRANDFATHER

Edmund Henderson Hunt - Arder - was a loving and proud pipe-smoking grandfather and a great raconteur of stories, many of them about Scotsmen, and some of which I still remember. With punch lines like, 'Dark as 'ell and stinks of cheese'; 'And a mighty poor show for Kircaldy'; and best of all the American relatives at the Grand Canyon who were trying to impress a Scotsman, whose response was... 'Aye, grand maybe, grand maybe,.... but for QUEER, we've a peacock in Paisley wi' a wooden leg'. It was Arder who first infected me with a love for Stanley Holloway's recitations I referred to earlier. He had been at Harrow with Winston Churchill, who was his junior by seven days; Churchill had been a bully at school, and for his whole life Arder disliked him intensely.

Arder had worked for much of his professional life in southern India, where he had been surgeon for the Hyderabad railway, which also included being personal physician to the Nizam of Hyderabad, said to be the richest man in the world. Arder was a keen tennis player, and they had a grass court at Cheniston.

I remember him telling us that the Nizam, as well as being exceptionally rich was a miser and an obsessive collector of pearls. It was said that he had enough pearls to cover a tennis court. We were never told how big the pearls were, why you would want to cover a tennis court with pearls, or whether it was a singles or a doubles court, which would also make a difference. One dinner party in India Arder overheard the man two to his left say to the lady next to him, 'I say, by the way, jolly interesting, don't you know, but my great grandfather died at Waterloo'. To which his neighbour said, 'Oh really, what platform?' The following week, at another dinner party he was talking to the lady on his right. 'You won't believe the conversation I overheard at a dinner last week.' And recounted the story to his bemused neighbour, who said, 'Good God, Edmund,...I mean, as if it mattered what platform!'

Granny Hunt (née Laura Buckingham) had been born in Assam, where her father Sir James Buckingham ran a tea estate. She met Arder while on the boat out to India to help her father, and the two were married in India, where most of their oldest five children were born. The youngest, Uncle Kenneth, was a home leave post-World War One afterthought. Granny Hunt had inherited Cheniston after Uncle Billy, a decorated military brother with post-traumatic stress and depression from the first World War, disappointed in love, had committed suicide. Another brother was James Buckingham (Uncle Jim), who was an inventor, and author of his own motor car. His most significant invention was the tracer bullet. Granny Hunt was a wonderful supplementary mother to us grandchildren at Cheniston. She taught us how to eat an orange without making any mess. You got undressed and into a hot bath, cut a square hole in the orange, pushed in a sugar lump, and then sucked the juice through said lump. Of course you did then make a mess finishing off the orange, but it didn't matter because you were in the bath.

ON THE EARWIG AND THE EAGLE

It was Arder who first encouraged my interest in biology. I spent hours catching ladybirds with different numbers of spots and putting them in matchboxes to show him; my record was 21 spots. A keen beekeeper, he had constructed a special observational beehive out of a hollowed-out rotten tree trunk, and this lay on its side on a stand in the upper reaches of Cheniston's large garden. I remember at the age of four asking him my first serious biological question, which thanks to the internet, seventy-three years later I have just had convincingly answered. 'Arder, can earwigs fly?' Earwigs are of course insects and are endowed with two pairs of wings. I remember coming in one day very excited from an earwig-observation session, convinced that I had seen one take off and actually fly, rather than just flop to the ground. Excitedly, I shared this, my first uncontrolled case study, with my grandfather. Of course, you now just use a search engine, and this is a summary of what you will find... Earwigs (of which apparently there are some 1,800 species worldwide) have two sets of wings, of which the hind ones are concealed by the fore ones, and are large, semi-circular, and fold outwards like a fan. Male European earwigs sometimes use these for flight, when seeking food or locating mates, but mostly they prefer just to scurry about. When preparing to fly, the insect typically climbs to higher elevations and flies down mostly for just a brief moment. So that is presumably what I had seen. An otherwise lazy male earwig looking for a mate and just having a go.

I think Arder, like most grandparents expected his grandchildren to hold him as more beloved than anything else, but he had not catered for the magnetic powers of *The Eagle*, a weekly comic born in the 1950 by an anglican vicar, Marcus Morris, with bible stories on the back and on the front the adventures of Dan Dare, pilot of the future, the asexual Miss Peabody, and the Treens. These were green extraterrestrials, under the control of the Mekon, who was a bit like Stephen Hawking; he was small, apart from an enormous head, super-intelligent and locomoted around on a personalised hovercraft (yet to be invented). I remember we really upset Arder one day, when on leave from the Pilgrim's School we tore into the week's copy of *The Eagle* before giving him a kiss, or even a 'hi'. I don't think he realised how near to destruction the Earth was that week from a massive meteorite called the Red Moon. Since then I have been fascinated by meteorites, as you will gather later.

DON'T WALK WITH YOUR HEAD IN THE GROUND, DAVID

As a child I was clumsy, a trait that I may have inherited from Dad, who Mum said had once knocked over a horse - an accusation he vehemently denied. Maybe it was just natural selection at work, but it has always seemed logical to me to spot things I might trip over before I actually did. At around the age of nine I got a real break outside Farnham station as I walked down the steps and my eye caught a bright blue sizable crystalline object, which I pocketed with some excitement. Arder found it would scratch glass, and identified it as an amethyst. We agreed it must have dropped out of a lady's ring, presumably as she tripped over the steps when looking up, not down. Miss Biggs the jeweler agreed, and as after three months no one had claimed it at the police station, I got it back finders-keepers, and she bought it from me for two pounds. That was a lot in those days, and I then strengthened my domestic position by splitting the reward with my three siblings. Thereafter I could always justify walking with my head in the ground, there only being birds and planes to spot up in the air.

A GODFATHER TO REMEMBER

My father had a lifelong eccentric bachelor friend, Rugby School's architect, Noel Russell. Uncle Noel was small, bald, had a glass eye from a wound in World War One, and suffered from a terrible stammer. This was, of course long before the days of speech therapy (*The King's Speech* excepted). Noel was asked to be my godfather, and with some reluctance - because he already had three godsons - as Dad was a prisoner of war, he accepted. He always took a great interest in his godchildren, and continued to take on new ones after me. He was unpredictable, eccentric, and it was almost impossible to second-guess what he was trying to say. Predictions of the outcome of his stammer were invariably out by 180 degrees. I soon learnt one just had to wait. He bought a baby Morris and took up driving in his late fifties, failing his driving test a record six times; and when he retired he went on interesting trips and safaris all over the world, which he documented in lined notebooks with exquisite drawings. He even had a great holiday in Tanganyika, and visited the *Ngorongoro* crater, which he had to write down. A regular educational trip with Uncle Noel was a day in the Natural History Museum in South Kensington. He told one marvelous story, which was greatly enhanced by his stammer, and so only he could tell it; it went like this.

'My youngest g-god ch-hild, David, is William, a....aged eight, and his parents asked me to ta... to ...take him to the N...N Natural History Museum the next Friday, as they were b... busy; and so being f...f...free I said y...y...yes. Then his m...m... mother t-telephoned me on Tuesday and said that little M..Mary, William's s...sister, aged five, would like to come too. 'She's a very good little g...g...irl, Noel, you know.' ... S...s... so I agreed. as long as William loo....looked after her and she be... be... haved. Then on Friday morning the mother phoned to say unff...fortunately W...William had been taken ill, but M....M..., ary was so looking forward to it, so could I st...st... still please take her? So with great re... with great re... with great reLUCTance I ag...greed. Right enough Mary was, t... true to f...form, v... very good. We traveled there on the u...u...underground, and w...went in, and I said, 'Ma...Ma....Mary, here we are at the N...N...Natural H...H...istory M....MU ...Museum, and there are all sorts of dead animals, and they're all stu.... they're all stu.... they're all STUFFED. There are st...stuffed lions, and stuffed c...camels, and st....stuffed gi...giraffes, and stu.... stu...stuffed eleph......stuffed elephants, and whales and t...t...tigers and all sorts of other stuffed animals, which would you like to see first?' And she looked at me and said 'p...please Uncle Noel, what I'd R...REALLY like to see ff...first is a st... a stu...... a stuff.... a stuffed Spi....... a STUFFED SPIDER, because I've never seen a STUFFED spider before!"'

So he spent all morning with her in the arachnid section of the Natural History Museum, pulling out draw after draw of stuffed spiders.

A SEVERE BRITISH WINTER SPENT IN INDIA

Soon after the end of the war, by some mystery the family expanded with the addition of a brother, Stuart, and two years later a sister, Margaret. They grew up from the start with my father, whenever he wasn't posted abroad, and so they were able to get away with being difficult, as children often are. I think my first formal school was a Parents National Education Union (PNEU) school, under the benevolent tutorship of Miss Strudwick, and I have a vivid memory of mastering the times-tables, up to and including thirteen. After a time at the War Office, and then in Germany translating for the Nuremberg trials, Dad, now a colonel, was posted to southern India as Chief Engineer. We went to join him, with a sixteen-year-old nanny, Doris, on the RMS *Andes*, traveling via the Suez Canal and Aden, where we were entertained on board by a gully-gully man's magic, and enjoyed our first Turkish delight. A fellow passenger bought a whole box for Antony from one of the bum-boats crowding the ship; when opened later the box was full of pure desert sand. No gully-gully magic would turn it into dessert, or disguise what a cad that bum-boatman was.

1946/7 was a bitter winter in England, but great in Wellington Cantonment in the Nilgiri hills, near Ooty where we lived in a nice bungalow called Glencoe. We learnt to roller skate on the rink with Doris, who later married Roy, Dad's driver. I remember there was a hole in the drive, and one day I saw what looked like a golf club stuck in it. Approaching to pick it up, I decided not to when I realised it was in fact a king cobra enjoying the view, and I ran like hell!

I went back to Wellington with my wife, son Bruce and niece Kate, on holiday in 1999, more than 50 years later, armed with notes from my brother's photograph album. On second take, and following Antony's instructions, I found the house, still named Glencoe, and now occupied by a Brigadier-general Rathore. Put off somewhat by the warning to beware of the dog, I was meditating what to do when a man drew up on a motor-cycle. 'Can I do anything for you, Sir?' he asked. Showing him the pictures, I said, 'More than fifty years ago I used to live here; my father was an army officer: could you tell me how I can contact Brigadier Rathore?' 'Just hop on the back of my bike and I'll take you to him', he said, and so I did. Rathore, at first diffident, was impressed when he saw the pictures, and invited me home for lunch. Little had changed - as far Is I could see the washing up was still not done, although the cobra sticking out of the hole in the drive had gone. There was an almost full list of occupants on a plaque, starting with the next one after we had left. I took advantage of that trip to go to the Pasteur

Rabies Institute in Coonoor, which I remembered Arder talking about; this visit was critical to my journey into rabies prevention, discussed later.

MEMORY OF THE DELHI RIOTS

Antony had earlier contracted dysentery, an event that was to come back to haunt us both, but especially him twenty years later. But later in 1947 we relocated from the Nilgiris to Delhi by train, past Madras. Uncle John Napier was stationed there with his family, and I remember swimming in shark-infested waters. In Delhi we lived in Aurangzeb Road and were aware of serious problems over the partition of India. I remember eating my first banana at the swimming pool, and learning to dive and then to swim - under water at first. Such is the touching faith children have in adults. And I have a vivid image of serious-looking bearded and turbaned sikhs sharpening their swords by the side of a tree-lined boulevard, and hearing that they had to draw human blood before they could resheath them. And of sleeping in sweltering heat in the garden, my father with a gun under his pillow. I remember my mother, who had had a crash course in obstetric nursing organised by Arder, going off to the Purana Qila fort as a volunteer to deliver babies; and her enrolling the support of Lady Mountbatten, to improve living conditions there; and stories of whole trainloads of Muslims being slaughtered on the way north to Pakistan. We had not been in Delhi long before being evacuated to a transit camp north of Bombay called Deolali, where one day Antony and I went out to find the balloon man. I took the high road, and he took the low road, and he was bitten by a rabid dog on his dick and I wasn't. I remember the horrific business of seeing him being immunised with injections, under the skin of the abdomen, of mushed up sheep's brain vaccine developed and produced in the Pasteur Institute in Coonoor. Fortunately he did not get rabies, but this memory was an indirect stimulus to my returning to rabies prophylaxis over fifty years later.

TO TANGANYIKA FOR THE GROUNDNUT SCHEME

We all went home on another troop ship, the *Empress of Scotland*, spent time in a rented house in Emsworth, and went to school in Havant. My sister Margaret was born in 1948. Not long afterwards Dad was posted to Tanganikya, as engineer seconded to build roads so the 'bush' could be tamed to grow ground-nuts. This was a rushed project of the Atlee Government and a much-despised Mr Strachey, which wasted £70 million, which doesn't seem so much nowadays. The idea was thereby to feed post-war Britain. Mum followed with the family on a smallish passenger rust-bucket called the *Llanstefan Castle*. The journey was meant to take twenty-one days, but instead took six weeks, as it was always breaking down. On the way, we met my Uncle Kenneth's father-in-law, the composer Albert Coates, on a day trip at Capetown. Then later, on the beech in Durban Antony and I were entrusted with our toddler brother Stuart, as we built a sandcastle. When Mum came back from changing Margaret's nappy she was aghast... 'Where is Sticky?' 'Well, he was here with us five minutes ago'. Panic spread as Stuart was searched for. What seemed like hours later, we went to the local police station to report a blond stolen toddler, and there he was. A well meaning lady had seen him playing on the beach apparently unaccompanied, and whisked him off to the police station in case he got kidnapped, which lots of children did. 'Mummy, can I go home now?' were his first words when he saw us. That lady provided my first evidence that being well-meaning does not necessarily protect you from also being extremely stupid.

Finally, via Zanzibar we reached Dar Es Salaam, where we were met by Dad, who drove us to Kongwa, which was the physical centre of the Groundnut Scheme. Dad, being seconded as Deputy Chief Engineer, was responsible for making roads. We enjoyed Kongwa, although Dad nearly died under the anaesthetic when having a hernia repaired. This was of course twenty years before cardiopulmonary resuscitation, but he survived intact. I have an excellent watercolour by him (see illustrations) showing the hospital, set beside a baobab tree; it is little more than a hut. Our major recreational activity was building a church, as Kongwa was, not surprisingly, church-deficient. This was where I first learnt how to mix cement. On his third birthday Stuart's footprint was ceremoniously set in a concrete block that was to serve as the foundation stone. The church was still incomplete when we were called home, because the Groundnut Scheme didn't turn out to be such a good idea after all. We went on safari at least once, and certainly saw zebra, giraffe, elephants and lions; we drove back to Dar, and spent a week on holiday in Zanzibar. This time we flew home in several hops, in a twin engined tub called a *Vickers Viking*. We were flying over Capri as I recall, and Mum was in the cockpit with Antony. When Dad and I went up, the pilot seemed less interested, because the starboard engine was feathering. The tub turned round and made an emergency landing in Naples. 'See Naples and die', my mother said comfortingly. A Naples taxi ride to the sea to see the fishes and sponges was much more terrifying than the emergency landing had been. The fault had apparently been a blocked fuel filter, which was cleared overnight, and we continued on our journey home.

SOME MILITARY RELATIVES OF NOTE

Mark Henniker was one of our favourite Uncles. He was married to Dad's sister Denys, like Dad he was a sapper, and was also posted to Malaya. He had had a very distinguished war. and was also an author of note, mainly writing for Blackwoods magazine. He wrote four books of memoirs, of which the best is *Red Shadow over Malaya*. For a year their two children, Adrian and Fiona were left with Mum, as it was felt to be too dangerous for them to go to Malaya. Adrian had the time of his life, as he went to the local Church of England School with Stuart and Margaret, but unfortunately child psychology had not yet been invented, and infant bonding was poorly understood. I don't think Fiona ever fully recovered from being parted at the age of two from Mum, when Denys and Mark returned, this time children in tow, to Malaya. We have recently seen a lot of Adrian and his wife Anne in Italy, as they have a holiday house a couple of hours drive to our north. Mark, unlike Dad, was wounded but not captured. He was seconded to the First Airborne Division for the invasion of Sicily. He remained with them until shortly before D-day when he disagreed over the plan to drop the Division behind enemy lines at Arnhem. General Urquhart politely asked him to leave First Airborne, giving him a note for General Thomas a couple of weeks after D-Day. 'Fine chap, Henniker, please give him a job. Good organiser, signed Urquhart'. The job he was given was to organise the dismantling and collection of the Bailey bridges as the forces advanced across France. Some six weeks later came the disaster at Arnhem and *A Bridge too Far,* and Mark was tasked with setting up a Bailey bridge overnight to rescue the remnants of his former comrades in First Airborne. Bringing up the rear was General Urquhart. 'What did you say, Mark?', I asked. 'Well, words were exchanged' was his reply! Mark was definitely our most eccentric uncle, and for a while drove his family around Farnham in a milk float, causing much confusion as they didn't have any milk to sell. His life's ambition was to build a perpetual-motion machine.

David Coussmaker Anderson

Another distinguished military uncle was John Napier, direct descendent of Robert, Lord Napier of Magdala. In the spoof history book *'Ten Sixty-six and All That'* he is immortalised as 'Lord Rapier of Ragdala', much to my schoolboy amusement. Uncle John came up with the idea of *Pluto*, which was code name for an underwater oil pipeline across the channel. He had a fight to be recognised for this vital idea for transporting oil to the allied forces after D-day, but was ultimately declared its author and received a prize of £500.

My father was the third of six children. His father, John, also an accomplished watercolourist, had been a barrister in India, and at around the age of forty-six retired back home and married Minnie Storr, known to us as Granny Andy. He died in 1930, and Granny Andy then moved from the south coast to a house called Pilgrim's Way, on the other side of Farnham. Among the nicest of the Andersons was Aunty Helen. She was a musician and singer, and apparently spotted the exceptionally talented and unique Kathleen Ferrier. Mum said Helen never got married because men thought she was too bright, which didn't make much sense to me. When she retired from music she took up watercolour painting with great enthusiasm. Dad's older brother Ted taught at Charterhouse school, later became an anglican vicar, and was greatly upset when his wife Muriel and their oldest son became Catholics. Aunty Muriel was always into some new fad. When I was a medical student it was magnesium and I recall her sending me an alliterative booklet *'Magnesium the Miracle Mineral'*. Dad's oldest sister, Ruth, had married Tom Barnard, a major in the army who when he retired became an artist. We saw a lot of them in their old age. Ann Arkel, their daughter, is still alive and in fine health. Ruth and Tom's son Rob was tragically killed by bandits in Borneo shortly after he went out there as a District Forestry Officer, and was posthumously awarded the Queen's Commendation for Bravery. Dad's younger brother Godfrey had poliomyelitis as a child, and so wore a caliper. He was director of British Aluminium for many years, and had married Jean Crompton who was late, large and very jolly. As young children we saw a lot of them and their two sons, Christopher, who was dyslexic, and Martyn who married and went to Hong Kong, where we will meet him again later.

HOME IN BOUNDSTONE, IN A HOUSE NAMED ST CHRISTOPH

On our return from Tanganyika we lived for a while in a house near Bordon called Brambletye, that had wonderful blackberries which we marketed, and a nice large field where we could fly our model aeroplanes. In 1951 my parents bought a small house in Boundstone, a hilly suburb near Farnham that was to become their intermittent home until Dad's retirement from the army, and from then on into old age. He was very much a do-it-yourself person, and removed the whole front of the house, extending ground and first floors, and in the process giving my mother a great deal of worry - (see illustrations). Arder died in the big 'smog' of 1952, and when Cheniston was sold Granny Hunt moved into a cottage. Antony and I were allowed to take over the room above the garage at St Christoph, which became our 'top room', where we installed trestles and packing cases all round and set up the 'O' gauge *Lord Nelson* railway set Dad had bought in India. In time our parents put a bungalow on the property, which became Granny Andy's home. She suffered from intermittent mania and depression, but lived well into her nineties.

A DISPLAY TO REMEMBER, AND FARNHAM PROJECTS

One New Year when I was at Rugby we had a superbly planned firework display on the front lawn of St Christoph, that all of us present must remember. The fireworks were placed out of harm's way in a baking-tin on the lawn, and the display began with a couple of large Catherine wheels nailed to two posts. They were impressive and lovely to watch as they sent out a stream of sparks a decent distance...oh dearie me... towards the tray of fireworks. 'Move those trays out of the way, would you David'... but it was too late, as first a volcano started to burn impressively, followed by the sparklers. Then the rockets began to shoot unpredictably and horizontally across the garden, another volcano erupted, more untethered Catherine wheels took off like low flying helicopters, and there was an emergency retreat into the house. The firework display didn't last long, but it was certainly in its way quite spectacular, as we viewed it from behind the relative safety of the hall's front bay-windows.

In later years my parents became very much a part of Farnham, and engaged in many projects, the most important of which concerned the Farnham bypass. Dad opposed this effectively by designing an alternative underpass project, which didn't divide the town in two. He built a scale model of the proposal which became the centre-piece of resistance to a project that would have ruined Farnham. Having won that one, he then devoted his efforts to the purchase and conversion of the Farnham Maltings, using volunteer labour. There was the odd near-disaster such as when he and some boy volunteers started to dismantle an empty tank left by Courages' the brewers, that turned out to be full of ammonia. There was no explosion and nobody died, but I believe it was a close call. The Maltings is now a multi-purpose centre right at the core of Farnham's cultural activity.

My parents in their retirement were undoubtedly a formidable couple, with Mum right at the heart of their musical activities, as she led the cellos, and was also a very well-respected and imaginative cello teacher. Dad enjoyed concerts, but would invariably fall asleep, and then often snore. He was of course, constantly tired from his work on the Maltings. I remember sitting beside him in Bourne Parish Church for a rendition of Bach's B minor Mass, which has some lovely obligato for the cello, but doesn't have a part for the snorer. As the music went softer, the snore got louder, till I had to dig him in the ribs. He awoke with a start, and expostulated in a loud voice, 'Why did you do that?!' Both my parents developed osteoarthritis of the hips, most of which were replaced at least once, as they became quite lame. Dad was a bad driver and oblivious of danger, while Mum was a good driver but developed cataracts, had a pacemaker, and a sixth sense that was especially needed when Dad was driving. For a while in old age they worked as a team with Dad at the wheel, until he had a serious accident at the foot of the drive when nosing out onto the main road, so the driving duo had to stop. They finally sold up and moved to Blackheath to be near my sister Margaret. Dad was also not keen to be helped on stairs, or anywhere else, and would shake off any assistance, on one occasion nearly throwing an unsuspecting helper down the stairs of Fairfield Halls in Croydon. Margaret said he needed a sign round his neck saying '**Warning! Help this Old Man at Your Peril!**'

Chapter 2

BOARDING SCHOOL

BECOMING A POXY PILGRIM

The Pilgrims' School is a boarding preparatory choir-school located close to Winchester Cathedral, where Uncle Ted and Aunty Muriel's son John had been a pupil and chorister. On returning from Tanganyika in 1949, Antony was immediately sent there, and I was to join him a year later. We were commoners, not choristers. That was where, after a year or two, I was switched from playing the piano to the violin. Mum's idea was to grow from seed a string quartet, starting from the top down. Our teacher was Miss Nellie Fulcher, a nice old biddy, but a hopeless teacher, who was unkindly nicknamed 'The Vulture'. I thoroughly enjoyed the Pilgrims' School, although early one summer term, I suppose it was 1951, while brushing my teeth I was spotted by the matron with spots, and on stripping they were all over my body. Otherwise I was perfectly well. The head-master's wife Lorna Salwey was called to inspect. 'This is chicken pox' she said, 'has anyone in the family had it recently?' 'Oh yes', I said, applying the diagnostic skills of a future doctor, 'my brother Stuart had it three weeks ago'. He had had three spots and I remembered Mum saying, 'It looks just like chicken pox .... but then it can't be, he is so well, and it's only three spots after all'. And very soon Stuart's spots went away and they were never spoken of again. I was only trying to be helpful, but it didn't put my mother, who was already under suspicion for being Aunty Muriel's sister-in-law, in the school's good books.

I was put into isolation because in those days that was what they did, and I can remember lying for hours imagining figures hidden in the patterns of the flaking ceiling. There was not much else to do. Of course for the first week I only saw adults, mostly the matron; and then to my joy the epidemic hit big-time and I was joined by other boys as the whole school went down with it. For the rest of the term the school could only play cricket with other chicken-poxy schools. This was serious because cricket was taken seriously. By half term I was almost spot and pustule-free, apart from two enormous scabs on the top of my head. I can still feel the scars. The school doctor had said the scabs would fall off in time, although there was thick hair matted through them. We were taken to Farnham for the day to visit my grandparents, and my surgeon grandfather Arder pronounced the GP's opinion to be ridiculous, and then painstakingly removed them. When I got back to school the headmaster, Humphrey Salwey exploded like Krakatoa (the red skies of his childhood of which Arder often talked). My mother's reputation had already sunk from low to zero for the sin of willfully letting a son catch chickenpox. It now dropped further to strong negative, and was only redeemed when the school was later chosen for Stuart, (whose fault it had been all along for catching *varicella* so mildly). As expected, Sally as we called him, got into a monumental 'bate'. These were well recognised, usually unexplained, and always lasted for about a week during which it was best to keep out of the firing line. In retrospect they may have been due to premenstrual tension, which women often blame on their husbands, but which was yet to be invented. Although beatings at the Pilgrim's

School were rare, they too were cyclical and conducted with a strange and flat but serrated butterpat. This was something I was to experience a year or two later when I had the gall one Sunday to describe Lorna's home-made jam as disgusting, so discovering that honesty doesn't always pay.

There was a thing at PS called 'bowling on the lawn', where you tried to land the ball on a biscuit-tin 'plate' a good length in front of the wicket, and if you did you won a penny, and if you got a hat trick you stood to earn a small fortune. James 2, who later became an eminent Professor of Geriatrics, once got a hat trick. James 1, (no relation), on the other hand, was expelled for cleptomania; it seemed he had a propelling pencil fetish. Funny the things one remembers. Otherwise, the school was good and in retrospect seemed paedophilia-free, although a fecophilic temporary teacher aged about sixteen called Inky Stevens disappeared fast when an epidemic of 'ploppers', of enormous adult size, started to appear on the toilet seats in the boys changing room. I doubt if he got any anti-plopper counseling. I still remember the jingle for all the monarchs of England since 1066, when history began, 'Willy, Willy, Harry, Ste,' and even the Duke of Marlborough's telephone number (BROM 4689), rote-learnt from Mr Paton (Patey's) date list (see Appendix). I wonder if they still teach like that now.

My brother and I occupied ourselves almost continuously during our spare time making aeroplanes with balsa wood, cement glue, tissue paper and 'dope'. We enjoyed the smell of dope, which you painted on the tissue-paper-covered wings to make them tense and waterproof, and I suppose we may well even have been a bit addicted. The planes were either gliders, or propeller-driven and powered by long rubber bands that extended the length of the fuselage. You twisted the propeller clockwise at least a hundred times, released the plane downwind, and they always flew well at least once. We especially cherished that first flight over and into the brambles of Brambletye. We later extended ourselves to jets, powered by tiny rockets I doubt if you can buy any more. In the summer we always went to the Farnborough air display, and on September 6th 1952, perched on a hill overlooking the runway got a prime view of the tragic DH110 crash of test pilot John Derry, who was killed as the plane disintegrated, and pieces flew into the crowd, with many casualties.

The first person important to me who died was Arder, on December 15th 1952. He was lucky to have lived into old age. I still remember him telling me more than once that as a young medical student he had contracted septicaemia and pneumonia, and through his coma he had heard the doctor say, 'He's not going to make it, this one'. So he had set out to prove him wrong. 'Don't forget that, David, when you become a doctor.' He was admitted that winter of '52 to the London Clinic and became one more victim of the Great London Smog. Antony and I were pulled out of the Pilgrim's School and taken to see him, frail and barely recognisable as the pipe-smoking story-telling honey-making Arder we knew and loved. He muttered something as he kissed us, two of his favourite grandsons, and then bade us farewell. We left and Mr Salwey told us two weeks later that he had died. My first contact with death was as simple as that, but I still miss him.

AT RUGBY SCHOOL

In the summer of 1954 I followed my brother and the earlier Anderson generation to Tudor House, Rugby School. When I got there it had been largely cleaned out of a bunch of bullies in the senior house, who had made Antony's first year hell. My father had been posted to Kuala Lumpur as Chief Engineer, Malaya Command and was soon joined by Mum and the two little ones Stuart and Margaret. During the holidays Antony and I stayed with Mrs Palmer, a war widow with two sons, one of whom had died in an accident. She was good to us, and her house was across the road from what was now the family home in Boundstone, which had been painstakingly rebuilt by my father. So we could continue our model-making and railway-building in the 'top room' over the garage.

I actually quite enjoyed Rugby, and only once experienced a sexual approach, from a particularly nasty boy nick-named 'The Runt'. When he tried it a second time I struck him on the chin, and got two green stick fractures of my right fourth and fifth metacarpals, which were strapped up round a rolled up bandage by the school 'quack', no questions asked. But it was definitely worth it and he never tried it on again. Later that year he was expelled for running a betting scam that I heard had netted £8,000. I wonder what happened to him in the end; such people rarely improve with age. After completing eight O-levels, I concentrated on the subjects necessary to become a doctor - chemistry, physics and biology, with one other option. I took German in the third year, and in the fourth year art, where I even won the Patterson Art Prize, in a year when art was distinctly weak. The masters were Mr R B Talbot Kelly, an eminent bird artist who had spent the war designing camouflage, and TK Barraclough, a sculptor with a beard and a squeaky voice.

It may come as some surprise to some, but until I was fifteen and started to study biology, I was quite religious, having been brought up as an Anglican Christian. Baptised early of course, I was confirmed two days after my fifteenth birthday, and started to take communion. But once I started to study A level biology, and learnt about Darwin's theory of evolution, any doubts I already had rapidly became set in concrete. It greatly upset my mother when I refused to take communion, or to attend family prayers, and finally to go to church altogether. I made an exception for carol services, because I liked singing. It is strange how the same information hits different people, but my two brothers remain Christians. There had been more than a hint, from my mother at least, that without a faith we would not know about good and evil, and then what would stop us from being bad?

Antony and I flew out to Malaya for eight week's summer holiday in 1954 to join the rest of the family. We flew out in a *Hermes*, and came back in a derivative of the *Lancaster* bomber, called an *Avro York*. It was slow, incredibly noisy and made several stops on the way. Being unpressurised it flew at a maximum height of 10,000 feet. Antony and I sat right next to the engines, and for at least three months afterwards I had tinnitus in my right ear, which has subsequently been deaf to high frequencies. Malaya was a great experience, and we did something different every day. Dad was engaged in building roads including a new one right across the peninsula. He clearly made a significant contribution to eliminating the terrorist threat, which was made easier by the fact the terrorists were Chinese, and the uprising did not involve the Malay majority. Dad was made CBE for his work as Chief Engineer, Malaya.

For my first three years at Rugby I was in the same house as my brother Antony. He is and has always been what you might describe as a boffin. He is very intelligent, but as a child was somewhat unconventional in his approach to study. He wanted to actually understand the principles behind solving problems, and with few exceptions was thought by masters at Rugby to be of below par intelligence. Later, after leaving school, he was to shine in his subject of electrical engineering. He was picked on by Mr Falk, our house master, probably because via Aunty Ruth in his first year he had exposed the extent of bullying by senior boys in Tudor House, so he was never even made a house sixth. Public schools then ran and probably still do, on the risky system of placing too much responsibility for the discipline of juniors on shoulders of senior boys. This breaks down if you have a bunch of unempathic bullies among the latter.

Dad was not impressed with my lack of keenness on things military, or its physical manifestation, the School Corps. John Carslake was a good friend with whom I shared a study for a time, where we kept a tank of creatures taken from Pond One, including a *Dytiscus* (Great Water Beetle) larva that kills by pumping its prey full of poison. Unlike me John was paternally obedient, keen on Corps, and passed Certificate A part 1 with flying colours, while I managed to fail, which was quite difficult to do. John had more trouble with the second part because he couldn't with certainty tell his left from his right. As a result he managed to march a platoon ...'Left right left right, left right... Company LE-E-E-FT TURN...', straight into the William Webb Ellis Memorial. My own main military distinction was when during Corps practice in Tudor Close in front of the Head of House, Tim Coghlan, who was a real 'Corps Gut', I subverted my platoon of A-Certified failures into giving a well-ordered demonstration of the goose-step. This was considered unpatriotic, and for this tasteless act of rebellion, which was actually done for a laugh, I was summoned into the housemaster Peter Falk's office. After a cliché-marked...'Now I'm sorry David, this is going to hurt me more than it hurts you'... I was given six of the best with a cane. It didn't hurt much as I had taken the precaution of going in well-padded with an extra layer of underpants. One week later Coghlan was caught swimming in the 'Tosh' at night with a crowd of other boys, and was rusticated for the rest of the summer term which, since he was an excellent fast bowler, took the cutting edge off the School's First Eleven.

APRIL FOOLS

I inherited from my father a natural propensity to play practical jokes. In Tudor House there was a system of queueing up to get chits signed by the House Master if you wanted food from the school tuck shop, or an item of sports clothing from Gilberts down-town. With practice I became pretty good at faking Mr Falk's signature. Furthermore, I was studying biology with him, and he wrote everything on the blackboard. On April 2nd 1957 there was to be a massive Hunt family get-together at Uncle Alan's house in London, and I had written a letter supposedly from Peter Falk on Tudor House headed notepaper to my father. The gist was that he thought David was doing very well generally, and was keen and attentive in class, but unfortunately he had got into the odd spot of trouble in relation to drinking. The other day had been found inebriated in the cellar with another boy, Frank Wisner - an American, and a detail included to make the story even more convincing - with an empty bottle of gin. But as this was only the second time this had happened he had let me off with a warning. It was dated April 1st, and posted to arrive on that date. (It was a good year for April fools, because I also pulled one on Mrs Palmer that same year). Well, the family party went very well, but Dad seemed a little subdued. On the train home he couldn't contain himself any longer and summoned me down the carriage. 'Yesterday I received a letter from Peter Falk, David, which....' 'Dad, what date was it yesterday?', and the truth struck to his embarrassment. I had inadvertently wrecked for him what should have been a joyous family gathering. Until his dying day he denied that he had actually been taken in.

My brother Antony and I got on well in the main, although I believe it was in retrospect a mistake for both of us to have been put into the same house at Rugby. Together we built a canvas-clad two-man canoe in the school workshop over two terms, with the intention, during the 1956 Easter holidays, of canoeing home, or at least as far as Oxford. It was extremely heavy, even before being overladen with clothes, food and camping equipment, but in the end it was locks and finally cows that were the killers. In the first three days we negotiated our way round numerous locks (to save money on lock fees) as the canal looped back and forth. Each time the canoe came out of the water it had to be emptied of all the gear. At the end of the third day we found a really nice looking large empty field, and decided to camp early. In the far corner of the field we could make out some tiny brown, black and white spots, and they could also see us. By the time the tent was shipshape, the herd of cows had arrived and started to molest us, butting the tent, and pulling out the guys. That was it. We cursed the cows, struck camp, walked off with canoe and stuff, found a telephone and phoned Mum, who kindly came and picked us up. It was not how it was supposed to end.

MY FORAY INTO OVER-ACTING

At Rugby there was a keen tradition of House Plays. In the Autumn of 1957, at the start of my last year at Rugby, one of the Deputy House Masters, a lanky, ultra-intelligent and somewhat goofy mathematical physicist called 'Loopy' Lupton was put in charge of the Tudor House Play. He chose Mary Chase's Pulitzer prize-winning play 'Harvey', in which the central character is Elwood P Dowd, who appears to be going mad, and who in our case was played by Mark Cheyne, who right up to the night before the performance was perilously word-imperfect. The second key character is the unseen but inferred Harvey, a six-foot-three-and-a half-inches tall white rabbit, who also has a crucial part, is Elwood's best friend, and with whom he converses all the time. There was no doubting Mark had the most difficult rôle, which would have been testing even if he had known his own lines, never mind Harvey's unspoken ones. Elwood P Dowd's sister is the formidable Veta Louise Simmons; I was cast in this rôle, and I knew Elwood's lines as well as my own, and so was sometimes forced to talk to myself. Her part is absolutely perfect for someone like me with a natural inclination to over-act. It was great fun, and thanks in large part to the prompter, on the night the play was a huge overacting success. Mum said that in drag I looked and sounded like the spitting image of her sister Elizabeth, and I must admit I had probably modeled myself on some of her more extreme mannerisms. Later that year, in the School play *Our Town*, by Thornton Wilder, I was rewarded with the rôle of a dead man. I had one line, which I underacted to perfection, and ever since I have stuck to recitations.

A NEAR-DEATH EXPERIENCE

Although I was not a natural sportsman, unlike Antony, who also had poor eyesight I did enjoy sport, especially 'rugger' and cricket. But I suffered as a child from severe hay fever. I remember while I was at The Pilgrim's School, Granny Hunt telling me Piriton the miracle-cure antihistamine had come on the market; it helped a bit, but made me very sleepy in the outfield. From May onwards the problem was such that in the summer of my final year at Rugby I took up swimming and joined the Swimming Eight, where I dived and swam breaststroke, both to moderate standard. It was at Rugby that I also learnt a dangerous swimming practice later almost killed me when, at the age of nineteen, I was working in a bacteriology laboratory in Philadelphia. The practice, common among schoolboys, is to deliberately over-breathe before swimming under water, because the main drive to surface is the rise in carbon dioxide level in the blood and brain. Over-breathing, by lowering CO_2 in the blood, reduces the drive while not increasing the partial pressure of oxygen, and you can become unconscious due to hypoxia. I still have a vivid memory of that evening, when my black friend Raymond Barlow's parents had given us a slap-up meal before Raymond and I walked through quite a dangerous part of Philadelphia, to the fifty-metre public swimming pool. I over-breathed and dived in at the deep end and swam the length under water. I still vividly remember seeing the end of the pool coming up.

My next memory is of fighting in the ambulance, its sirens blaring, against people of all shades who I thought were trying to kill me. I even broke a restraining strap. I remember finally then telling a nurse that my pupils were normally dilated, so not to worry about that. I understood later that Raymond was nearly arrested for attempted murder. Fortunately the life-guard (who I later went back to thank) had actually been paying attention and spotted my body on the bottom of the shallow end. I was discharged home and coughed up blood for two days. Many years later I heard of a boy who died in Hong Kong doing the same thing, so it has still not been erased from schoolboy mythology. My uncle Dr John Hunt, who later became the founding President of the Royal College of General Practitioners, wanted me to write a letter to *The Lancet*, but I let him down. He was eventually made a life peer, and one day someone came up to him in the Palace of Westminster and asked if he was the Lord John Hunt who had discovered the North Pole, to which he replied, 'No, Madam, and I am afraid you have got your wires completely crossed'.

Back to Rugby School; I think Dad felt I was somewhat undisciplined, and sent me during my final Easter vacation, with my erstwhile disorientated friend John Carslake, to the Ullswater Outward Bound School. This was a good experience, the principle of which is to try to build character by pushing you near the limit, with rock climbing, wall scaling, abseiling, canoeing, bollock-naked ice-cold morning lake-dipping, sport and camping in the hills. For the two-night hike and camp I was in charge of three others, one of whom, Nick, was aged twenty and from a disadvantaged background, (while I was only seventeen, and from an advantaged one). I was supposed to stop him getting into extreme trouble, to which he was prone. We got on pretty well in the mist, damp and cold, and I remember his uneconomical language in which every other word was 'f*ckin', so all his sentences were double the required length just for emphasis. Despite deliberately setting off the fire alarms one day, I got a gold medal at the end for leadership, with a bronze, the lowest, for sporting prowess.

CHAPTER 3

MEDICAL SCHOOL IN SCOTLAND

For financial reasons my parents did not want me to stay on at school any longer than was educationally necessary. Having got the required A and S levels I was well enough qualified to leave school and start to study Medicine, which I wanted to do without delay. Dad had been posted to York, and I was also awarded a City of York Scholarship. As expected, I applied to, and was interviewed at, St Bartholomew's Hospital (Barts) which had a strong family pedigree; a grandfather and two uncles had qualified there, and one of the latter - Alan Hunt - was the senior surgeon. The interview went well and having been accepted, out of the blue my parents came up with another idea, namely to go to St Andrews University in Scotland. I was pretty much a passenger in this process, but as my brother, who had completed a pre-University apprenticeship, was to study engineering in Queen's College, Dundee (which was still part of St Andrews University), I went for interview. I was accepted into the second year, provided I passed the summer resit of the First MB ChB degree, which I understood was pretty much equivalent to S-level physics, chemistry and biology. Barts, in the person of Uncle Alan, not surprisingly went ballistic, most firepower being directed at my mother, but some also at me.

I did warn the reader that this story might wander about a bit in space-time. Some twelve years later I was appointed as Lecturer in Medicine at St Bartholomews Hospital, and had pleasure when asked if I was a 'Barts man', to be able to reply, 'No, but I did turn down a place here'. Barts, I later found, had a reputation of seeing itself as a cut above other London Medical Schools, and certainly all Scottish ones. There was a popular saying among other London schools that you can always tell a Barts man, but you can't tell him much. One weekend when I was covering for the Senior Registrar, and was responsible for the medical admissions, I saw a woman who had been admitted to the medical ward with abdominal pain, and I made a confident diagnosis of acute appendicitis. I called the duty Surgical Senior Registrar, who quizzed me in a distinctly irritating way. 'Look, I've seen the patient and you haven't, and in my opinion she has all the features of acute appendicitis, including a classic history, a positive Rovsing's sign and rebound tenderness. Are you going to come and take her over or not?' I was probably even ruder than that, but I clearly made an impression, so he started to be nice. 'I say' he said, 'can I just ask? Are you a Barts man?' 'No, I'm not' I replied'... ... 'n-n-not that it mattered if you weren't!' came the reply. I am glad to say my diagnosis was correct, and she was successfully operated on that night.

So now, back to St Andrews. As this exam loomed during the summer vacation of 1958, I looked at the curriculum. I found to my horror that I had great pockets, nay black holes (which were yet to be discovered), of relevant ignorance, especially in chemistry and physics, where the First MB syllabus was much wider than the AS level one. The fateful time came, and I stayed for two weeks in St Regulus Hall, where I met one of the other 'bright boys', Timothy J Peters. Tim, who is still a good friend, is one of the smartest people on the planet, and knew a depressingly large amount in my fields of cavernous ignorance, especially in carbohydrate chemistry. As we sat the chemistry and physics exams he was kind enough to help me cram in some essentials, but by the end of the week I was sure I had failed. The second week we were joined by Jo Nicholson, who had taken two subjects in the summer, and only had Zoology and Botany to do. Tim had been very helpful, but that did not do much for my teenage pride. This, however, was restored a little when we got to the softer biology subjects. I well remember the zoology practical. Now I had dissected a crayfish at school, and knew its anatomy well; this had been the subject of the 1st MB practical in the summer, so Tim was confident it would not come up again. He had done the stats, and was extremely cocky in this assertion. The night before, I repaid some of his patience with me, by saying that he had to have some idea of the main parts of the eminent crustacean, just in case. And right enough the next day, there it was - 'dissect and display the main parts of the crayfish'. At the end of three hours, mine looked respectable, while Tim's looked like the remnants of a hastily eaten seafood meal. But we both passed, possibly on the grounds that as a composite we had pretty much covered the syllabus. I think in truth they wanted to try us three out as a kind of experiment.

A GOLFING NEAR-DISASTER

The Second MB course my first year was in human anatomy, physiology and biochemistry, but especially anatomy. We literally dissected the whole human body, (and were proudly told by Professor Walmsley we would double our vocabulary in the process), learning things we would never need to know again. We had practical examinations every three weeks. I suppose there was some point to it, and I worked hard. It really didn't leave much time to enjoy University in the sort of way arts students did. However I played the oboe in the University's orchestra, run by Cedric Thorpe Davie, and started to play golf with clubs that my Dad had given me, that were definitely time-expired. Students could play on the main courses for very little, and sometimes we would go out late on a summer's evening and play a few holes on the famed Old Course, for nothing. One such evening towards the end of term I was on the eighteenth tee, and hit a belting drive maybe 200-plus yards, but with the biggest curving slice you ever saw. I saw it strike one of the buildings on the right where very wisely the windows facing the tee were protected with mesh screens. There was obviously no need for such protection for those facing the eighteenth green. My ball, a Dunlop 65 No 3, had different ideas but in the end bounced back onto the fairway. As I approached it I was met by a large, middle-aged, irate American male. 'Is this your ball, he said?'. 'A Dunlop 65, No 3, yes I do believe it is.' He pointed up to the second floor window, facing the green, which I saw was shattered... 'Look what you did, you nearly killed my daughter; she was sitting beside that window until five minutes ago'. The ball in its curving flight had hit a buttress to the green-side of the window and bounced back so shattering the unprotected glass. I was of course profusely contrite as he took me upstairs to see the damage, which was complete. 'You'll pay for this he said'. 'Yes I will, and I am only glad your daughter had just moved'. I promised to go back when the window had been repaired, price three pounds. I did so three days later. 'Aw, you're a nice kid', he said, 'just forget it'.

SUMMER IN A COLONIE DE VACANCES

In 1959 I don't think my parents were that keen to have me around all summer, so Dad came up with a bright scheme. It was for me to learn a foreign language by the military deep-end-throwing-in method. Four years previously I had taken 'O' level French, but had done none since. 'I think you should learn French, you can go to France and work in a children's summer holiday camp'. Not one to argue over the sense in this, I had one or two lessons of spoken French, and was dispatched to France, where I spent a couple of nights in the 'Baby Hotel' in the fairly sleezy *deuxième arrondissement* of Paris, before going for one week's crash-course on how to become a *Colonie de Vacances Moniteur*. This consisted of intensive sessions where we learnt songs, games, and all kinds of activities designed to keep small French boys occupied. At the end of the week I still didn't have a placement, but one of the senior people there, a *Monsieur L'Abbé l'Oiseau*, seemed to think I had shown the right spirit. Furthermore I was aged at least eighteen, which was important to him, because it meant I could be left in charge of a contingent of small boys. His youngest *moniteur*, Alain, was only fourteen and needed cover. A day later Mr Bird the Priest contacted me by phone at the Baby Hotel, with the offer of a place in his *Colonie de Vacances* in the Vosges, at a place called Bussang, for free board-and-lodging and a Sunday off every two weeks. So next day I met the party at Boissy-la-Riviere, and we travelled by coach to Bussang. (The *Colonie* was, incidentally located at the very source of the river Moselle, something of which everyone was proud). I have never learnt a language so fast in my life. I had a group of eight-to-nine-year-olds, specially selected for their indiscipline. But by joining up *équipes* with Alain, who was good but under-age, we managed somehow. Every evening there was a thing called a *Veillée*, where half an hour of games and entertainment were followed by a religious five minutes with the Lord's prayer, and in my case some reflective mumbo jumbo. I became very good at abusing the rhetorical question. 'So as we stand here, and we marvel at the sky, and we say to ourselves, 'how about all we see around us?' and we think for a minute, and ask ourselves, 'did this all happen by chance?' And maybe we answer, 'probably', but isn't it great anyway?'

We used to go for long walks through the Vosges, one of the French killing fields of World War One, and on one occasion came across an unexploded shell, which we didn't take back, but reported. After three and a half weeks, and before the end of the *Colonie*, I left with some regret, and, now even dreaming in passable French, went to a music summer school at Canford. There I joined a friend Bill Oram who was a very accomplished horn player, and his clarinetist sister Jean, who was my 'Senior Woman' at St Andrews, and of whom I have fond memories. We all went on an intensive chamber-music camp under the guidance of the famous bassoonist Archie Camden. Music camps were in my mother's blood, but this was the only one I went on. The main thing I remember about Bill Oram is that he was red-headed, as skinny as a rake and completely fearless. That year for a bet Bill had taken a prolonged swim in St Andrews harbour next to the famous pier. Once a week after chapel, students would join the pier walk, clad in the classic red St Andrews University gowns, whose position on the shoulders declared whether you were new (a bejeant) or something more senior. Eventually it trailed along the ground, which denoted untouchable seniority. Anyway, Bill, in his second year had no subcutaneous fat, and shivered bravely while he trod water at the bottom of the pier's steps watched by me and another friend. I was the medic, and the one to insist after twenty minutes or so, and before the bet was won, that we fish him out as he was clearly about to expire from hypothermia. I remember it took several hours of slow warming in a bath at Sallies (St Salvators Hall), our hall of residence, as we gradually topped up from cold, with warm water to restore him to what passed for normal. Bill had battiness down to an art form. And he also played the French horn very well.

CLINICAL YEARS IN DUNDEE

At the end of five terms we sat the 2nd MB exam, which I passed respectably, and Tim Peters passed with honours. He then did a year's basic science for a PhD and left our year. The summer term of 1959 we travelled to Dundee for the start of our clinical training, and our year suddenly doubled in size. That was when I met Jennifer Calderwood who was one of the Dundee crowd - and being close alphabetically we were in the same clinical group. Our first bedside teaching session, on a case of mitral stenosis, was given by 'Beautiful Pete' Robertson (who knew everything, it seemed, but may have been less bright than he was beautiful. There was a second Peter with the same surname, called Squeaky Pete, to whom the obverse applied). By the bedside and while Beautiful Pete talked about mitral stenosis, my future wife fainted. Nearly sixty years later, and after fifty-four years of marriage to me, Jenny still has a slow pulse, lowish blood pressure and occasional dizziness. I wondered as she collapsed how she was going to cope, but I slowly discovered she was made of sterner stuff. Having gone to a one-gender public school, I was still pretty scared of the opposite sex, terrified actually, though in my final year at Rugby I had summoned up courage and taken Tatton-Brown's sister to the summer ball, and could manage a *Foxtrot* and a *Dashing White Sergeant*. Anyway Jenny seemed to be accounted for, and we didn't start dating till eighteen months later, by which time I had had a couple of quite diffident heterosexual experiences which we don't need to go into. I had then actually just been jilted by a lovely technician called Frances, after my twenty-first birthday. As I was getting over this insult to my pride, I suddenly realised Jenny Calderwood might be the one. As well as being fun and beautiful she also had a half-share with her brother in a small Wolseley saloon called FUV, and she expressed an interest in skiing.

ROMANCE AND SKIING

Now I haven't mentioned yet that when Mum, Stuart and Margaret had joined Dad in Malaya in 1954, that Christmas Antony and I had gone to München Gladbach in Germany to stay with Uncle John and Aunty Buf (Elizabeth). Leaving the younger Napier cousins behind, after Christmas we were driven with our wartime sibling cousins Rob and Jane, to a small resort called Mittelberg, near Öberstdorf. When we arrived, well after dark, we found our booked accommodation had been taken and instead were forced to trek up the hill to an extremely cold farmhouse. The only source of heating was a small herd of cows next to the toilet and below the living quarters. Icicles grew on the toilet taps. Antony and I had vestigial neolithic skiing equipment - to wit our parents' pre-war skis. Antony had to saw a foot off the back of his. The bindings were insecure springs, and we wore corps boots with a groove cut out of the back. We had good fun mastering the stem turn, in which you forced the legs apart with the ski tips together, and put weight on the lower ski, except that when hurtling straight down a slope I couldn't work out which the lower ski was. We depended a great deal on the kick turn. Uncle John was by then Lord Napier of Magdala, having inherited the title given to his Victorian great-grandfather, the General who had punished the mad Emperor Theodore of Abyssinia in 1868. Like my father he was a seasoned sapper, and so this was not a holiday for softies. As soon as we could slither down a nursery slope we went on expeditions. On the main one, where we slept sardine-style in huts, we climbed a decent mountain called the Höher Ifen, most of us using skins on the bottoms of our skis, grain pointing backwards. My aunt, however was walking and trailing her skis behind her, and as we went up a ridge, one of her skis came loose. We were well above the tree line, and there was one small bush on the whole slope below us. Fortunately the ski turned round and headed for it, impaled itself in it and my cousin Rob heroically retrieved it. But for that bush it would have taken itself all the way to Mittelberg and beyond.

With that background, let me fast-forward to early April 1962, and Jenny and I plan a weekend skiing. In Airlie Hall there was a Russian student called Boris Oleinikov, who we presumed was a spy, and who claimed he was a proficient skier. He leapt at the chance to come with us. We stayed for a weekend in the disgustingly named Spital hotel at the Spital of Glenshee, and the following morning drove up to the top of Glenshee equipped with skis and boots. To my surprise it turned out that Boris had never been on a coathanger lift before. Never mind, after falling off a couple of times, I managed to get him up to the top of this steepish and icy slope, and into the usual dense Scottish cloud, when I realised what was wrong with Boris Oleinikov. He had never skied downhill before, there being an absence of hills next to his home on the Volga. So there I was stuck at the top of the lift with a Russian spy who had only ever skied on the flat. But thanks to Uncle John I was proficient at both doing and teaching the kick turn, and by dint of traverse, kick turn, traverse, kick turn... we got down about an hour later. That is the last I remember of Boris Oleinikov, although we must have brought him back to Dundee after the weekend. But that evening Jenny and I had a memorable walk in the cold, and I discovered that she was as keen on me as I was on her.

For several Easters thereafter we used to join the Napiers for a week's skiing in the Cairngorm mountains, staying in a cold house in the small village of Kincraig. This was a ritual which - along with highly competitive racing-demon that Rob always won - continued for years. There was one chair lift up the White Lady, but we preferred to ski in the gully behind, called Coire na Ciste, which regularly filled with snow to a considerable depth. After taking the lift up the White Lady we would climb to the top, ski down to the bottom of Coire na Ciste over five to ten minutes, and then take off our skis and solemnly walk back to the top. On a good day we got in three whole runs. The equipment had improved somewhat from Mittleberg days and we now had things called Marker bindings, but the ski boots were still quite soft, and the bindings did not release on impact. I never broke any limbs, but on one occasion I did manage to do a complete summersault and break the same hickory ski front and back. The day's ritual started with porridge, and if any was left over this was to be mixed the next day with new porridge. Wartime habits had still not died in the Napier household. My aunt ate and thought like a sparrow, which was unfortunate as it was she who dispensed the picnic lunches. She would bring a single block of dates which was solemnly cut into however many pieces there were people in the party. One trip some years later I got into trouble by buying twelve such blocks and apportioning one to each person, and she was furious.

For two years while I was at Rugby our summer holidays were spent on the island of Sark, where we camped in a remote farmer's field; the second year our parents old green canvas honeymoon tent was blown away in a hurricane, which put paid to camping that year but not of course to sketching. We also had two excellent Anderson family winter holidays in 1959-60 and 60-61 in Gerlos in Austria, where Dad had skiied before the war, and where he met up with Herr Moser a ski instructor friend from over twenty years before. The first was the occasion for writing an epic poem - *'The Hunting of the Ski'* - based on Lewis Carroll's *'The Hunting of the Snark'*, written mostly by Dad, and expertly illustrated by him (see illustrations). The family car, an old coach-built Wolseley saloon (NPE 792), had been bought in and brought back from East Africa in 1949. In 1962 Mum was coming up with my sister and brothers to join Jenny, me, and the Napiers skiing in the Cairngorms. Antony was driving when they were run into head-on by a young woman out for an illegal spin in her boyfriend's sports car, on a straight stretch of road immediately outside Bridge of Earn hospital. Fortunately no one was killed, but this was in the days before seat belts, and Mum, in the front passenger seat, sustained horrific facial injuries that needed expert surgery and months of splinting. That certainly put paid to any more skiing for her.

Many years later Uncle John invited our son Kenneth to join them, and Ken became prematurely so keen and confident that shooting down out of control he managed to knock over a whole ski class like a line of dominoes. I am sure he got a good military dressing-down for that. John Napier had a heart of gold, and once as a student and short of cash I borrowed five pounds from him while staying in Edinburgh. When I later offered to pay it back he told me to give it to someone else when I was older who needed it more than I did. Sadly he died in a car crash in his eighties with his dog Marco when he fell asleep after lunch at the wheel on the road north to Edinburgh, and ran into the back of a parked lorry.

'OLD MAN RUDDLE' AND HIS DAUGHTER

Arder had a friend from India days who in old age we affectionately called 'Old Man Ruddle'. He lived locally with his daughter, who had been Granny Hunt's god-daughter, and who in her early forties adopted a baby girl. Mum became the godmother and took a lively and sympathetic interest, as did we all, in Mary and her infant daughter. Tragically, when the latter was aged only four, Mary died suddenly and unexpectedly, and Louise then went to live with her unsuitable guardians who already had three children of their own. When the guardian family abandoned their charge and left for New Zealand, Louise was ultimately welcomed into our family at around the time of Jenny's and my marriage (1964), when she became my second sister. To their great credit our by then elderly parents gave her the loving home she needed. After leaving school she trained as a chiropodist, and then emigrated to Australia. In Melbourne she set up a thriving chiropody practice. Family continuity was maintained there by Uncle Kenneth and his family, and she became a passionate and skillful horsewoman. While we were in Hong Kong Jenny and I kept in close touch, we had a joint holiday together, and with great pleasure in 2003 went to her wedding to Andrew Child. I remember this as a joyous family occasion which took place in a park by the beach beside a cycle path, to the sound of passing cycle bells.

THREE MONTHS IN THE USA

In the summer of 1960 I had another interesting trip, this time to the United States. I have already mentioned how I nearly drowned and had that distinctly memorable near-death experience. I actually went there on an immigrant visa, so I could get a paid job when there. My godfather Uncle Noel, - he of the stuffed spider story - had generously sponsored the £60 for the flight, which was with students from the Oxford Union, and I was well looked after by distant Anderson relatives, Len and Peggy Marshall, who lived in New York, and who had a beautiful weekend holiday home beside Candlewood lake. Somehow via home contacts I got a job in the bacteriology lab at the Hospital of the University of Pennsylvania (the HUP), where I worked under Professor Robert Norris on a thing called the bifidus factor, which had something to do with the benefits of breast feeding. I was paid $600, had fun and stayed in the Phi Chi Fraternity house, which was free but filthy. I made a good friend with a more senior medic, John Brown, and succumbed to some other abortive amorous attempts best left in the recesses of distant memory. John was definitely more successful in that regard, while I was keen, but clueless. This was also my first experience of American Christian evangelism, when a philandering anaesthetist invited me home for dinner, and treated his wife like dirt. He told me I was on the fast track to hell fire and damnation unless I found Jesus. He was not a great advertisement for salvation.

SOME MEMORABLE TEACHERS IN DUNDEE

We were fortunate to have some excellent teachers, among whom was Willie John Tulloch, the chain-smoking seventy-four year-old Professor of Bacteriology, who early in his career had done some significant research on typhoid vaccination. His love of alliterative language was epitomised by a jingle I recall about the transmission of typhoid, which was spread, he told us, by 'the filthy feet of fecal-feeding flies, dirty drains, and suspect water supplies'. Other memorable teachers included the Professor of Psychiatry, Ivor Batchelor, later knighted, whose lectures were a model of clarity and insight, and who introduced us to Hervey Cleckley and the concept of psychopathy. Then there was Mr Smellie, (pronounced Smiley) who was an authority on knee trauma on which he had written a textbook. He told us that two of the main causes were the American Football tackle, 'The main purpose of which is to rupture the medial ligament of the knee'; and skiing, 'which in most places is carried out on snow, but in Scotland takes place on rocks and heather'. In his teaching clinics he had an uncanny ability to predict what the patient was wearing, just based on the referral letter and his knowledge of the GPs; and he did the interview and examination standing up, as it wasted less time.

In the summer of 1961 I did a long clerkship in Arbroath with an Austrian doctor of Jewish extraction, Walter Strauss, who spoke with a strong Austrian accent and insisted that his housemen and anyone else like me who came along did their own blood tests. I had to learn to do pretty much everything. Blood counts, blood films, platelet counts, urea and electrolytes - and give him the results in the middle of the night. This was definitely in the days when consultants could write the rules as they went along.

In Dundee, clinical skills were taught in theory, but the way to get actual experience was to do clerkships, where you stood in for junior doctors when they went on holiday. Or you could get attachments on specialised units or with GPs. In the summer before final year, 1962, Jenny went off to the USA for an attachment in Minneapolis. I was allowed to use her car and I remember stopping, with some trepidation, in Birmingham on the way past, and meeting her (Northern Irish) parents Pard and Elizabeth, and her sister Jayne. The latter was studying Law, and gave me a legal inspection, which I apparently passed. Later that vacation I worked for three weeks on a neurosurgical unit at Bridge of Allen, and did a stint of similar length with a medical couple in Leeds, Alastair and Joan McKinnon, who ran a joint general practice. Joan was one of the daughters of Ramsay McDonald, the first Labour prime minister, and we were distantly related on my mother's side, a connection our family, being good Tories, for the most part kept under covers. The young MacKinnon son John was extremely keen on insects, and eventually became a world-renowned biologist and wild-life campaigner, who we caught up with in Hong Kong many years later. While I was there Alastair, an excellent golfer with a good sense of humour, got into hot water by saying on a radio show something about recommending unhappy men to take up golf or have 'an innocent flirtation'. This was inflated in the American popular press to, 'English doctor recommends his patients to have extra-marital affairs', and the press hounded him for weeks afterwards. *Plus ça change*!

A SECOND BAPTISM

As medical students we had to put in a certain amount of time delivering babies, and in all I think we had to deliver eight or ten. These were done under supervision of a midwife, of whom the most daunting was Dundee Royal Infirmary's Sister Kiddie. She seemed to take an instant dislike to me, until one morning I was doing a vaginal examination on a heavily pregnant woman under her hawkish eye. I was suddenly hit in the face by a shower of amniotic fluid, as the membranes ruptured, and Sister Kiddie was greatly amused as she said to all within earshot, 'Oh nurse, he's been baptised, he's been baptised!' After that it was a standing joke, and she seemed to treat me like a human being, quite possibly even a true Christian. She would greet me after I had qualified with, 'Oh you're Dr Anderson, I remember you - you were the student I saw baptised!'

For my last two years at Dundee I joined an *al capella* choir, called the Phoenix Madrigal Group. There was, as always, a distinct shortage of tenors, in fact there was only one when I arrived. He had a rather abrasive voice, and I felt that mine being more muted served to dilute the raspiness of the tenors somewhat. I was tasked with organising a concert tour in the summer, and much to my surprise and relief it went off pretty well. We sang our way south from Dundee and finished with a concert organised by Mum in Farnham Castle.

MEDICAL FINALS

For my final year I left the residence Airlie Hall, and took a flat nearby with my brother Antony, who was working on his PhD, and two medical friends Sandy and Jim. I passed finals with Commendation, and was kept on along with two other fellow students for the Medicine prize examination, which to my surprise I won. I sat it with an extremely bright and keen girl, Greta who always came top of everything but for some reason fell apart during the ordeal; and a really nice north-country lad called Robin Kell. At the climax of this prize exam we had vivas, and one question we were asked by the external examiner, Professor Melville Arnot, was, 'If you were the Almighty and re-designing the human body, what changes would you make?' I don't remember my own answer, but I do remember Robin's. He had a dry north-country sense of humour. He thought for a bit, and then said with a straight face, 'Well I think if I was God I'd make the whole thing a good deal simpler, so it were easier to understand.' I think I got the Medicine prize by default.

While on the subject of exams, another friend in an earlier end of term exam, had chosen to answer a short notes question. He had not attended many lectures, and I remember one of the topics was the *Venturi mask*. This is in fact a breathing mask through which pure oxygen is blown, which then draws in air from the sides by the Venturi principle, so reducing the oxygen concentration in a controlled way to a safe level. Mike didn't know this, but got one mark for inventiveness when he wrote... *The Venturi mask is a curiously passive mask-like facies seen in cases of bilateral facial paralysis, first described in 1796 by the Italian physician Venturi.*

There was a custom to stay up late the night before the results were posted, and drink plenty of beer. I remember painting a car park space marked 'Princ' in wet flour outside the Principal's house; and in the early hours we went and played a round of golf on Carnoustie Golf Course. I don't remember how we got there. Jenny and I had both passed, but I had to stay on for a week for the above examination. We then went and visited both sets of parents, and having long before decided to get married I don't remember making a formal proposal. But I do remember formally asking Pard, Jenny's father, in the drawing room of

David Coussmaker Anderson

their house 'Titcombs' in Sheep Street, Burford, if I might take the hand of his daughter, and he seemed delighted. In fact with his permission I took the whole lot. Then, after a brief holiday camping in Andorra, with a friend Walter Turck and my cousin Jane, came the house jobs. Walter had studied classics before deciding on a medical career, a foolish but brave move. I later became atheist godfather to his son Richard.

Chapter 4

AT LAST A DOCTOR

IN AT THE DEEP END

Jenny and I both started our House Officer jobs in Dundee Royal Infirmary (DRI), she with her surgical and me with my medical one. For the first six months we were paid at a rate of £630 per year. It was then increased a bit, and by dint of complaining we did eventually get free board and lodging. I worked on the professorial wards and my boss was Professor Sir Ian Hill, who had been knighted as he was the Queen's Physician whenever she came to Balmoral. He was a small man, but packed a considerable punch, and didn't suffer fools gladly. His wife had been a nurse, and was a heroin addict. When she eventually died he married his first cousin, and had a happier retirement. There was another cardiologist called Dr Gordon Clarke, who had the wards below on the first floor, and he and Sir Ian had completely different attitudes to medical advances. Gordon was distinctly unacademic, and used to refer to Sir Ian as, 'The wee electrician upstairs.' I liked Gordon Clarke all the same, and when Jenny and I started to become a visible item in final year we took out life insurance policies, and I was examined by him. He clearly had views on relationships between the sexes, especially for brighter students. 'You're friendly with that Calderwood woman aren't you?' he said. 'Yes, Dr Clarke'. 'Now my advice is don't rush into anything foolish, son'. 'I won't Dr Clarke'. One year later, as a qualified doctor, for some reason I had a further insurance examination. 'You used to be friendly with that Calderwood woman, weren't you?' 'Yes, Dr Clarke, as a matter of fact we're engaged to be married.' 'Oh well, never mind,' came the response, 'it's not too late to change your mind'. Two years later, in the course of taking out a further policy we went through the same ritual... 'I seem to remember you used to be friendly with that Calderwood woman weren't you?'... 'Yes, Dr Clarke, as a matter of fact we're now married'. Looking disappointed, this time he held his peace.

MY FIRST HOUSEJOB - DUNDEE ROYAL INFIRMARY'S PROFESSORIAL MEDICAL UNIT

Professor Hill had two senior lecturers, Ken Lowe ('Uncle Ken'), and Donald Emslie-Smith ('Bumble Nose'). Donald was an expert on vector cardiography, and had a somewhat otherworldly view on life. I recall one teaching round in winter when he looked out of the window and saw white flakes falling. 'Good God It's snowing', he said. Ken Lowe had some endearing traits too. He would sometimes point at a small brown mark on the chest below the nipple. 'What is that?' he would ask a generally perplexed student. No response, or at best, 'It's a mole, sir'. 'It's an accessory nipple', was the response', and then... 'I make a habit of looking for accessory nipples'. Of the three, Uncle Ken, who had been a high-flyer at the Hammersmith Hospital, was undoubtedly the most intelligent of my senior bosses, but he was also the laziest. My immediate superiors were the two registrars, respectively the Squeaky and Beautiful Petes Robertson. This house job was my introduction to the 'throw-him-in-at-the-deep-end' approach to postgraduate medical education. There was a dangerous amount of responsibility entrusted to young doctors just out of medical school, and there was nothing resembling formal postgraduate education. In any case, there would have been no time for it. The medical firms at DRI admitted patients on two days a week, which on the Professorial Unit were Wednesdays and Saturdays. We also admitted every third Sunday. The same applied to Gordon Clarke's unit downstairs, while the other two units, at Maryfield Hospital, each took admissions once a week, and one Sunday in six.

One houseman (I was paired with Robin Kell) took the men's ward, and the other the women's ward, and we each regularly had ten or more admissions in twenty-four hours. If the ward was full, beds were put up the centre, and if that was full, out in the corridor. I remember getting a stinking cold around the end of October, and a patient with gross myxoedema (from an underactive thyroid) grunting at me as I walked past wearing a mask. 'Heh, heh, Doctor, Doctor!' she called in her husky hypothyroid voice, and the same five minutes later as I walked back, 'Heh, heh, heh, Doctor!!' 'What can I do for you, Mrs McGee?' I asked. 'Doctor, ah see yer in desguise', she chortled', 'are yer guisin for the Halloween!?' She taught me that an underactive thyroid does not destroy a sense of humour - it just slows it down. Many of the ward sisters seemed ferocious, and Sister Farquhar (Farkie) particularly resented me at the beginning, as I looked and indeed was, too young. Actually, towards the end of my three months on the female ward she started to become quite nice, after she had reduced me to tears on one occasion. I have no idea how many people I inadvertently killed, but at least I didn't mean to, and if I did so I wasn't found out, or at least no one reported me. At that time on the professorial surgical ward a very keen young surgeon did Dundee's first open cardiac massage, on a man whose heart had stopped on the operating table, and miraculously the patient survived. Then people started to write about closed-chest cardiac massage. One man came in with a heart attack, and suddenly died - or underwent what we had formally equated with death. I called the passing pinkie (trainee nurse) and we placed him on the floor and I started to thump him on the chest. We had no defibrillators at that time, but his heart miraculously restarted after nearly twenty-five minutes of chest thumping, and in the end we wrote it up as a letter in *The Lancet*. Ken Lowe proudly dictated the discharge letter to the GP for the secretary to type, and I recall he said, 'On examination he had a very prominent *arcus senilis*' (referring to the band of cholesterol deposited in the cornea). The secretary typed this with some inventiveness as, 'On examination he had a very prominent *arsus sensitis*.'

On the professorial ward we got one half-day off every three weeks. On admission days the houseman had to examine and write up all ten or more admissions (sometimes helped by the Registrar), that is to say one of the Petes, who would do a ward round on Thursday and Sunday morning followed by Professor Hill or one of the other consultants. Days after admissions and before the next were busy with treating and discharging the sick. As we were both on call every third Sunday, that left two out of three Sundays when we were not admitting. On one of these I got the afternoon and night off, and on the other Robin Kell did. I remember being so tired that on one occasion, the following morning, I became very cross with the night nurse who was about to go off duty. 'Who on earth told you to do that?' 'You did, when I phoned you at four o'clock and asked you to come and see him, and that was what you told me to do before going back to sleep'.

Jenny was engaged in something pretty similar on Messrs Sturrock and Soutar's surgical ward, (where there was also a very keen neurosurgeon called Joe Bloch, who, however, had no beds). So she and I rarely met. Mr Soutar's wife (Ma Soutar) used to anesthetise for her husband's morning list. She would regularly go off in the middle of the list to put the lunch on, with the anaesthetic apparatus and hypoxic patient left in the even more incapable hands of the houseman or theatre nurse. Patients who woke up afterwards were not always all there.

PRESIDENT KENNEDY'S ASSASSINATION

I well remember on 22nd November 1963 meeting Jenny in the corridor and her telling me with horror that President Kennedy had been assassinated. Kennedy's death was felt particularly personally, but maybe would have been less so had we known more about his philandering. His murder was followed a day or two later by the assassination on television of chief suspect Lee Harvey Oswald, followed by that of Oswald's killer, Jack Ruby. Jackie Kennedy of course, had been trapped in a failing marriage, and not long after her husband's death, for doubtful reasons she married the Greek shipping tycoon Aristotle Onassis. Many years later I heard Dr Michael O'Donnell (editor of an excellent freebie medical journal *World Medicine*) tell a probably apocryphal story about when Mao Tse Dung was visited by a delegation of Irish doctors. He was in a good mood and welcomed the visitors into his bedroom. 'You are especially fortunate that Chairman Mao is in a good mood and will answer one question from each of you'. After some fairly bland questions about Traditional Chinese Medicine and Sino-Irish medical relations, the final delegate said, 'I would like to ask Chairman Mao what he believes would have happened if Krushchev had been assassinated and not President Kennedy?'. His reply eventually come back through the translator. 'Chairman Mao thanks you for your question and says that if Khrushchev had been assassinated and not Kennedy, only one thing is certain. Aristotle Onassis would not have married Mrs Khrushchev.'

That reminds me that ten years or more later I had a brief period when I used to write short satirical articles for *World Medicine*, which Michael O'Donnell seemed to like. I remember seeing a film sponsored by Schering on female sexuality, which was topical at the time due to the work of two people called Masters and Bates (or maybe it was Masters and Johnson). This led me to write an article which I entitled '*Sheer, Boring, Schering Porn*'. I tried to describe in print what was shown, using neologisms in place of offensive words - for example I described how this naked lady was shown to modulate herself up to and including the Oregon. Arguing that it was really not necessary to claim this was a serious scientific study I wrote; "Because it is there' may be a good reason to climb Mount Everest, but hardly to film the *Mons Pubis*.' This incensed a humourless female sexologist enough for her to accuse me in print of being, 'Ill at ease with his own sexuality'. Actually, by then I no longer was.

One of Professor Hill's mildly irritating quirks was that after his ward round he expected his housemen to accompany him down to his car. My predecessor had been Charlie Wardrop, who had managed to upset the Prof in many ways including failing to say why he was going off one weekend - it was to get married - and refusing to take part in the car park ritual. This had inflamed in Professor Hill a profound hatred for Charlie, of which I, as next houseman, was a beneficiary. I was in any case not going to fan the flames of a small but otherwise benign boss in this way, unless some life or death occurrence was taking place on the wards. He had enough problems of his own at home with a heroin-addicted wife.

A SECOND (AND SURGICAL) HOUSEJOB; EVEN DEEPER IN.

My second house job was surgical, and at Perth Royal Infirmary. Generally, plum professorial surgical jobs were reserved for any new graduates who were seen as potential surgeons (of course by actual surgeons, thus ensuring the cloning of this fearlessly incisive type of doctor). Despite my impeccable surgical family pedigree I did not fall into this category. I think I used to ask too many questions. So instead, I took a busy surgical job at Perth Royal Infirmary with a certain Mr Conal Charleson. I remember Tom Heyworth, who preceded me at Perth, saying it was a great housejob for getting experience with managing surgical emergencies, for the simple reason that Mr Charleson had been in every emergency imaginable, generally of his own making. I thought he was joking, but he wasn't. Conal would sometimes get completely the wrong end of the surgical stick, though he was certainly competent at some things, such as the Polya gastrectomy. His opposite number, Mr Kirkpatrick preferred the gastrostomy and pyloroplasty - these were the days way before the discovery in 1982, by an Australian doctor called Barry Marshall, that stomach and duodenal ulcers were caused by a micro-organism, *Helicobacter pylori*, and should mainly be treated with antibiotics. In my student days it was known that ulcers were caused by stress, and in an exam to say they were caused by an infection would probably have caused you to fail. One of the standard treatments for an active peptic ulcer was to put up a milk drip via a tube in the stomach. Full cream of course.

I soon learnt that despite the fact that Perth Royal Infirmary received a fair number of head injuries, Mr Charleson had some strangely passive ideas about the simplest neurosurgery, and in fact knew even less than I had picked up in my three-week clerkship at the Glasgow's Neurosurgical Centre. We were just three surgical housemen, Jo Nicholson, myself, and a slightly better qualified SHO who in the daytime ran Casualty. We covered each other's off duty, and during the early hours of February 6th 1966 (theatre day) I was called down to Casualty to see a young man who had come off his motorbike, and had been knocked unconscious. He had blood coming out of one ear, and had recovered consciousness, but this didn't last long. He had a classical lucid interval, before lapsing into unconsciousness again, an obvious indicator of a ruptured middle meningeal artery, and extradural haemorrhage. I called first the Senior Registrar, Dr Chandra Chud, but he was busy, so I contacted Mr Charleson, who was about to start his cold case list. He was not going to interrupt his plans to remove a lady's gall bladder, for the opinion of a new and untried houseman. He did not want to do a burr hole on a dying man, on such slender evidence as a classical history, blood coming out of an ear and a dilating pupil. I was told to infuse hypertonic saline or something, and then to do a lumbar puncture to see if there was blood in the CSF - an absolutely elementary error, but something that was necessary in order to persuade my boss. He had some crackpot idea that if after a head injury there was blood in the (subdural) CSF it would exclude bleeding into the extradural space. My lumbar puncture was with the finest needle for the shortest time ever used, and to my relief I avoided causing coning of the *medulla oblongata*. Not surprisingly there was blood, so Conal was reassured for the wrong reason.

When I got out of theatre the patient was dead, and I found Chandra had actually issued a death certificate. Furious, I called the relatives and said there had been a clear misunderstanding, and that we needed to learn any lessons from their son's case. They agreed to an autopsy, which next day revealed a ruptured right middle meningeal artery, a massive extradural haematoma, and a very contrite Conal Charleson and Chandra Chud. This was in the days before audit, but word definitely got back to the neurosurgeon at Dundee Royal Infirmary, where the bedless neurosurgeon Joe Bloch was furious. My boss was not held in the highest regard by his surgical colleagues in Dundee. I should have known when Tom Heyworth had warned me. 'One day Conal was operating on a femoral hernia and he nicked the femoral artery. Somewhere he had read that the right thing to do was to clamp it off, and then to cut it across to make it easier to suture! Where he got this from I have no idea. But he phoned Prof Douglas, at DRI. 'Hello, Charleson here, just had a spot of bother - nicked the femoral artery doing a femoral hernia repair - might have happened to anyone - but not to worry, I am sending him across by ambulance. By the way, I've done the right thing, I've clamped it off and cut right through the artery to make your job easier.' 'You did WHAT?!!!'

Funny to think how six months of nightmares early in one's career comes flooding back more than half a century later. Like later on, when I had a similar casualty experience to the February one, and another patient with a skull fracture and deteriorating consciousness came in. There was for some reason no senior back-up so, helped by Jo Nicholson my fellow houseman, and with the patient dying, I did a burr hole myself. It revealed that the patient had massive brain damage, astronomic intracranial pressure, but no extra-dural, and of course he still died. Conal was shocked, but very nice when I told him, still feeling contrite about the patient he could so easily have saved had he listened to me. He had a word with the Procurator Fiscal, and no action was taken, because I had meant well, I suppose.

A PATIENT GIVES ME A WEDDING PRESENT

There is one final Perth Royal Infirmary story I must record. This was three weeks from the end of my job, and so in late

June (since I had stored up two weeks holiday). Jenny and I were due to get married in Burford Parish Church on July 18th. By now I had grown to know when to ignore my boss, and although I was clearly no surgeon (neither it had turned out was he), I was on the way to becoming a reasonable physician and knew a bit about fluid and electrolytes. As I have said he liked doing gastrectomies and this particular private patient, a lady, had had a pyloroplasty done elsewhere for an ulcer, and her stomach pain was no better. He decided to convert it into a Polya gastrectomy, his preferred procedure. (Don't worry about the details, just accept that given the premises in question it made some sense). At surgery, the peritoneal cavity was full of adhesions, and so the surgical field was a dense fibrous fog. He first closed off the outlet of the pyloroplasty, and as the position was confused decided just to leave the stomach draining through the duodenum (which was also obscured) as normal. Post-operatively the patient started to vomit. I put a nasogastgric tube down, and an intravenous drip up to replace lost fluid and minerals. I kept a close eye on what one patient called her 'electric lights'. I was on medical home ground. Next morning Conal told me to take the drip down. I did so, but her vomiting continued, so I infused her again overnight, and took the drip down before the ward round next day. After five days of this clandestine night-time infusion we are at the weekend. The Senior Registrar Chandra Chud knew what I was doing, and said, 'Leave it to me at the weekend'. When I came back on Monday, Chandra was chortling with glee. 'What happened?' I asked. 'You aren't going to believe this. She continued to vomit, and on Sunday he took her back to theatre, and guess what? He had closed off the only exit from the stomach and had just left a blind pouch! It had been a Polya not a pyloroplasty all along.' When the patient left the ward she kindly gave me five pounds as a wedding present for saving her life, (though she may not have known it).

Conal invited both housemen and the Casualty doctor to his home for a farewell dinner. He was a keen gardener, and loved his roses, and there was a ritual, where the men all went out after dinner, stood in a line, and sprayed the roses with cheap natural liquid nitrogen-containing fertiliser. He gave me a silver propelling pencil as a thank you present for looking after all his private patients, and saving some of their lives. One thing I learnt from my surgical house job was that it is not enough just to have a good bedside manner, as he had. In fact, when push comes to shove it is better to be rude but competent, than pleasant but incompetent. Best of course to be both nice and competent.

CHAPTER 5

EARLY MARRIED LIFE

JULY 18TH 1964, BURFORD PARISH CHURCH

Meanwhile Jenny was doing her six months in Medicine at Dundee Royal Infirmary, on the same professorial firm as I had. We met occasionally - basically one Sunday afternoon every three weeks, for reasons already given. But though exhausted, she was also young. We invited Professor Hill and his two consultants to come to the wedding, which might have encouraged them to give her an extra day off, but didn't. And we drove FUV down to Burford on Thursday afternoon, July 16th. We were to get all of two weeks off before returning to new jobs, me as Registrar in Renal Medicine, and Jenny as Senior House Officer in Ophthalmology.

The wedding took place in Burford's spectacular church, presided over by Uncle Ted, Dad's brother and an anglican vicar. From photo albums we both look remarkably fresh and happy (see illustrations). We were to take our honeymoon in Yugoslavia (Croatia as it now is) in Korçula for the first week, and then Dubrovnik. This was booked through an unreliable travel agent called Yugotours. It seems mad with hindsight, but after the wedding reception, lunch and speeches, we changed clothes, left by taxi and took a train to London. There we stayed the night in a cheap hotel and flew off early the next morning. Complete insanity that, to miss one's own wedding reception party, which everyone said was very good; indeed so good that one of the guests woke up in a ditch. We flew to Dubrovnik and caught the late ferry to Korçula, arriving at 3 am. I had booked a room overlooking the sea, but by the time we got to the hotel (lugging suitcases through the dimly lit town), we found we had no room. After much fuss in German, we were given a room with a single bed, and the occupant's luggage and clothes still in the cupboard. We did eventually get a double room all to ourselves, but Jenny spent three days sick from honeymoon cystitis, which newly wed women got in those days.

We spent the second week of our honeymoon in a hotel on the outskirts of the spectacular town of Dubrovnik, which had been strongly recommended by my parents. I blush when I recall how irresponsible I could be back then. Not much has changed, I suppose. A long distance off the hotel beach, the best part of a mile away, was a small uninhabited island, and I decided to swim there, and then of course back again. Jenny was impressed with my swimming ability, but nothing else, as I got out of the water an hour later, tired but elated. Years later I read that this part of the mediterranean is a favourite breeding-ground for the Great White Shark. Of course even now you won't read that in the tourist brochures. When we got home, I expended some energy on an acrimonious correspondence with Yugotours over not getting what I had paid for in Korçula, and was accused of being a fascist; but at least I got a small refund.

We began our married life in a rented flat at the top of Airlie Terrace with no lock on the door, and a proprietor who lived downstairs. I think she had an old-fashioned view of when and where young newly-weds got up to hanky-panky. I remember one or two narrow escapes. I started to work as Registrar in

Renal Medicine at Maryfield Hospital with Dr W K (Bill) Stewart. The hospital had a couple of Kolff haemodialysis machines, and I soon introduced the technique of peritoneal dialysis, which was still in its relative infancy. I got on well with Bill, who had a reputation of being beastly to his staff, but was good to me. He was a great one for research ideas and had an assistant, Lorna, whose job it was to put them into effect. I got involved in lots of projects, far too many in fact, as it was made clear that serious academics would pass their Membership examination with minimum fuss and maximum speed.

HOW TO GET A NERVOUS BREAKDOWN

Jenny, meanwhile, was doing sensible things like getting trained, working on the Eye Unit at Dundee Royal Infirmary. We didn't want to delay starting a family, and fairly soon after a precaution-spent six months, without difficulty she became pregnant, and we decided it was time to buy a house. We bought one that was being built, in Cults Gardens, on a new estate just outside Dundee. Still having done no further studying for the MRCP examination, my mind full of projects and building up a small Renal Unit, we took our annual holiday in my in-laws' house in Burford. Rather than relax and play golf with Pard, I decided to swot, a decision that was to prove disastrous, because over not much more than a week I couldn't sleep and developed a severe anxiety state. I soon developed severe depressive thoughts, and guilt became overpowering. The pressure of becoming a father, being an academic failure, and half-baked research studies took its toll as I passed into a severe and acute depression. These were the days before anxiolytic drugs such as Xanax, with which I would now cautiously self-medicate if a similar situation arose. I was soon having suicidal thoughts, and realised that I was becoming a danger to myself, so I pushed to be seen by the Senior Lecturer in Psychiatry, Dr Peter Aungle. After a couple of days, by now profoundly depressed and contemplating suicide, he had me admitted as a voluntary patient to Liff Hospital.

RECOVERY AND A MAN CALLED JOHANN

I won't say having a self-driven depressive illness is something I would recommend, but this experience undoubtedly gave me a new perspective on life. As I recall, I was treated with imipramine and quite soon I found that I had periods where I felt back to normal, alternating with a return to severe depression. I even prayed once or twice, but it didn't last. Dr Aungle was very positive and reassuring, and I got a lot from the other patients, some of whom were really away with the fairies. I remember with affection a German-speaking Pole, called Johann Mowinsky, who had, like many Poles, married a Dundee lass. Johann was hypomanic and extremely paranoid about another patient, a Ukrainian, who he probably correctly read as being a vicious Nazi. Johann had an interesting wartime story, having been recruited by the Germans, and sent into Russia with the Polish army, to spy. He was a major, and one of twelve officers infiltrated in this way, but got on well with his men. After capture the Russians wanted to sort out the Polish army officers (who were then led off to be massacred in the forest of Katyn). The captives at first refused to denounce the officers, and so were lined up and every tenth man was taken off and shot. The man next to him asked Johann to swop places, because he had a wife and children, and Johann obliged. But the man had miscounted by one and was shot, while Johann was spared. They then inspected each captive's hands. Smooth hands marked you as an officer, but he said his were smooth because he was a butcher (he had worked on his uncle's farm). 'Prove it'. 'Give me a sharp knife and that cow'. He slit the standing cow's jugular vein, and proceeded to drink the blood spurting from it, (as he had seen done on his uncle's farm);

and that convinced the Russians he was telling the truth. The ordinary soldiers were released to work in Russia, and Johann picked up some information on troop movements useful to the Germans, eventually escaping before the German invasion, on a train back to the border and into Germany. His information was so useful that he was invited to have a cup of tea with Adolf Hitler, who he described as the most charming man he had ever met. Of the planted German-Polish officers he was the only one to return. I kept up with Johann on discharge, and was saddened when he died of a lymphoma a couple of years later. I still have a passably good water-colour portrait I did of him when I was recovering (see illustrations).

Jenny was terrific, and soon after my discharge and moving into our new house, our first son, Kenneth, was born. After this mental breakdown I think I felt under less pressure at work, as it was realised I was human. I now studied more sensibly, took time off, and when on holiday played golf with Pard. But renal medicine was still stressful. We had a nurse who was over-confident and I remember a ten-year-old girl was being dialysed; at the end the blood in the machine was returned to the patient by running saline into the system, which had no safety mechanism. The nurse wandered off, forgot what she was doing, and I was called from the office in a panic to find the girl was unconscious and the best part of a litre of air had been pumped into her circulation. For lack of any better idea I started to do external cardiac massage, and amazingly she gradually responded as the frothy blood was forced from the right ventricle out into the lungs. Miraculously the little girl recovered from this disaster apparently unscathed, only to die later from her chronic renal failure.

I wrote a paper on declotting arterio-venous shunts, with my classmate Tony Martin, who was working on the much more sophisticated Renal Unit in Edinburgh. Three years after qualifying I took not one, but two MRCP examinations - in London and in Edinburgh. Professor Sir Ian Hill was President of the Royal College of Physicians of Edinburgh, as well as the Queen's physician, and it would not have looked good just to take the London one. I took the Edinburgh exam with the special subject being renal disease, and passed both without difficulty.

ON ALCOHOL, SAILING AND CAPSIZING

There was another old Rugbean, who I had met again when I went to Dundee. He became a good friend, was studying Scottish Law, enjoyed sailing and in those days still had an Old Rugbean wild streak, which his girlfriend, who was a daughter of the Manse, distinctly lacked. She was single-mindedly out to tame her man, something I thought was never going to work. For a start, she was teetotal, and Paul was the opposite. When they got married, the reception was held in a 'totally tee' Dundee hotel. After the service we went with the groom's father to the pub next door; then later, gently alcoholised, we toasted bride and groom with concentrated orange juice, which I interpreted as some sort of *Wee Free* compromise drink - 'It's not alcohol, but at least it's disgusting'. My friend was a keen sailor, and shortly after they married, but before his wife had given up alcohol for him, he was caught out in the open sea in a storm, and had to be rescued by an Air Sea Rescue helicopter from RAF Leuchars. Wanting to reward his rescuers, some weeks later he bought a case of whisky for their mess Christmas party, which of course he also attended. I think it was cheaper than paying the Air Sea Rescue fee. Jenny and I once visited them as newly weds in Edinburgh, and knowing Paul enjoyed whisky, we brought a bottle of the finest ten year-old Glenfiddich Malt. His now-beloved saw it and without a moment's hesitation poured it straight down the kitchen sink. Who says an alcoholic has to give up for himself, and no one else can do it for him?

Many years later, we went and looked them up in Fife. He had become a revered and staid solicitor in a small Scottish town, was a completely reformed one man alcohol-free zone, and a perfect example to his three Wee Free children. He was barely recognisable, but I guess that's what being a lawyer does to you.

A CAREER MOVE TO LONDON AND THE HAMMERSMITH

For some reason I was regarded as being a suitable candidate for Professor Hill to recommend to Prof Christopher Booth, a former protegé and Dundee whiz-kid, and by then head of the Royal Postgraduate Medical School, at Hammersmith Hospital, London. This was a well-trodden path, and I had been preceded by Alastair Breckenridge, who was regarded as the brightest student to come out of Dundee. It was said unkindly that anyone who doubted this had only to ask him. I was advised that I needed more general training, as it seemed I was specialising too early in my career. So I applied for a job as Registrar to Professor T Russell Fraser, a renowned clinical endocrinologist. The Appointments Committee at the Hammersmith interviewed for twelve registrar posts at the same time. After the interview, I was informed that I had been successful, but instead of Russell Fraser's job, I was being offered one with Dr Cuthbert Cope, a world authority and noted author on the adrenal cortex. So, slightly bemused, of course I accepted. It would have been more than my life was worth to do otherwise.

Jenny was by now well on into her second pregnancy and about to give birth to what turned out to be our second son, Bruce. She had not been idle, had passed the Diploma in Ophthalmology, and seemed set on a career as an ophthalmic surgeon. We sold our Dundee House and bought one in Princes Gardens, West Acton, two stops down the line from the Hammersmith Hospital, in East Acton. Cuthbert Cope was in many ways the antithesis of the Hammersmith academic, as embodied by Russell Fraser, Chris Booth and Professor Dame Sheila Sherlock. Cuthbert greatly resented change, and regarded newcomers to his Unit with immense suspicion. He thought I was both too young and too keen, and this seemed to be reinforced by my predecessor as Registrar, Chris Burke, who used to stand at the back of ward rounds muttering agreement whenever I had transgressed in Cuthbert's eyes (which was frequently). My opposite number Colin Beardwell was very congenial, and helped me by pointing out many of the do's and don'ts one had to pass through as part of one's initiation.

HOW TO UPSET CUTHBERT L COPE

Now, from the point of view of clinical medicine the job was not exactly arduous. As far as I recall, we had one admitting day a week, and usually had about 5 patients on each of the male and female wards. Cuthbert did two ward rounds a week, one on the male and one on the female ward, and though there was also a houseman, every communication with Cuthbert had to be done through the registrar, who was a sort of primary filter. You had to have a very good reason to tell Cuthbert about a female patient on the day of the male round and vice versa. He would give a very good opinion if information was given to him at the right level - but he would go intercontinentally ballistic if asked about something lesser, which he classified as a 'registrar decision'. Other things he would not tolerate included discussing research on a ward round, which was something that was obligatory on all other Units. He would go mad if he wasn't told about a problem, and equally mad if he was. There was a delicate path to tread, and if in doubt it was useful to warn him that he was going to go mad, as this would have some restraining effect. I counted eighteen ways to make this otherwise genial old man furious, tried each of them at least once, and just before the

Christmas party, when attacked for something else, tearfully told him what I thought of him. To be fair, this did lead to some subsequent restraint, but I was mainly saved by Colin taking on a research job, and being replaced on the wards by a Dr John Wales. John was a definite whizz-kid, who was so whizz that he was appointed without his membership (MRCP). He had spent several years doing high-powered research in the USA, something referred to as getting his BTA - (Been to America). You were supposed to get the MRCP first.

EARLY ENDOCRINOLOGY RESEARCH

Cuthbert was quite old-fashioned and was approaching retirement, and expressed distress at my wish, which was in fact a Hammersmith survival requirement, to do research. 'Anderson wants to do research, but what's the point?' he would mutter at the back of the ward round, and Burke, who was moving from a year of house-rebuilding, to research on a clever technique called steady-state gel filtration, could only agree. I wanted to measure Vitamin D, but that was too difficult so in the end went for testosterone, using a method called competitive protein binding. I also worked on a method to measure sex hormone-binding globulin (SHBG), and got some mediocre papers published. There was a very keen lad called John Marshall, working for Professor Fraser, and we did some things together because he was developing a radio-immunoasay method for measuring luteinising hormone (LH). Together we worked on what was called a clomiphene stimulation test, which involved taking high doses of the drug clomiphene citrate that turned out to drive you mad over a week. This plunged me over a period of seven days into another profound depression, which I later recognised to be the nearest to premenstrual depression that a man can get, clomiphene being an anti-oestrogen. I recovered within days of stopping it, to find that John Marshall and Chris Burke, who had both also been normal subjects taking this pernicious drug, had come to blows and nearly killed one another. I don't think either had the insight to blame the drug. Never mind, in the end John and I published a paper on the blood results. He had a fearsome car called an AC Cobra, which could do 0 to 60 mph in three seconds or less. John took Cuthbert out for a ride in it one day, and the old boy nearly died of fright.

It was the arrival of John Wales that definitely saved my professional life in the eyes of Cuthbert Cope. John was off to a bad start by not having his Membership, but despite my giving him tutorials on the do's and dont's before each and every ward round he still managed to try out the eighteen infallible ways of driving him mad from a standing start, many of them more than once. By then I was the one to be trusted, for the simple reason that although I was still judged to be too young, he had got used to me. When Cuthbert retired, his beds were taken over by Professor Chris Booth, and then donated to another very keen gastro-enterologist, Herman Dowling. His attitude was the exact opposite to that of Cuthbert, so I had to relearn bad habits, such as discussing research on ward rounds.

One of the excellent things about the Hammersmith was the Wednesday Grand Round, where in turns it was every medical registrar's lot to present an interesting case to the whole of the assembled Medical Departments. I enjoyed this, and also developed a technique for asking questions, which was very simple - to write them on my notes, and put a circle round them. I have never had a problem with ideas, and Chris Burke once complimented me by saying I was an 'ideas man' while he saw himself as a 'hole-in-the-road man'. I hadn't until then realised how often, when you see a hole in the road, you will find a man at the bottom willing to answer questions.

David Coussmaker Anderson

A FAMILY NEAR-DISASTER

You may recall how I had decided to become a doctor at age five, after my surgeon uncle had removed my acutely inflamed appendix, and so got rid of my tummy pains. I made my mind up then and never changed it. It was only when I was working at the Hammersmith twenty-four years later that I experienced the flip side of a willingness to treat sick relatives. I do not mean that you should wash your hands and ask no questions, as one colleague in the Hammersmith did when his infant son developed severe diarrhoea, and he stood by while fellow doctors let him die from dehydration. In my opinion, your role when confronted with a sick relative, unless you are the only person available, is to direct them to the best colleague you trust to deal with the problem, then to stay informed and continue to use your brain.

In the summer of 1969, my brother Antony had been chronically unwell for some time and was attending doctors in Dundee. Our mother was understandably concerned, and when Antony came home she phoned her brother, who was indeed an eminent surgeon, but that is not the point. He was seen and almost immediately admitted to Barts where his appendix was removed. He was discharged home but then developed a high fever, and had to be readmitted. Despite antibiotics and further surgery for a suspected subphrenic abscess he became progressively sicker. I was throughout obviously in an invidious position as a concerned medical brother. Meanwhile my uncle, unknown to us at the time, was himself ill with leukaemia, from which he died within the year.

Increasingly worried, I connected directly with the surgical Senior Registrar at Barts, Mr Rothwell Jackson, who handled a delicate situation decisively but with great sensitivity. I remembered that Antony had had dysentery as a child in India. And I was fortified by having not long before seen and diagnosed a case of liver abscess in Dundee, based on an unusually high serum alkaline phosphatase level, which Antony also had. Those were the days before abdominal ultrasound, let alone imaging by computer tomography. Eventually a massive liver abscess was drained, and Antony recovered completely on the anti-amoebic antibiotic metronidazole. The probability is that all along he had had an undiagnosed amoebic liver abscess.

While at the Hammersmith, as well as conducting research I also improved my knowledge of basic biochemistry, which was distinctly rusty, by going to Chelsea College one half day a week for two years on an MSc course. I went with another Hammersmith registrar, Ted Gordon-Smith, who was on his way to becoming an eminent haematologist. We used to start with lunch in a wine bar, which meant that if the lecture was especially boring I could fall asleep undisturbed. Somehow I got a distinction. Ted worked for Professor Dacie, who had a reputation as being a rather humourless man, but in his spare time was also an eminent entomologist. I understand that when he retired his staff gave him a book entitled *Advice for Expectant Moth-ers*.

DANGERS OF A LITTLE KNOWLEDGE

I said I would write some stories against myself, as I have had at least three seriously embarrassing memories, but on second thoughts I think I have already said enough. The only other one I'll give you now is when I was in Glenshee with my brother Stuart, in our old Singer Gazelle, and it was very cold and we came off the frozen slopes very late. When the engine finally started it was spluttering and large volumes of water were exiting from the exhaust. Not wishing to run the risk of a burst gasket, which I had read about, and maybe even seen, I phoned the nearest garage in Blairgowrie, for breakdown assistance, which arrived an hour later. We were hoisted up and towed, nose in the air, to the garage, to find on arrival that there was nothing wrong that condensation did not account for. If you want to hear a more detailed and entertaining version ask Stuart, who remembers it better than I do. But the punch line is that a little knowledge is a dangerous thing.

FINALLY A JOB AT BARTS

When a Lecturer in Medicine post came up at St Bartholomew's Hospital I was encouraged by the Barts-based endocrinologist Professor Mike Besser, to apply. I think he was impressed with my work on testosterone and sex hormone-binding globulin (SHBG). So in 1971 I finally ended up in Barts, quite possibly the only person to do so having had the affront to turn down a place there as a medical student. At Barts I continued mainly to work in the lab, and wrote with Chris Burke what may well have been my best-regarded paper, entitled *Sex Hormone-binding Globulin is an Estrogen Amplifier*. Actually, the conclusions were probably in the main wrong, but by the time I had spotted the fallacy it had been published in *Nature*.

The Department of Medicine was under the direction of a Professor Eric Scowen, a rotund little man with a sliding gait. I remember the Outpatient Department had very thin walls, and a very loud but observant elderly lady leant over the table and in her penetrating voice said to me, 'Professor Scowen, doctor?' 'What about him,?' I whispered back. 'Professor Scowen,' she repeated loudly...'is there something wrong with him?' She was right, there was, but I was curious to know what she meant. 'What do you mean, Mrs Smith?' I asked. 'Well' she replied, again in a penetrating voice heard throughout Outpatients, 'It's when he walks - he sort of slithers along'. It was indeed a perfect description of a gait as if on runners of this eminent,

Where Angels Fear to Tread

but distinctly slippery old man, who wore a white coat that was two sizes too long. He was later knighted, because he ran the Safety of Medicines Committee, which had been set up in the wake of the Thalidomide Disaster of a decade before. Professor Sir Eric Scowen expected that his lecturers would go on his ward rounds, where he prided himself on his clinical acumen, and used to engage in diagnostic mind games with his juniors from the bottom of the bed. After being given a brief history he might say... 'Is it what it sounds like or the other thing?' It was important to reply obliquely. 'Well quite surprisingly there's no eosinophilia', might come the most intelligent cryptic reply. 'Ah, and the Babinski'? 'Negative, Sir Eric; so should we do an LP?' 'Let's talk about that over coffee'. We would then repair for coffee to talk about other things. His ward rounds were as incomprehensible as they were short. He was once described as being a legend in his own lunchtime.

At Barts I spent most of my working days in Professor John Landon's laboratory in Bartholomew Close, a stone's throw from Smithfield meat market, working on sex hormone-binding globulin, and also giving work to a keen young scientist called Roy Fisher. I was trying to finish my own thesis, which was taking for ever. There were some very clever people there, not all of whom were as bright in their extra-curricular activities. They were definitely soft targets for females with a predisposition to acute under-garment divestment. This applied especially to an absolutely ghastly woman called Julia Popovic, who I understood was wife of the Bulgarian ambassador, who had come to study something to do with sperm motility. She would sidle up to Roy and me and say, 'Oh David I so interested in sex-binding-globulin, please will you show me'... 'No not now, Julia; and by the way it is called sex **hormone**-binding globulin'.... 'Never mind', she would say 'plis you show me jus the same'! We were all convinced she was a Bulgarian spy. Anyway she was extremely bad at science, so her talents must have lain elsewhere, maybe upon locked office floors after hours or during coffee-breaks. It was rumoured on good authority that she didn't wear knickers; at the Christmas party Roy and I did a sex-binding-globulin skit with me playing the part of a visiting research fellow called Julia Poppanickasoff.

MEMORIES OF THE SOCIETY FOR ENDOCRINOLOGY

Once it had become clear that my career was now headed for endocrinology rather than renal medicine, I was invited to join the Society for Endocrinology, which was a typically low-key British organisation, and in those days dominated by zoologists. Once a year it met for its Spring meeting in the London zoo at Regent's Park. Every second year it also held a meeting jointly with the Dutch Endocrine Society. One such year, after we had returned from the USA, I went to this joint meeting in a small town called Domburg. The meeting was held in the Bad Hotel, which was actually quite good, but was due to be demolished the week after our meeting. One of the simultaneous sessions was conducted in a room with a bar at the back, accompanied by the clink of beer glasses. The following week Jenny and I drove with Chris Burke to Hamburg for the International Society for Endocrinology meeting. Chris's marriage was on the rocks, but at the meeting he found a nice young woman endocrinologist who was also bored with life, and the four of us booked for the Conference dinner. Chris and I were both horrified to hear of the cost which was something like forty Marks per person, and that didn't include drinks. Wine was due to cost sixteen Marks a bottle, and he and I schemed how to survive. The prospect of Germanic conference speeches was bad enough. So in the end we went to an off-licence, bought three bottles of riesling at four marks a bottle, and put them in the fridge. I booked us on the table immediately next to the distinguished speakers. I then went out to look for a cork screw, and found a promising-looking hardware store. 'Ich möchte eine Korkenzier kaufen, bitte', I said in passable German with an English accent. 'Wie bitte?' came the irritated reply. 'Ich möchte eine Korkenzier kaufen, bitte', I repeated. 'Are you Enklish?' he replied, clearly annoyed. 'Yahwohl' I replied. 'Zen vot is it you vant?' Whereupon I gave up. 'I would like to buy a cork-screw, please', I said, meekly giving in. 'So you vant a cork screw??? Zen vy didn't you say so in ze first place?'

So we now have three bottles of cheap wine, a cork screw, a plan, and two definitely embarrassed young women (one a wife, one an Other). We are sitting right plonk next to the dignitaries in an already overpriced conference dinner, with three bottles of cheap but cooled riesling concealed in two bulging conference bags under the table. I summoned the head waiter from the high table, and produced as if by magic a bottle. 'I am so sorry, but would you please be good enough to cork this bottle of a riesling which I particularly like'? At first he refused, but seeing a potential row brewing close to the dignitaries he said 'It is highly irregular, but I will - it will cost you ten marks!' 'Done!' I said and handed him the money. Thereafter when no-one was looking, or during the speeches, I would remove the now empty bottle, exchange it for an unopened one from under the table, and remove the *korken* with said uncomprehending *zieher* and deftly put the new bottle on the table, like Elijah's widow's cruise but at a profit, and filled with wine rather than oil. We enjoyed a good, but overpriced dinner on a table that was now both happy and impressed. And by my calculations we had saved forty-eight marks, less the cost of the cork screw which I may still have.

THE CHAIRMAN'S ROLE

As one's Endocrinology career advanced, even quite junior endocrinologists were asked to chair obscure break-out sessions, held in rooms in remote parts of the grounds of the London Zoo. On one such occasion I was designated to chair the last session of the day in a small remote lecture theatre, within howling distance of a cage of bemused gibbons, and the theme was sex hormones. Whenever I was chairman I always noted down questions as they came to me during the presentation, feeling that the speaker deserved at least one, and there was no guarantee than anyone else would ask it. The last paper of the day was given by a very nervous young Middle-Eastern lady research-fellow on the effect of the contraceptive pill on liver function, which seemed a relevant topic at the time. The audience consisted of me as chairman and about twelve others, most of whom were asleep. Her title was *The Effect of Oral Contraceptives on the Rodent Liver*; and in her introduction, Miss Sarfat spoke at length about how and why the rat was an excellent model for the human liver. She then proceeded to describe a series of experiments on the mouse liver, so I noted down my default question. It seemed that her results showed that there was no effect in the mouse. 'Thank you, Miss Sarfat, are there any questions from the audience?' No obliging hand was raised. 'Well, in that case I would like to ask one from the Chair. You said at the start of your talk that the rat is a very good model for the human liver, and you then proceeded to describe the effect of the oral contraceptive on the liver of the mouse.' She giggled a bit. 'So, Miss Sarfat', I continued, 'is the mouse also a good model for the human liver?' 'No', she replied, 'he is wery bad model'. Scenting chairmania I went in for the kill. 'If the rat is a very good model and the mouse a very bad model, why did you choose the mouse?' She looked a little embarrassed and then replied with a blush, 'I choose ze mouse because I am not scared of him!'

AN AFRICAN HOLIDAY TO REMEMBER, AND INTO A CONRAN'S HEART OF DARKNESS

I wasn't entirely happy continuing with academic medicine, and had always had a hankering to work overseas. I toyed with the idea of taking a job in Chandigar, a new Medical School in north India, but nothing came of that. Then in early 1972 my brother-in-law Rupert Hughes came to lunch one Sunday with a good friend of his, Kevin O'Sullivan. Kevin, who ran an engineering survey company called T P O'Sullivan and partners, had found the love of his life, the famous Shirley Conran, and was due to marry her in six weeks or so. She had recently rid herself of her first husband Terence, and was later to write a titillating best-seller entitled *Lace.* Anyway, Kevin's company TPO had just completed an important project called the Trans-African Highway Study, with the ambitious task of mapping out the best road across five countries in densest, darkest central Africa, from Kenya in the East, through Uganda, Zaire, and the Central African Republic (CAR), to Cameroon in the West. They had used two Land Rovers to execute the survey, and the report on the different options was almost complete. One of the Land Rovers had been driven back to Kenya by the survey team, while the second was parked in Bangui in the CAR ready to be driven back later. In less than a month Kevin was due to fly to Bangui to present the report, and he had planned to drive the vehicle back, accompanied by his mother, who by all accounts was a formidable woman; but she had fractured something so couldn't come. 'So are either of you interested in joining me?' asked Kevin over Jenny's excellent Sunday lunch. Well, it certainly had some appeal, but there were three problems. First was taking two weeks off work, which did not seem insuperable. Second was paying for the airfare. And the most serious was that Jenny was about to leave her ophthalmology job and join a General Practice, a spousal career change that was not to be taken lightly.

Well, the decision was made easier by my mother who jumped at the idea and offered me £250 as a gift for the air fare. I must admit, it was an extremely (many would say typically) selfish decision, but with some pressure from Rupert and Kevin (eg, 'We'll need a medical member of the team after all, and you would be ideal, as you also speak good French'), with some fake hesitation I took it. And, persistent guilt aside, I never regretted doing so; now forty-five years later, I think my wife has forgiven but she has certainly not forgotten, (or is it the other way round?) Kevin went on ahead as he had the all-important conference to attend; but as he was about to get married he needed to put some things in order for his upcoming career as Shirley's second (and ultimately her most despised) husband. So one Sunday morning I was charged with taking some stuff round to her flat somewhere in the posh part of London. I was greeted at the door by a bleery-eyed and somewhat tetchy woman a nightdress, who did not strike me as the glamour-girl in anyone's mind's eye. She seemed to be distinctly unamused at being woken by this medical squit-friend of her beloved-to-be. I said who I was, delivered the goods, and parted without a cup of coffee. It was not a good first impression (or indeed last one, as I'm not sure we ever met again). Later, somewhere in a jungle clearing Kevin was waxing eloquently about Shirley, when I tactlessly asked, 'But have you seen her in the morning?' Apparently he hadn't.

LOST LUGGAGE AND LATERITE ROADS

I hastily pulled together mosquito nets from the Army and Navy Stores, and a medical bag of time-expired drugs from Barts Pharmacy, for needy Africans and missionary doctors, as well as some in-date ones for ourselves. And in no time Rupert and I were off on a flight to Bangui via Chad. When we were met by Kevin in his swish TPO Land Rover we discovered that our luggage had been left behind at check-in at Victoria station. We had no option but to hunker down in a tall hotel overlooking the river Oobangui. This delay was a blessing in disguise, or so it seemed, although it threatened to delay Kevin getting back to Shirley Conran's, from Joseph Conrad's *Heart of Darkness*; but it did allow us to get used to driving on laterite roads. Now laterite is hard and red and dusty, and under the persistent vibration of vehicles it forms a wavy surface like corrugated iron. We discovered that you have two options - to drive at less than ten, or at more than forty miles an hour. Anything between, and you were juddered to death. So we went for more than forty, or in Rupert's case fifty. Rupert and Kevin next day spent a considerable time buying up all the wine and whisky stocks in Bangui. The conference had taken its toll on Kevin, who was by nature on the introspective side of hypochondriacal, and had been told by a French doctor that he had, 'Un syndrome neurovegetative'. I told him it meant he should take more vegetables, which seemed to satisfy him.

THE LUGGAGE ARRIVES AT LAST

The vehicle had an English, *Transafrican Highway Study* side, (the left), and a French *Étude sur la Route Transafricaine* one (the right). The Central African Republic (CAR) is, of course, part of francophone Africa, and at that time was under the dictatorship of a particularly nasty man called President Bokassa, whose mother was for some reason adulated by Uganda's Idi Amin. Finally, after three days our luggage caught up with us and we were able to load up the vehicle and depart, driving eastwards parallel to the river Oobangui. We had to cross the river into Zaire at a place called Bongassou. We spent the first night in a Two Star hotel, where there seemed to be a lot of night-time activity and which we discovered doubled as a brothel. We left after breakfast, and made good progress on day two, stopping for a leisurely and scenic lunch by a waterfall. it was Kevin's

David Coussmaker Anderson

birthday, and we ate an excellent picnic, washed down with two bottles of good French white wine, and then Rupert took over the driving. I was seated beside him on the left side of the right-hand-drive Land Rover, and we were traveling fast (to avoid the judder).... down a hill.... into a right-hand bend ... with a negative camber... and before you could mutter merde, we were pitched straight on into deep jungle. *'Merde!'*, I expleted. 'Shit, Rupert!' said Kevin, whose French was poor. Fortunately we were English side down; this was the side I was on. As we clambered vertically out of the French side of the vehicle we were miraculously joined by a crowd of some fifty Africans, and it became clear that this was a local business, probably part of the tribal business-plan. I imagine that any attempts to eliminate the negative camber bend would have been heartily opposed by locals on economic grounds.

We were well-equipped, notably with an axe and a chain. But to expose them and lighten the vehicle we had to unload our luggage, which included an enormous volume of alcohol. Kevin and Rupert had worked on a bottle of Scotch a day for two weeks and we also had a lot of soda, several cases of wine, and some lemonade. So all that was stacked with our luggage on the jungle floor as we set to work. That is to say, as the women set to work, because the men obviously needed to give instructions. Finally we were hacked, levered, pushed and hauled backwards, up on to the road, and by some miracle the vehicle still worked, although we had to wire up the doors on the English side. It was then payback time with a clamour for whisky, of which we parted with two bottles for the men. We nearly started a riot, when we offered the women lemonade. I think we had to give them a bottle of whisky too. Then, bruised, battered, but unbowed we continued on our way to Bongassou.

THERE MAY BE ANOTHER SMALL PROBLEM

As we camped in a clearing over dinner, Kevin broke the news that there might be another tiny problem. To pass between countries in recently war-torn francophone central Africa the vehicle needed a document called a *Carnet de Passage*, which had to be stamped at each border post. Ours had been stamped on the way out to Cameroon, but the team had driven it back into the CAR after 6 pm, when there was no one to stamp its return. That was three months ago, and it still wasn't stamped. So what were we to do? The following morning when we arrived at Bongassou, Kevin got on the phone to raise high profile government officials, who said they could do nothing, but that it shouldn't matter. I remember we met a nice middle-aged Frenchman who was shacked up with a willing American lady hitch-hiker, and they gave us an excellent lunch, for which we provided the wine. Then we went to the border post, where eventually, after further telephoning to someone in authority, the official let us out of the CAR without stamping the *Carnet*. The logic was that you can only let a car out if it has previously come in. But at least we were allowed to cross the River Oobangui into Zaire, apparently in a vehicle that had been paddled up the river from Cameroon as if by magic.

So now we are at the water's edge, but with no ferry. The problem was that the ferry's battery was either flat or stolen or both. No worries, the Land Rover has a battery. So as team's doctor, and therefore its most dispensable member, and maybe also because I spoke French, I was given the battery and was solemnly paddled the mile to the other side of the Oobangui in a dug-out canoe, with this precious cargo wedged between my legs. Somewhere in the Anderson archives there is a standard-8 cine film that soundlessly records this heroic and scenic journey. Once on the other side the mechanic was summoned from a nearby village by tom-tom, the battery was placed in what turned out to be only half a ferry (the other half having been ripped up and burnt as firewood). The half ferry was started, and off we went back, with the Zaire border official (who had malaria). Once on the CAR side, the ferry engine was left ticking over, the battery removed and replaced in our vehicle, and we drove on. I gave the grateful Customs man some outdated Barts chloroquine, but he too was not to cleared to stamp the *Carnet de Passage.*

Now that part of Africa is repeatedly crossed by rivers running East to West. Once in Zaire we had to negotiate several. The normal ferry had been sunk a couple of weeks before, because they had tried to squeeze on a lorry behind a mini, but the ferry was too short for both. So as it was 6 pm, the ferry was left with the front wheels of the lorry on board, and its rear wheels on land. Overnight a storm blew up and the ferry sank, mini, lorry and all. We were therefore diverted sixty kilometres to the west, to take another ferry. We camped overnight, and next morning were about to drive on. We were turned back at the water's edge, and sent to the nearby Customs Post, where we approached with the French side facing the Post, as in Africa first impressions matter. It was so lucky the French side was still pristine. We were met by a suspicion-riddled dignitary who was being shielded from the sun by a man with an umbrella; we explained how important we were and told the story about the *Carnet.* Eventually, with Kevin pulling rank again we were allowed on, with a piece of paper which said he was not responsible, and which referred us on to the next Customs Post.

COOKED LUNCH AND COLD BEER

It was now early afternoon, and we were hungry, so imagine our joy at finding a restaurant that advertised chicken and cold beer! It was irresistible, so we didn't resist. We stopped and we were the only customers, so we ordered. The owner clearly had ambitions, and there were men smoothing out a new cement dance floor. One hour and two warm beers later, we still had no chicken. We should have twigged and left when an extremely athletic old rooster emerged from his pen at high speed, ran all over the wet cement, and was finally caught twenty minutes later by a fast teenage boy who clearly played rugby. The squawks died down and a further hour-and-a-half later we shared a chicken and potato stew with the bar owner and his family. It tasted good, but was the most athletic chicken I have ever not eaten. We paid and left, camping in another inviting clearing amid beautiful wild lilies and spectacular butterflies. A storm was brewing, the tent was small and Kevin generously volunteered to sleep in the vehicle. An hour later the tent was flooded in torrential rain, and amid protestations, Rupert and I were allowed to join him inside the Land Rover where we seemed less likely to die from a lightning strike.

I think we mostly followed the favoured Transafrican Highway route, but it certainly needed a lot of work. Since this part of Zaire had seen white mercenaries only a few years before, we found several villages where it was clearly unwise to stop. We finally took a left turn at a place named Buta, which had a post office, from which Kevin sent his humour-deficient beloved a testing telegram which said, 'What-ho, am in Buta, love Kevin'. Other memories of Zaire include meeting a group with a broken-down vehicle who had been there for a week, and spending a night with some missionaries, who were pleased to receive the out of date medicines. We also shared whisky and another night with flying ants and two Greek businessmen - the Greeks seem to get everywhere. Finally, we crossed into Uganda, drove to a town called Arua, and it seemed like a return to civilisation. At least we were in anglophone Africa and from then on no one cared about the unstamped *Carnet de Passage.*

David Coussmaker Anderson

GREAT RELIEF AT REACHING AMIN'S UGANDA

You can imagine our relief at sitting down for a meal in an excellent Asian-run restaurant in Arua, where in an adjoining room an unmistakeable and affable Idi Amin was dining with a group of army officers, presumably planning genocide. This was a couple of months before Amin decided to kick out the Asians. Anyway we knew nothing of what he was scheming, ate our meal, paid, and left to look for a campsite. A couple of miles out of Arua we found a nice flat bit of open ground on which we pitched our tent and enjoyed a good night's sleep, to wake up the following morning to find we were camped in the middle of a golf green. We hastily packed up and left for Murchison Falls National Park, where we got a tourist boat all to ourselves which took us up the crocodile- and hippo-laden Albert Nile to the falls, for a memorable side trip. We camped that night near the waters' edge, leaving generous spaces between tents for the hippos to walk to the water. This was before Amin took to feeding dissidents to the Murchison Falls' crocodiles.

Kevin then rather foolishly left us to fly home from Kampala to get married, and in retrospect agrees that even being cornered by a crocodile might have been a better bet than being conned by a Conran. Rupert and I were given responsibility to take the damaged Land Rover back to Nairobi, and spent a few great days in game reserves at Lake Nakuru, where we saw flamingoes, and Masai Mara where we saw lazily copulating lions. That night hyenas ruined all our tin plates and mugs, which we had foolishly left outside the hut. We concluded by staying with a generous coffee-farming Napier relative in Nairobi before returning the TPO vehicle for repair and flying home. Nobody at Barts seemed to mind that I had had to take an extra week. And Jenny and the boys seemed to understand and looked relieved. They may have forgiven, but they have not forgotten.

CHAPTER 6

CALIFORNIA

TO THE USA FOR A YEAR IN LA JOLLA, CALIFORNIA

I have already said that I wanted to leave London, and Jenny and I decided that once I had finished writing my MD thesis it would be a good idea to spend a year in the USA. She had settled down in general practice in Ealing, continued to do some eye clinics, and felt she too could take a year out. Our three boys would also benefit. I decided to contact Professor Samuel S C Yen, a rising star in the female steroid hormone field, and when I met him at an endocrine meeting in London he was both charming and enthusiastic. So with his support I applied to the Medical Research Council, and was awarded a Goldsmiths' Traveling Research Fellowship for a year. Panic buttons in full action I completed my MD thesis on Plasma Androgens and Sex Hormone Binding Globulin in Health and Disease, and submitted it to my newly renamed *alma mater*, The University of Dundee. MD theses are read by the writer, the typist (in those days we had typewriters), and two examiners. A copy is placed in the library, and never looked at again, though the author is expected to get a few papers out of the work. My thesis, looked at the best part of half a century later is not a world-shattering document, but it was awarded with commendation, and career-wise it did its job. In late July 1973 I posted three copies to Dundee, the week before we sailed in the SS *Oronsay*, on her final voyage, for the west coast of the United States. A beneficial effect of my year away was that Michael Thorner took my place at Barts under Professor Michael Besser, and he became an eminent and serious world-renowned endocrinologist. In middle age he was rendered paraplegic when a tree fell on him, but he continued to do important research; he and his wife Prue remain good friends of ours, and a few years ago visited us in Italy.

We rented our house to the Zaire embassy in London, which may seem an odd decision, but they promised to pay well, and for the first few months payment came into our account from an Irish estate agent called Murphy, who then started to syphon off funds. Chris Edwards, (now Professor Sir Christopher Edwards), a Barts rising endocrine star who had just got his BTA, recommended buying a right-hand-drive Volvo, and having it shipped out to the USA for fifty dollars. After a year you could bring it back without any import duty. So we did that, and planned to pick it up in Los Angeles a month later. It was a traumatic departure, with an unnecessary but short-lived family row, and we were seen off on the SS *Oronsay*'s last trip, by my parents from the quayside at Southampton. The journey cost £700 and we had a cabin on F deck, at a perfect level for sea-sickness during the stormy first five days. We stopped at Bermuda, Nassau, Panama (with a memorable trip through the canal), Acapulco and finally Los Angeles. There we stayed with my old friend John Brown, now an eminent orthopaedic surgeon, and his wife, Kay, who was a singer. She was hospitable in a slightly enigmatic Californian, 'We've had trouble with house guests recently', sort of way. We picked up the car and drove to La Jolla, where we found it was Labor Day weekend, so we said, 'Hi' to Sam Yen, met the estate agent and looked at the house she had found for us in La Jolla Shores.

We then headed off via Phoenix, Arizona, (where a window was smashed in and had to be repaired), and the Grand Canyon.

The right hand drive Volvo certainly caused confusion, and although it could still be broken into it was not of interest to joy riders. Volvos seldom are anyway. One day Jenny drew into a gas station, and the attendant was dumbfounded to find there was no driver. He finally spotted Jenny on the right, and came round, looking confused. When Jenny had explained we were taking it back home after a year, he was interested to hear that in England we were forced to drive on the wrong side of the road. 'Say, where do you guys come from?' he asked, spotting a strange accent. 'England' replied my wife. 'Gee, that's fascinating - what language do you speak?!' 'Well, what language do YOU speak?' 'English, of course'. It seemed he had never connected the dots.

MY FIRST CHINESE ACADEMIC FALLING-OUT

Sam was the first but not the last Chinese medical academic I was to fall out with. When we got back to La Jolla, he and his charming wife Kay invited us with our children round to their house for a barbeque, and all seemed fine. That, however, was the last time we were invited. A day or so later we met Bill Lasley, a veterinarian research fellow, who sounded incredulous that anyone would deliberately come from England to work for a year with Professor Yen. Bill invited us to a farewell lunch for a Rockefeller Research Fellow who, unable to stand Sam, or maybe fired by him, was leaving. In fact this turned out to be a great boon, because the pound was about to crash and I was paid in pounds sterling, but the rent and everything else went out in dollars. After a month or so of increasing impecunity, Sam offered Jenny a half-time post at $4,000 a year on his Rockefeller grant, which brought our combined earnings up to an acceptable $14,000 a year (the MRC had finally pegged mine at $10,000). For the first six months things in La Jolla seemed to be going swimmingly. The gynaecologist Howard Judd, whose immediate ambition was to write a paper a month, and was Sam's right hand man, told us something of his past. Born in mainland China, he had flown jets for Chiang Kai Shek, against the communists. Upon the defeat of the nationalists he had escaped to Hong Kong in a boat where passengers were chained together to be thrown overboard if the Chinese communists intercepted. He studied Medicine at Hong Kong University, where he was spotted by a famous US professor who was impressed and finally recruited him to the USA. Sam was ruthlessly ambitious to succeed. He did not speak brilliant English, but I noticed he often exploited this to facilitate jumps of supposedly erudite but actually illogical thought.

The lab was run by a very nice man called Bill Hopper, who was very good technically but had no genuine interest in research. His real interest was property and real estate, and he was no intellectual threat to Sam. He helped me set up the techniques to measure eight related steroids at once, and Sam was enthusiastic. For further help or materials Sam would suggest writing to a colleague, saying, for example, 'Davie, you write Mort Lipsett, he verygreatpersonawfrenofmine'. I tried this once or twice, but his supposed very great personal friends never replied. Sam had tens of freezers full of old serum samples that he would resuscitate for new analyses whenever a new paper was needed. Bill Hopper used to keep Sam happy, by repeating analysis of any outlier whose result was anomalous until it fell into line, so by the end his data always looked perfect.

I REFUSE TO LEAVE

Sam and I fell out after seven months when he asked me to submit a paper on sex hormone-binding globulin to the Pacific Gynaecological Research Society meeting, but then when I asked for departmental travel expenses he refused. I said I thought that was unreasonable, since he had asked me to do so. He smoldered for two weeks, and in early January on returning from a meeting on the east coast called me to his office and said, 'Davie, I been thinking what you say the other day and it not acceptable, so you can GO!' Just like that! 'Well, I'm going nowhere Sam,' I replied. He was not in a strong position to fire me for two reasons. First, he was not paying me, and second, Jenny was working for him, and he could hardly fire her for my perceived misdemeanor. Actually there was also a third reason. Neil, our youngest son, went to a Montessori school with Sam's youngest daughter, and Jenny and Kay Yen shared driving duties. They remained on civil terms throughout, and never once discussed their husbands' fight.

I went to the Faculty office to report what had happened, and showed them the letters of invitation etc, and for the last five months of my fellowship I worked better than ever before, and ultimately produced two good papers in respectable journals. I was helped in this because Sam never gave Jenny any more work, so she worked as my technician. Alan Lane, his deputy head, and Howard Judd said I should apologise, and Alan tried to get Jenny given some work, but to no avail. Meanwhile Bill Lasley worked day and night to get data Sam needed for a prestigious lecture he was due to give at a Gordon Conference in the summer. Bill had come to work on subhuman primates, and ended up working on women; as it turned out they were the only primates Sam had access to. On leaving I wrote up my research, and put Sam's name on the papers. I never got any comment from him on the drafts, but many years later he told me that for any paper on steroid methodology from then on he just wrote, 'steroids were measured by the method of Anderson *et al*', even when they were not measuring the same steroids.

LATER MEETINGS WITH SAM

Of course I met Sam in later years and we got on superficially like old friends. The first time was in Florence, and we had dinner with Sam and Kay, and a Welsh endocrinologist, Picton Thomas. I had told Picton about our falling-out, and my being fired and refusing to leave. All was going well, but over dinner Sam went ashen grey and staggered off to the toilet, followed at Kay's request by Picton and myself. It seemed he regularly bled from a duodenal ulcer. 'Picton, this one's for you' I said, as Sam had a massive haematemesis into the toilet bowl. 'If I look after him and he dies no one will believe it wasn't murder.' Sam gave a characteristically incomprehensible talk two days later, on Bill Lasley's ground-breaking research. A year or two later, when I was getting established with a research team of my own in Manchester, I took my Fellows with me to Sheffield where Sam was to speak. They were Stavros Manolagas, David Large and David Child. 'Oh hi Davie,' Sam greeted me with a smile, 'good to seeing you here. Nice paper you wrote in JCEM, how you doing?' 'Fine, Sam, thanks;' and we exchanged pleasantries. 'Sam, I'd like to introduce three young doctors who are working with me. This is Dr David Large'. 'Hi, Davie Large, very nice to meeting you', and they shook hands. 'And this is Dr David Child'. 'Hi Davie Child, good to meeting you too'; and I could see he was starting to detect a size-based Davidian pattern emerging. 'And finally, let me introduce Stavros Manologas'. Sam looked puzzled and said, 'Oh hi Stavros... you called Stavros? In't that a little confusing?'

I had clearly left an indelible imprint on Sam, and remember meeting him in 1991 at an American Endocrine meeting; a fellow and eminent British reproductive endocrinologist Professor Steve Franks was chatting to Sam, who said, 'I just meet Davie Anderson... he very difficult man, you know, Steve', to which Steve replied with a straight face, 'Oh, that's funny, Sam, because he has just said the same about you!' 'He did? - why he say that?' came the response. At the same meeting I met up with Sam's really nice technician Gail Laughlin, and we agreed to meet for a drink at a bone research meeting I was planning to attend in San Diego later that year. So when I arrived I phoned her. Sam lived in a house he had designed himself above the La Jolla cliffs, which looked like a giant upside down snail. He loved it, and I believe when his marriage to Kay broke up he had had to sell it, but he later bought it back. 'Sam's giving a party in his house', said Gail. 'I've got an idea, Sam says I can bring any man I like, so would you like to join me? It will be fun to see his face'. So I accompanied her. It was a good party, and to be fair if he was shocked when he saw me at the bottom of the wine-bottle-cork-lined inverted snail staircase, he didn't show it as we chatted like old friends.

TERRETORIAL IMPERATIVES

All things considered we had a good time in the USA, and made some lifelong friends. Mostly these were couples of whom at least one was from Europe. These included Skip and Eliane Johnson - he was a cardiologist, and refurbisher of classic cars and Eliane was Lebanese and also excellent company. Several years earlier, I had read and much enjoyed a controversial book by Robert Ardrey, *The Territorial Imperative,* which ran somewhat counter to the general views of anthropologists. One night we were invited to the Johnsons for dinner and to meet a couple, of whom the wife was an eminent anthropologist.

David Coussmaker Anderson

As I recall she had spent two years living with her young child with tribes in the Amazon basin, and she had strong opinions about our species. When I mentioned Ardrey it was like putting a match to tinder, but I stuck to my territorial theme; next day Skip said he was delighted that I had lit up the conversation with a good dose of biological controversy. We often went camping with friends in the Mojave desert, and twice went down to Mexico's Baja California. On one trip we were with a large group walking in the heat among hills covered with enormous rocks the size of houses, and Jenny, Ken and Neil wanted to go back to the car, while Bruce decided to go on with the rest. Little did I know we were like ants finding our way in a crumbling chocolate cake. Over an hour in the intense heat we managed to walk full circle. We climbed to the top of a large boulder, erected my tripod and put Jenny's blue hat on it, and, children dehydrated, with only one orange between us, sat and waited. Fortunately one of our party out looking for us spotted the hat, I shouted back and he came to find us, just as the sun was setting. We had not paid enough attention to unfamiliar territory as we had left with the rest of the party, and returning had missed the road and the cars by fifty yards. You don't mess about in unfamiliar desert, especially with young children and inadequate amounts of water.

We tried marihuana once and it had absolutely no effect, so we never tried it again. A chap called Gary in the Department on the other hand was permanently spaced-out. And while we were there a President called Nixon said famously, 'Your President is not a crook', while the San Diego Union, a paper distinctly to the right of the truth managed to scrape up the headline *Tapes Emphasize Nixon's Concern*. Our three kids also loved the year in California and we had some memorable trips to red rock-country - as well as the Grand Canyon, we went to Monument Valley, Bryce Canyon (where the children experienced altitude breathlessness for the first time) and Zion. We once camped overlooking Death Valley, and also in Yosemite National Park in the snow in April. And we went up the coast road to San Francisco. I was offered a job in the Scripps Institute, but it would have involved changing to work on diabetes. Jenny and I spent a week in Hawaii, leaving the boys with friends, and we stayed with another British endocrinologist, Fred Greenwood, who had some good advice for anyone thinking of moving to the United States as he had done. 'What you need to remember', he said, 'is that the advantages of moving to the States are very obvious, and the disadvantages less so; while with Britain it's the other way round.' Kenneth, aged eight, went to a camp, and was as pleased as Punch when we got back that no one had worked out he was not American. He later took up acting.

We had lived all year in a small house just up from the Seven Eleven shop on La Jolla Shores, humming birds drinking from the hibiscus, barbequeing in sunsets with Bill Lasley and Cedric and Linda Prys-Roberts and their family on the beach. On special nights we caught grunion fish in our bare hands after they had laid their eggs in the sand, on the grunion run. The house was for sale for $180,000, which unfortunately we didn't have. Worth millions now, it would have been a good investment.

AND SO BACK TO BLIGHTY

But we returned as expected to the UK, in that summer of 1974, me to Barts, and Jenny to her Ealing practice. We did have a spot of bother evicting the Deputy Ambassador of Zaire from our house. Our neighbours were accused of racism when our friend, near neighbour and defender Margaret Rice told the women to stop cutting down a tree in our small garden. The head man claimed diplomatic immunity, our house now being Zaire territory. In fact at first they refused to leave, claiming

David Coussmaker Anderson

we weren't coming back, and it took nearly three months to convince them, partly because our estate agent was trading on the dodgy side of Murphy's Law; eventually they left at the end of July. The Deputy Ambassador and his friends left a large bin filled with empty gin bottles they had consumed to celebrate the World Cup, for which Zaire had qualified. One day I went to the embassy to claim some money for a ruined freezer they had left full of water, and spoke in French, for reasons of face. The reply, also given in French, was then translated for my benefit into English, for me to reply in French again. We shook hands at the end like lifelong friends, agreeing that Margaret Rice could be difficult at times.

CHAPTER 7

MEDICINE IN MANCHESTER

MANCHESTER ROYAL INFIRMARY, AND THE CASE OF STEFAN KISZKO

It was not long before I had applied for and been appointed to a Senior Lecturer and Consultant post in the Department of Medicine at Manchester Royal Infirmary. I moved to Manchester in September 1975, and I had only been there for a few days when David Child took me to see a patient called Stefan Ivan Kiszko, on the haematology ward. Kiszko, who was in his midtwenties, had the body proportions of a eunuch, and pea-sized testes. He lived with his mother in Rochdale, on a vegetable-free high-cider diet, and was grossly anaemic from folate deficiency, so much so that he had needed a blood transfusion. I made a confident diagnosis of Klinefelter's syndrome, and prescribed half the normal dose of testosterone depot. I warned him that his sex drive would develop, and he would start to masturbate, and he might become a bit more assertive. I put him on a half-dose because I always started therapy with this normal male hormone cautiously, after an experience with an androgen-deficient patient at the Hammersmith. He had become a little aggressive with his wife, and had taken time to adapt to adult levels. I was fully trained as an endocrinologist, but though I attended and worked in the odd Endocrine Clinic, I was not incorporated into the Endocrine Unit itself, which was run by Dr Donald Longson. On 11th December I saw Kiszko again, and he was effusive with his thanks. There was not the slightest suggestion as to what was about to unfold. However late in the afternoon of Christmas eve, 1975, I received a visit from two police officers from the Criminal Investigation Division, who said that Kiszko had sexually assaulted and murdered a little girl. The rest of the story is recounted in my joint book *Three False Convictions, Many Lessons - the Psychopathology of Unjust Prosecutions,* written forty years later. Suffice it to say here that the accusation and trumped-up charges against Kiszko, and his subsequent conviction for the murder on October 3rd 1975, of eleven-year old Lesley Susan Molseed, is one of the major stains on the English Criminal Justice System. Ultimately, and much too late to help Kiszko, this case was to have a major impact on my own life.

STAVROS THE GREEK

I enjoyed working at Manchester Royal Infirmary, home of the University's Medical School. We settled for a house right next to the railway station in Bramhall, and quickly became immune to the noise of passing trains. After the tremors of California they were nothing. Indeed since then in Umbria, Italy, where I am writing this in retirement, I have had no difficulty sleeping through earthquakes. 'That was an earthquake', my wife opined next to me in the early hours of August 24th 2016, as somewhere nearby in the Appenines was shaken to bits, but I merely detected a passing train.

Bill Stanbury, my notional boss, was a world authority on calcium disorders, and had some very good people working in his lab, notably Dr Barbara Mawer. Robert Cryer, who had worked with Professors Scowen and Besser at Barts alongside me, lived just down the road from us, in Bramhall, and worked as Consultant Physician at Stockport Royal Infirmary, when he was not breeding quail at home. And he had taken on as his SHO a very ambitious and persistent Greek doctor, Stavros Manolagas, who desperately wanted to work with me; he put me under a lot of pressure to try and find a research post for him, which in the end I did. Those were the days when keen up-and-coming academics could quite easily get research grants from the Medical Research Council or the Wellcome Foundation, and Stavros left Bob Cryer, and came to work on the effect of steroids on bone.

Stavros did some clinical research in Glasgow with Bob Lindsay, who was hot on steroids and osteoporosis. But our main claim to fame came when we started to work on the embryonic rat's skull bone, and found that glucocorticoids were necessary to maintain Vitamin D receptors. In the general run of research this was pretty low key, but it served to get Stavros launched into academic hyperspace, where he turned out to have big ambitions. He had been to medical school in Greece, where things had definitely gone downhill since Hippocrates. But, helped by ideas from me, (and hindered by an Australian cousin of mine, John Hunt, who came to work that summer, and spilt a tray of his tubes, so destroying a crucial experiment), Stavros advanced. He needed a lot of protection at meetings, but ultimately went off to California to work with Professor Len Deftos, and so onto the launch pad of a stratospheric research career. Over the years I fell in his eyes from celestial star to embarrassing failure, as he was now up with the big boys. At one meeting, many years later, he said to me, 'You could have been so good, David, (unspoken thought - 'like me' -) if you had just stuck at one thing, but there you are all over the place'. 'Stavros,' I replied, 'if I had been like the others, would I have taken on an untrained Greek doctor who knew nothing except that he wanted to go up? I take some pride in your success, as I took you on when no sane person would have even considered you.' I am still not sure if he took my point.

I just mentioned my Australian cousin, John Hunt, which reminds me that his godfather was our common medical uncle of the same name, who founded the Royal College of General Practitioners and became Lord Hunt of Fawley. Now hyper-eminent, as well as hyper-busy, as a practical move senior John Hunt foisted junior John on me for the England section of his pre-Medical School world walkabout. We had a lot of fun with him in our boyly family that summer, but we never beat him at table-tennis. Afterwards I lent him my second car, which looking back was a rather embarrassing vehicle, although one up from my earlier scooter. I was going through some sort of eco-conscience crisis at the time. It was a bright yellow plastic shell on three wheels, called a *Reliant Robin*. When overloaded with a man too many in the back, the front wheel came off the ground so it could no longer be steared. Leaving a fuming Stavros behind, John more or less reliably drove the Reliant round the Lake District, until he managed to let it run out of petrol, something you only do once. I believe he hailed a passing driver who helped him fetch a can of petrol and for gravitational reasons they had to tip the Robin half on its side in order to pour in the magic fuel. I presume this was therefore a three-man job, two to tip the Robin, and one to pour the petrol. He never let the Robin run dry again.

JENNY'S PRACTICE IN BRAMHALL, THREE GROWING SONS AND A STRAWBERRY PATCH

Jenny worked at first for the local single-handed Doctor Davidson, who probably should have been struck off the register he was so bad; but then she moved into the main

Bramhall practice across the road, before finally starting one of her own in the village. Our older two boys went to Stockport Grammar School, which was excellent, while Neil went to local day Prep Schools and then, having being turned down for Stockport by the new headmaster, to Rugby as I had done. He hated it. But one does the best one can, and so much depends on our individual personalities, which by and large we are born with. One of the strongest arguments for the absence of a controlling deity, I suggest, may be the chance system chosen for procreation. You take more or less equal amounts of random DNA from two fairly compatible people interested in sex, mix it together, and hope for the best. (Actually, to change that would have been quite a good answer to Melville Arnot's question in my Finals Distinction viva). Still, on the whole we get on well with our three sons. Neil was the only one interested in classical music. He took up the cello, taught by an ex-pupil of my mother, and we often played cello-oboe duets together. In fact he and Kenneth are both quite musical, and now more serious about playing than I am.

We do not, however always agree. On leaving Rugby, Neil went away for a while and found religion in the form of Catholicism. But he still kept in close touch. We both remember, and can even laugh about, the strawberry-patch debate. I should say that in Bramhall, right beside the railway line we had a wonderful garden. I had taken back an area of asphalt from the deserted school playground next door, covered it with soil and manure, planted some marvelous and productive cherry trees, and there we also grew raspberries, potatoes and parsnips. In another area I had a magnificent strawberry patch, with straw supporting succulent berries, and covered by nets. The strawberries were unbeatable. One lovely summer's day, Neil was back from the monastery in the south of France, and came out to pick on his atheist father, who in turn was picking strawberries. We had this surreal discussion, where my recollection is that he said he was as sure of the existence of God as he was that I was standing there picking strawberries. He may have been even more certain. But at the end of a heated discussion it was I who had picked all the strawberries. To his credit, he did help eat them. Three years later in Hong Kong our near neighbour Joe Boyle, who was an ex-jesuit priest who had left to get married, thought this story was hilarious, and taught it as a parable whenever he preached. 'I'd like to tell you the parable of the believer son, the atheist father, and the strawberry patch...'

We made some excellent friends at Manchester Royal including Ray and Liz Carroll and their three children. On one occasion, after I had moved to Salford, we met up with them at Lake Annecy, where we were camping. Their youngest, Katherine, was just six, and we played a round of silly golf. The silly man running it said Ray could not share his club with his small daughter, and I got into an argument with him in French. Finally, I told him to 'piss off', and walked away, and miraculously that was the end of the trouble. Apparently this made a big impression on Katherine, who a week later in their holiday was being troubled by an irritating small boy of her age. Exasperated, she went to her father and said, 'Why don't you just tell him to piss off, Daddy?' On the same holiday, I disobeyed instructions and went for a tandem paraglide, which Liz thought was highly irresponsible. But hell, if you can't be irresponsible at forty, with a wife and three children, when can you?

NO LUCK WITH PETS

Jenny and I both like animals, and our house and garden on the face of it were ideal. I had long since become allergic to my parents' cats. Then Kenneth developed asthma from contact with his uncle's dogs. So we went for rabbits, until Bruce became allergic to them. Undeterred we got a pair of budgerigars, which happily yielded two budgie litters in a cage in the dining room, and they went down well until Neil started to get budgerigar-fanciers lung. I built an aviary for them beside the garage and they never bred again, so we settled for goldfish which are actually pretty boring. The aviary was used once by a baby tawny owl called Ziko, (he was spotted on the window ledge watching Ziko score in the 1986 World Cup). We fed him road kill till the man from Bird Protection said tut-tut and on his recommendation we opened the aviary and he flew back to his family across the railway line.

A CUP OF TEA WITH A MEDICAL LEGEND

As already mentioned, while we were in California for that memorable year we tended to socialise mainly with other families of European descent. These included our good friends the Thiels, who were German and of whom Hjalmer was a world authority on the *benthos*, which is the top 3 inches of the bottom of the ocean. He worked at the Scripps Institute of Oceanography in La Jolla, just beyond the naked bathing beach, and they had two sons and a daughter. His wife Marin was to train later as a doctor. I remember that, as with many Germans of our age, they were very self-conscious about the wartime family history, and especially that an uncle had been a member of the SS. As a consequence after the war Marin's father had lost his job as a Professor of Pathology. They lived in Lübek, and a year or two after our return I went to a medical meeting in nearby Hamburg, and took our two older boys Kenneth and Bruce, who stayed with their Thiel friends. After the meeting I went to pick them up and was taken for tea to visit Marin's parents. Her father was no less than Friedrich Wegener, whose seminal paper in the 1930's on the disease, a form of granulomatosis, that bears his name had just been celebrated by the journal *Deutsche Pathologische Gesellschaft*, which had even published a facsimile copy of his paper, which he showed me with justifiable pride. They rated it as one of the most important papers the journal had ever published. He had lost his University professorial post in pathology after the war, because of his SS brother, and thereafter had worked as a jobbing pathologist in Lübek. Enough academic punishment for such a man you would think. I note on checking on the internet that there is now a posthumous witch-hunt going on because of doubts about his wartime past, with a proposal to drop the disease's eponymous name. I remember him as a nice, but proud man, and I really doubt the sense or the justice of posthumous sanitation of the medical literature and its nomenclature because of disputed political views and actions by a man who died in 1990. Better, surely, to learn the real lessons from a horrendous psychopathic regime that doubtless put countless professionals under pressure to compromise, and study how to prevent such horrors for the future?

THE MOVE TO HOPE HOSPITAL

While at MRI I also looked after the long-stay patients at nearby Barnes Hospital, which I enjoyed and gave me a first-hand experience both of geriatrics and terminal care. I had been working at MRI for just over two years when I heard that the Medical School had advertised for a Senior Lecturer in Medicine with an interest in endocrinology at the newly designated teaching hospital, Hope, in Salford. I contacted the Department head, Professor (now Lord) Leslie Turnberg, and asked for details. I think he had thought I was well settled where I was. By this time the post had been advertised, so I had to go for interview; the other candidate, Pat Kendall-Taylor, was obviously not pleased when I was appointed. Anyway, in October 1979 I moved to Hope, and after about six months I suggested to Leslie that it might make sense for me to join forces with an NHS consultant, Dr Harold Cohen, who ran the Diabetic Clinic. Harold was delighted, especially when I applied for funding for a research fellow to work on home blood glucose monitoring, to try and measure its benefits in improving diabetic control. We got a very keen young doctor, Peter Winocour, who made a big success of this project.

HUGH HUNT, FORTRAN AND SOLVING THE PYRAMID PUZZLE

One of the most intelligent people in our family is John Hunt's brother Hugh, now a distinguished Reader in Engineering at the University of Cambridge. Hugh, was likewise on his Aussie world walkabout, when he joined us for a few days in Annecy the summer we camped there with the Carrolls. Jenny's mother Elizabeth was incredibly inventive when it came to Christmas presents, and that year she had given us The Great Pyramid Puzzle. The pyramid had four faces and thirty-six triangular pieces that fitted on, nine to a face, and with symmetrical red and white geometrical designs, which had to match up with those on the adjacent pieces. The designer was offering one pound for each puzzle sold, to the first person to solve the puzzle. (In the end he sold 24,000). It was said to be impossible to solve with a computer, but Hugh said, 'Nonsense'. Well, that Christmas I had spent a substantial time trying to solve the puzzle manually. Of course it was easy to get thirty-three or thirty-four pieces in place. I then made a triangular board to help speed up the process. Then Hugh came to stay, and he reckoned it could be solved by computer using *Fortran*, and it so happened he was going to work at Great Ormond Street, to design a programme for recording the volume of newborn babies. He finished that in a week or so, and then fed the progress to his boss by degrees, so he could work for the rest of his time on the pyramid puzzle, using a clever programme he had written in Fortran. Meanwhile I had worked out one face with an image of the sphynx on it, which was clearly not random. It fitted with various clues that were coming out in the press at intervals. Using his *Fortran* programme Hugh solved the puzzle, just before coming to Annecy, but when I saw it, it was clearly just a random solution. So on my insistence he then fed in the face with the sphynx, and bingo, a unique solution! Hugh did this in 3 hours tying up the Great Ormond Street Hospital's main-frame computer. We knew we had won, but alas, we hadn't. What I believe we had solved was the designer's original, non-random, design which he had then scrambled, designating as winner someone who stumbled on one of many random solutions. Someone much less deserving than us, we felt, had won the £24,000. But then the designer had warned us that it couldn't be solved using a computer.

PAGET'S DISEASE OF BONE; TREATMENT AND RESEARCH

One of the things about endocrinologists is that no one else really knows what they do, except that it is vaguely to do with hormones. With few exceptions people don't come with an endocrine diagnosis written all over their faces. There are many conditions at the fringes of specialties, which no one else is looking after, and one of these in Greater Manchester was Paget's Disease of Bone. There were literally hundreds of patients dotted all over the North West of England, which was clearly Paget's Disease capital of the world. Professor John Evanson at Withington Hospital, was interested in studying the natural history of Paget's disease, but not in improving its treatment. The Professor of Rheumatology at Hope Hospital, Malcolm Jayson, was interested in joints rather than bones, and certainly shied clear of trying any new treatments. There was a hormone called calcitonin, discovered and developed at the Hammersmith Hospital, which had some temporary effect, but certainly didn't cure the disease. I had been interested in it since Dundee days, when we had written a case report of a lady with Paget's disease of one radius, and overactivity of the parathyroid glands. So I saw all these patients with this extraordinary disease which seemed to pick bones out at random, as a big challenge.

I then met an enthusiastic Dutch professor, called Olav Bijvoet, who was trying out a new bisphosphonate drug called pamidronate, for treatment of Paget's disease, and claimed excellent results. The drug had been developed as an additive to washing powder. I expressed interest to Olav, and he gave me no less than one kilogram of pure powder that he had obtained from Henkel, the manufacturer. To cut a long story short, Judy Cantrill, the young pharmacist attached to our firm (who was very useful to our clinical research programme), got it checked for purity by gas chromatography. The Pharmacy Department then had it made up, dissolved in saline, into vials for intravenous infusion. We got authorisation from the local Clinical Research Committee (those were the days), conducted a prospective trial, and found it worked much better and was better tolerated than calcitonin. It is poorly absorbed by mouth, so giving it by slow intravenous infusion in saline was much better. Eventually we pushed the dose up for some of the more disabled patients. And, based on long-term bone scans we definitely got some permanent cures. Finally, thanks to our data and documentation, Ciba Geigy in 1991 marketed pamidronate for the treatment of Paget's Disease.

A STRANGE PAGETIC INTRODUCTION TO OPERA

Before I left Manchester my Research Fellow Dr Peter Richardson was working with a Ciba Geigy researcher on the analysis of our treatment data. This took us to Switzerland for three days for a meeting. One of my many musical cousins is the baritone opera singer Rupert Oliver Forbes and he was singing with Basel Opera. He and his wife Elizabeth kindly put us up and we asked him if he could get us opera tickets. Peter had never seen an opera before, and my cousin warned us that this production might not be the best place to start. It was an ultra-modernistic performance of Verdi's *Falstaff*, a comic opera written when Verdi was an old man. The music, as expected, was great, and as a comic *buffo* baritone, Rupert, who was excellent, also made some obtuse sense. However the opera was set in a modern Geriatric Ward and included a true Falstaff, and a false Falstaff, who was apparently the senile and hallucinating Giuseppe Verdi himself. It was completely incomprehensible and therefore probably not the greatest introduction to opera as a musical art form.

DOGS, DISTEMPER AND A BRITISH LION

So what was the cause of this disease? It clearly affected the resorbing cells, bone's multi-nucleated osteoclasts, which become ultra-large and ultra-active. I had long felt that it was caused by a single point in time blood-born infection, that settled out in these cells, and was then propagated locally, by recruitment of more precursor cells. There was data published to show that in Paget's disease the osteoclasts contain an RNA virus similar to measles virus. But to me it obviously wasn't measles. It seemed to be concentrated in the north-west of England, in middle aged and elderly people, so I wondered whether it might instead be caused by the related canine distemper virus (CDV).

In the early eighties I was joined by Dr John O'Driscoll, one of the famous Irish rugby-playing O'Driscolls, whose elder brother Barry was a good friend of Ray Carroll. Barry had approached me, and I put in a good word for John to get a Senior House

Officer post at Hope, and he was appointed. He had just finished working on my Unit, and was doing six months on the Respiratory Unit, when he received a call inviting him to join the 1984 British Lions tour of New Zealand. It was felt by some colleagues, notably Annie Holmes, a renal physician, to be bad enough that he was taking days off for Irish internationals. So she viewed three months unpaid leave in New Zealand to play rugby, with extreme disdain. I remember her raising a lone voice of objection at the Division of Medicine meeting, using the spurious argument that a pregnant woman could not take three months unpaid leave to have a baby. As well as being untrue, it also ignored the fact that half the population is designed to have babies, whereas very few are called upon to play for the British Lions.

Upon his return from New Zealand John asked me for a project. We dreamt up doing a survey by questionaire, of dog ownership among our patients and a control group, and also asked about known exposure to CDV. There was a significant difference in favour of having dogs, and unvaccinated ones at that, among our patients. Amazingly, we got the study published as a paper in *The Lancet*. But of course this was just a nice hypothesis, so as well as extending the study by using a more detailed questionnaire I set about getting the local molecular biologists interested in doing *in situ* hybridisation on biopsy samples, from patients with Paget's disease of the pelvic bone, which is a common site. Margaret Gordon had been a very good research fellow working on a steroid project, and she took this on, under Dr Paul Sharpe, a molecular biologist, so we had quite a team, supported by research grants. When I left for Hong Kong, one of the negative factors was leaving the Clinic and the Paget's research behind. I know several other people, including Paul Sharpe and Andy Mee, a vet working on large dogs, believe in the work and the central thesis. The theory is that distemper was rife at the time when there was a lot of Vitamin D deficiency, and consequent over-activity of the parathyroid glands. In humans it caused a transient viraemia, seeded out in osteoclasts in bones at random, and then spread progressively through them, but never to other bones.

In those days there was a scientific Society called the *Bone and Tooth*, which I nick-named the *Tooth and Claw*, because there was quite a lot of seemingly vicious discussion. Professor Alan Boyde was a member, and ultimately became a good friend. He was always interested in ideas, such as my canine distemper theory, and much later was game to help with some research on jade and Hongshan glass. But he did seem to take a spurious delight in the self-defeating game of trying to upset distinguished people. One year I went with Jenny to the Gordon Conference in New England, where he seemed to have it in for another and very nice osteoclast man called Steve Teitelbaum. The two were going at each other fairly amicably during the meeting until Alan's invited lecture, which he started thus...'Mr Chairman, Ladies and Gentlemen, Steve Teitelbaum'.... It is always possible to overstep the line between banter and insult.

BEETHOVEN AND A SICK POODLE

The most famous person suspected of having Paget's disease of bone is Ludwig Van Beethoven, and when I was due to give a lecture on the subject I was interested to find that among his earliest compositions at the age of nineteen, was the *Ode to the Death of a Poodle.* He had been very attached to the Breuning family's poodle, which became ill and died. This was in the late eighteenth century when the first epidemic of Distemper ran through Europe. Beethoven became deaf in later life, and drawings, as well as his autopsy findings suggest he had Paget's disease of the skull. In fact his developing nerve deafness had a major influence on his career, and he had to stop playing the piano and concentrate on composing. I felt able to entitle my 1990 presidential lecture to the Endocrine Section of the Royal Society of Medicine, *Paget's Disease of Bone, from Fido to Fidelio*.

A SAD CASE OF BARRY MANILOPATHY

An unkind definition of Gynaecology is that it is the most complicated endocrine system in the body looked after by the simplest type of doctor. Furthermore in the past many gynaecologists were obstetric surgeons, and themselves rather looked down upon by their mainstream surgical colleagues. They had little or no endocrine training, and some endocrinologists came to manage the disorders of ovulation rather better. Better still, there evolved an increasing tendency to run joint reproductive endocrinology clinics, as I did with Dr Gordon Falconer, at Hope hospital. In such clinics the endocrinologist in turn ends up with any patient bordering on psychological, for whose management he too is not properly trained. I remember well one such underweight and fixated young woman, Margaret, who was referred to the clinic because her periods had stopped, and whose particular variant of anorexia nervosa included a mega-crush on the popular singer Barry Manilow. It soon became clear that she was one of a crowd of older but still screaming women who lived for Barry's concert tours, which in turn fed the blurring in this sad young woman's mind between dream and reality. Furthermore post-concert contact with the singer was compounding the fantasy. Eventually I contacted Barry Manilow's UK agent, who listened sympathetically as I asked her to explain to Barry that Margaret had convinced herself that he would see that she was the one, and in the end marry her. I suggested that he might write her a letter explaining that he was already accounted for, and he did this, which probably just further fanned the flames of her delusional Barry Manilopathy. I note, incidentally, that the stalwart singer, who is three years younger than I am, is still going strong, and in 2015 married his long-term, and male, manager.

AN INTEREST IN MODERNISING MEDICAL EDUCATION

I was always interested in medical education, and had ambitions to change the system of teaching in Manchester. In particular I could see that specialists were directly teaching students new things that they now regarded as basic, but that even their colleagues in other specialties didn't know. In the Final Examination there were clinical cases, short and long, but some particularly narrow-minded Professors would mark down a student for doing something the 'wrong way', which was in fact how that student had been taught by his co-examiner. So I decided it would be a good idea to create a series of video teaching films, with specialists showing their method; these would then be available for their colleagues to use and also to learn from. This would be the 'Manchester method'. We had an excellent Medical Illustration Department at Hope, under the direction of one Robert Mitchell, and we tentatively started on this project. I was always keen also to film classical clinical cases, for the same reason. Occasionally we strayed a bit and I would co-opt Rob to film a discussion with an entertaining patient. I recall filming a pathological body builder, who was narcisistically fixated Putin-style on his body beautiful, and who also took every drug under the sun. He told me he had won *Mr United Kingdom* one year, and had only been runner up in *Mr Universe*, which was a disappointment I suppose as no martians were running.

Much later, when in Hong Kong this idea had blossomed into my *MediVision* teaching film series, I took some films to a medical education conference and came face to face with some self-opinionated Professors of Medical Education. One expressed incredulity when I said that I had made a film of tetanus and diphtheria, filmed in Vietnam and the Philippines, which showed ten cases of tetanus and four of diphtheria. 'Well', he said 'they don't need to know about tetanus - it's too rare, not on the list of 200 cases for our skeleton curriculum, and they'll probably never see a case'. He looked blank when I said this is only because of First World immunisation policies that kept these diseases at bay. 'Tetanus spores are everywhere, waiting for an open wound, and how can a doctor argue for maintaining immunisation against a horrific disease whose features they can't describe? Do you really want the first case a doctor sees to be the first case he misses?' He just looked blank and walked away.

A FIGHTER PILOT'S CLAIM TO FAME

A lovely and somewhat dishevelled elderly man, the husband of a patient who had just been admitted, was standing outside the ward one day, and I asked him how he thought his wife was (she had had a stroke). 'Well to be honest, Doc, she seems a bit disentoriated,' he replied. That seemed to me to be a perfect neologism and I have used it ever since. He was wearing a soup-stained RAF jacket, so I continued... 'I see you are wearing a 46th squadron jacket, Mr Jackson, were you a fighter pilot in the war?' I asked. 'Yes I were' he replied. He had presumably been a non-comissioned pilot. 'What did you fly?' 'I flew 'urricanes and Spitfires, Doc.' 'And which did you prefer?' (I was beginning to get into my Battle of Britain mode). 'I preferred the 'urricane' replied Mr Jackson. 'And why was that?' (I had no idea what was coming). 'Because they float better', was the reply... Now myself a little disentoriated, I decided to change tack. 'Mr Jackson, I hope you don't mind me asking, but just out of interest how many aircraft did you destroy in the war?' 'I destroyed six,' he answered, and then added, 'and they were all ours.' 'Please talk me through it, I said... 'Well, the first, it were a rogue pilot, who were strafing our troups, so I were sent up ter shoot 'im down, and I did'. 'And the other five?'... 'Well, then it were Norway, and Jerry were coming, and me and me mate was told to fly to Norway and destroy any of our planes left on the ground, so Jerry couldn't use 'em, and there were two left there, so we landed and set fire to em.' 'And then you flew home?' asked. 'Well, by now we was short of fuel and we'd 'ad instructions to land on the *Glorious*; but unfortunately by the time we got there the *Glorious* had bin sunk, so we 'ad to ditch 't plane. And that were when I were glad I were in a 'urricane, (because they float better). Eventually we was picked by a destroyer that were looking for't *Glorious*, but found us instead'.

So now Flight Sergeant Jackson is back in Blighty with no plane, and he still has two more aircraft to destroy. 'Tell me what happened then, what about the other two?' I asked. 'Well, to be honest Doc, it were a bit embarrassing. I were put on barrige billoon duty, but being inexperienced-like, I flew them up to't wrong height, and unfortunately two of our planes flew into 'em before I realised me mistake.' I presumed that was the last time he flew anything, but at least he still had his 46th Squadron jacket.

CIRCADIAN RHYTHMS, DEATH OF A FRIEND, AND HIS QUESTIONABLE SAUDI LEGACY.

The Professor of Chemical Pathology at Hope Hospital was John Daly, who sadly died in 1980, in his mid-fifties, of liver cancer caused by hepatitis B he had contracted from a needle-stick as a young doctor. The adrenal hormone cortisol, is important in controlling many day-night rhythms, and in the early days of global jet-setting there was much interest in how these changed with jet lag. John told me of his experience undertaking experiments to look at circadian changes, in which BOAC had cooperated. A team of endocrinologists was traveling to an international meeting half way across the world, and their study involved collecting timed urine samples. So the right hand toilet was reserved for endocrinologists, to pee into a measuring cylinder, take an aliquot and note the time, volume and name on the bottle. John was at the front of the queue, when the left hand toilet became available. He said to the man behind, an American, 'You go - it's too complicated to explain, but I have to use the right hand toilet'. The man looked perplexed, but when he came out and saw John still there, he had a smile on his face. 'I got it', he said, 'you got a right-hand thread!'

John Daly was a kind man, and when he died his kindness came back to haunt me. Under pressure from the Faculty administration, in the form of Dr Bill Beswick, John had agreed to take on a lesser member of the House of Saud, Mr Abdul Redhwi, who wanted to get a PhD. Apparently quite a lot of oil money for the University depended on his success, so John agreed to supervise his thesis. Actually, not only was Redders, as he was affectionately known, quite old and not very bright, but he also had extremely poor English, and John, who had been endowed with a saintly streak, used to give him private English lessons in his office. I had repeatedly urged him to concentrate his efforts on real science, but to no avail with regard to Mr Redhwi. Anyway, John was now at home in the final stages of liver cancer when he asked me to visit him. It transpired that as I knew something about Vitamin D metabolism, which Redders' thesis was concerned with, he was going to bequeath him to me in his academic will. 'Please, David, you are a good friend, promise to do this for me'. I promised to do what I could. After John's funeral, I got a summons from Bill Beswick. By this time I was hardening my heart, but in the end I agreed to take Mr Redhwi on for three months on appro to see how it went. And I suppose he could have been worse; he was also being helped by Barbara Mawer and doing a Sephadex fractionation of vitamin D metabolites extracted from blood plasma, which was not easy. I recall reviewing his results one day, and I asked, 'Mr Redhwi how do you know that this peak is 1,25 dihydroxy D3 and not 24,25, or something else altogether?' His eyes lit up and he replied. 'Dokitor Anderson, two months ago I am showing same results to Professor Daly, and he asket me exact self-same question, and he say to me, 'Mr Redhwi I wanter you to go away and do more speriments with GC mass spec and column chromatography', and I go away, and do exact same speriments he ask, and I am coming back with results, and finally I PROVE that peak is 1,25, not 24,25, or something else, and I am wanting to show Professor Daly that I am right, and I am ready to show him, AND THEN HE DIED!' Well, I have no idea how, but eventually by dint of a kindly external examiner Eric Lawson, much re-writing, explanations that he was never going to harm anybody, and the importance of his result to University funding, he was awarded his PhD. So I could hold my head up, and I presume copious funds came the University's way though regrettably not to me.

A GREEK VERSION OF BALLESTEROS

After Stavros I had two other Greek research fellows, one of whom worked hard and wrote a good thesis, but lacked a sense of humour. He was called Panos and he was the absolute spitting image of Severiano Ballesteros, who was at the height of his golfing career, and idolised by almost everybody, although not by Panos, who had never heard of him. The British Open Championship that year was at nearby Lytham St Annes, and Andy Robertson and I organised a lab outing to go there for the day. On the way I explained to Panos a bit about golf and then warned him that he might find people came up and asked for his signature, because he resembled the much-loved golfing legend Seve Ballesteros. I had, however underestimated just how alike they were, and he was literally swarmed with kids asking for his autograph. He was extremely angry, instead of just standing there and obligingly signing 'Panagiotis Petsos'. I was somehow blamed for some cunning Anglo-Saxon golf plot against Greek honour. Andy tried to placate him, but to no avail. His successor, Kostos Mavroudis, was a more charming man, but unfortunately also rather less ambitious, and to his later regret, and following Panos' advice, did not complete a PhD.

SALFORD, THE NHS AND REORGANISATION

I was a member of the Salford Health Authority for several years. The head when I had first arrived was one Duncan Nicholl, later knighted for services in reorganising the NHS, which in retrospect seems premature. But in 1979 he was not there yet. I needed funding for a research technician, so I went to him and asked if there was any NHS money to pay for one. Salford was skint, but also on the make, being the latest Manchester teaching hospital. There was a big refurbishment programme, (and ultimately a brand new hospital, now called *Salford Royal* which looks like a space station from *Star Wars*). 'I see no problem,' he said, 'I'll fund it through slippage'. But nine years later, Nicholl had ascended into the stratosphere, and the hospital was under the direction of a man called Frank Burns, which was appropriate as it seemed to be going up in flames. The problem, quite simply, was that we were too good, and so attracting too many patients, and slippage was no longer *de rigeur*. For example, we were **treating** patients with diseases like Paget's, which others were just studying.

So our Area Health Authority was overspent to the tune of a million pounds a year, which actually doesn't seem much now. One of the things about the NHS in those days was that General Practitioners could refer their patients to whichever specialist they fancied. Word got around, and at Hope many doctors, especially clinical academics, had good reputations, were attracting patients, and so running up bills for the hospital and the Area Health Authority. Even bad GPs want their patients to be treated well, and they culled advice from better GPs, so it seemed to me that all that was needed was to measure what was happening. Then the Regional Health Authority would divert money to Salford, which was doing the work, from, say Stockport, which wasn't. And then try and improve things at Stockport. I called this pursuit funding, but obviously it was too simple. One day the Minister of Health, Kenneth Clarke came to visit us, and the Professor of Geriatrics, Ray Tallis, (who is also an eminent philosopher-author) and I had half an hour with him. Clarke was courteous, intelligent, caring and listened patiently. I asked him why they had not adopted such a simple system, rather than adding yet more strata of administration. He said they could have done it that way, but they hadn't thought of it, and had been advised by the likes of Duncan Nichol to go for more bureaucracy and create glorious NHS Trusts. A quarter of a century later I understand the NHS is still subject to eternal funding crises and slippage.

When the NHS had been created after the war, under Labour's Aneurin Bevan, he bought off the Consultants with a system of Merit Awards. 'Stuff their mouths with gold' he had said. That system continued, and I myself was a beneficiary. Committees were set up by the Consultants to decide who should get an award - C, B, A and finally A plus. They were mainly determined by research papers, which left the consultant who was just a good doctor rather neglected. The system also ignored the fact that someone good at research might run out of steam or want to do more clinical medicine. The obvious solution would have been to allow someone to move their award from Research to Clinical, by dividing the senior awards into a teaching and a research/academic component. But no one likes giving anything up, especially not money, and especially if ones pension at retirement is decided by the income right at the end of your career.

A change I made which I believe still bears fruit, was in the way in which house officers were selected across the region. Previously it had been entirely in the hands of the consultants, so juniors would be appointed to house jobs just for their perceived prestige. I designed a computerised matching system whereby the new doctors had a major say in who they worked for, and the teaching hospital academic units, some of which had got bad reputations could not just take the pick of the best students. The programme looked for the best two-way match. Needless to say, this was regarded as fair by most colleagues, but as outrageous by those with the worst reputations.

WORKING WITH ENDOCRINE SOCIETIES AND JOURNALS IN THE UK

Shortly before John Daly died I was approached by Professor (now Dame) Lesley Rees, a friend from the Hammersmith and Barts, and asked if I would consider working with her as co-editor of the relatively new journal *Clinical Endocrinology*. I decided to accept, and found this an interesting and not too taxing task, which I took on for four years. Some of my colleagues were incredibly prolific researchers, the trick being to get into a new field, especially one where there were lots of new hormones, and work yourself and your juniors to the bone. At the Hammersmith hospital I remember sitting in the Endocrine Investigation Unit one day, talking to a keen young houseman of impeccable endocrine lineage called Stephen Bloom, who wanted to know what I thought of his going to work with Professor John Nabarro at the Middlesex Hospital to develop an assay for the hormone glucagon. I encouraged him to do so, little knowing that this would be the start of a meteoric career in the new field of gut hormones. When ten or so years later Professor Booth retired from the Hammersmith, Steve, now a shining star, succeeded him and the last time I heard he had published, or co-published more than 700 papers. I presume he must now have exceeded 1,000, where most of us were happy with a hundred and a bit. He has now been knighted, and made a Fellow of the Royal Society (FRS), which latter especially is an hyper-admirable achievement. However maybe at times he went a smidgeon too fast. While I was editor of *Clinical Endocrinology,* one paper submitted by his team and on which he was a co-author, was judged by the reviewers to be full of holes, and was sent back several times for extensive revision and some new experiments. His laboratory was noted for its speed, further experiments showed it to be wrong, and another paper was submitted to another journal and published by the fast track. Not knowing this, eventually we did publish a revised version of the original paper. Unfortunately due to a time warp, the paper with the data now accepted as correct appeared earlier than the one that was wrong. I don't know if anyone in the field was as confused as I was, but there must be a moral in it somewhere.

I was also active in both the UK Society for Endocrinology and the Endocrine Section of the Royal Society of Medicine, of which I was Secretary from 1976 to 1980, and finally became President the year before I left for Hong Kong. There was a lot of fragmentation of endocrinology into smaller Societies. In 1980 in the process of putting together a bid for the next International Society of Endocrinology meeting in Montreal, due for 1984, which we lost partly through lack of support of our

UK member Roger Short, we came up with a plan to establish an annual meeting of the British Endocrine Societies The first took place in Edinburgh in 1982, and it has taken place annually ever since. Upon retirement I set up the Senior Section with Professor Gavin Vinson, with the idea of providing continuity upon retirement, encouraging continuing participation of senior members with the main society, and sustaining depth of understanding of past work and ideas. This has been a qualified success.

RETURN OF THE KISZKO CASE

I mentioned earlier the case of Stefan Kiszko, a patient of mine at Manchester Royal Infirmary who in 1976 was convicted in Leeds Crown Court of the horrific murder in early October 1975 of Lesley Molseed. I had been called to Leeds Crown Court to meet his defence team under David Waddington, but was not asked to give evidence at his trial. If I had been cross-examined in Court, the outcome might have been different. I had later been contacted once by his lawyer, but felt there was little I could do to intervene. In fact I had been made to feel partially guilty myself, since I had prescribed the testosterone replacement, said by others to have stimulated aggression in a latent paedophilic psychopath. Many were the occasions when I had mentioned in lectures the lesson I believed I had taken from this case. Then in the summer of 1991, I was phoned by a Police Inspector called Trevor Wilkinson, who wanted to interview me, as they were reviewing Kiszko's case. He said this was routine whenever the convicted man continued to protest his innocence, (which is not in fact the case). We met in my office in the Clinical Sciences Building at Hope hospital, and he told me that they had found evidence that sperm heads had been left on the little girl's clothing. Knowing that Kiszko could not have produced sperm, I said that this meant he was innocent. Shortly afterwards I met Wilkinson with Kiszko's lawyer Campbell Malone. I have written at length on the Kiszko case in my book *'Three False Convictions, Many lessons'*, so I won't say more here. Two police officers actually came all the way to Hong Kong to take a written statement. I remember Jenny was very concerned that one of our sons might have got into trouble back home. But this was my first real indication that all was not well in the world's justice systems.

Ten years later, based on incontrovertible DNA evidence, and a perfect match on the UK DNA database, Lesley Molseed's real killer, Ronald Castree, was convicted. It transpired that not long after Lesley's murder he had been convicted twice of abducting small children in his taxi, for which offences he had been fined by Magistrates' Courts a sum of twenty-five and fifty pounds respectively! The first of these took place at around the time of Stefan Kiszko's trial; the abducted small girl had escaped, and had actually identified Castree as her abductor.

PAYBACK TIME AT TWICKENHAM

Let me conclude this chapter with something lighter than injustice! Kieran Moriarty was a gastroenterologist and friend at Hope, who had played a practical joke on me at his Unit's Christmas party, and I felt he was owed one in return. It so happened that John O'Driscoll, had offered me two tickets for the 1988 England-Ireland game at Twickenham, and I only needed one of them, so he said he would offer the other one to Kieran. It was my custom for years to take my father to International Rugby matches, and we would meet other family members and friends at a pub in South Kensington and then take a taxi to the match. Eilon, son of our good friend Charlie Kenchington needed a ticket, so I gave him the O'Driscoll one, and after lunch he joined Dad and me in the taxi to the ground.

I told him of a scheme I had hatched. I knew Kieran was vehemently against ticket touts, and that he felt I was basically honest, but he might just believe that I would sell a ticket for a profit for the benefit of a charity. I worked closely with a local Paget's Disease Foundation and he might just swallow the idea that I would sell one for Paget's disease research. We agreed that after the match we would meet at the foot of a set of steps outside the stadium and that he would bring Kieran.

'Are you a friend of David Anderson, then?' asks Kieran. 'No, why do you ask?'. 'Well, I wonder how you got your ticket - I hope you don't mind me asking?' 'Oh, I didn't have a ticket, but was desperate to see the match, and I met this guy who had a ticket he wanted rid of'. 'How much did you pay for it?' 'Oh, he said he was selling it for research... something like Paget something, some sort of Foundation, so I was delighted to pay a bit over the top...' How much did you pay?' 'A hundred pounds, but I was really happy'! Silence. At half time the score was 3 nil to Ireland. Then the game changed, England ran in 5 tries, all converted, and the final score was 35-3. So Kieran had a miserable second half. 'Wait till I see that bastard... I'll get you your money back... where did you say he was meeting his friends?' 'Oh, come with me... it was right here'... and as I appeared, Eilon slipped away, and I was confronted by a furious Kieran, 'Good match wasn't it Kieran' I said 'and didn't England do well?...' 'You bastard, David, you give that money back right now to this young lad (who had just disappeared).' His humiliation was amplified as we all then went and joined John and Barry O'Driscoll and some other Irish rugby greats for a beer, and everyone thought it was hilarious. What a cad I can be at times.

CHAPTER 8

MANCHESTER, MUSIC, MUSICIANS AND ARTISTS

SOME EXTRAORDINARILY DISTINGUISHED FAMILY MUSICIANS

There are many corners of our family where great musicians lurk, one of which resulted from Uncle Kenneth's otherwise failed first marriage to Tamara Coates, oboist daughter of the composer Albert Coates. Kenneth, a mechanical engineer and professor to trade was also a brilliant clarinetist, and they had identical-twin daughters, Elizabeth (Libby) and Tanya, who became respectively a violinist and a cellist, both of great distinction. Marian, Ken's second wife, also a cellist, became a great friend of my mother and they used to go to string-teacher conferences together. Libby was later nurtured by Mum's pianist sister Mary Forbes when she first came to England to go to the Royal Academy of Music. Mary had married Watson Forbes, viola player and founder of the Aeolian String Quartet, and they had two sons we knew well, and who are both distinguished musicians. Sebastian, the older, is an organist, composer, and was Professor of Music at Guilford. He played and his *al capella* choir sang at our wedding. And Rupert Forbes (who we knew as children by his middle name

Oliver), as already mentioned, was a distinguished opera singer for many years with Basel Opera.

At the Royal Academy of Music, Libby Hunt met and ultimately married Raphael Wallfisch. He became a superlative solo concert cellist, whose father Peter was a brilliant pianist, and mother Anita Lasker-Wallfisch was also a renowned cellist. Anita is an Auschwitz survivor, who survived because she played in the Auschwitz 'orchestra', which was looking to improve its strings section. She and her sister Renate, now aged respectively ninety-three and ninety-six, are probably the oldest such survivors, and she recently addressed the *Bundestag*. Anita refused for fifty years to go to Germany, but since Peter's death she has become the most important advocate for less fortunate Auschwitz victims, educating the next generation to understand as far as possible what happened in the holocaust.

Peter and Raphael Wallfisch often came and stayed with us in Bramhall before and after their BBC radio concerts. Peter was quite absent-minded, and one day just before a concert mistook the door into the cellar for the door into the hall, and plunged headlong down the stairs into the void, fortunately into a bag of golf clubs, which softened the impact. After that I painted a perfect cadence on the door to remind him on future visits. On another occasion I arranged two concerts, one at Hope Hospital, and one at Stockport Grammar School. Peter and Raphael played with the clarinetist Anton Weinberg, and Hope had just spent £1,000 on a reasonable upright piano. After their rehearsal Peter said, 'David, how can one play on such an instrument? You actually paid **money** for it?... It is dead... it has no spirit...' The concert, which featured Brahms' exquisite clarinet trio, was excellent. I confidently reassured Peter that the school piano, a Bechstein grand, would be better the next day. After the rehearsal I asked him what he thought of the piano. 'How can the head of music call himself a musician and allow such a piano to exist? - it is dead, it has no life, no spirit... give me the piano I played on yesterday!' Again the concert was a great success.

Libby and Raphael have two sons and a daughter, and all three are musicians. Ben is a conductor and distinguished composer of film music and right hand man to Hans Zimmer. Simon is a highly entertaining singing cellist and operatic baritone; and Joanna, who is based in New York, is a great jazz singer and lyricist. So maybe the Almighty's sexual attraction and random DNA mixing method wasn't such a bad one after all, at least when it comes to musicians!

ON SINGING AND SAILING

In Manchester I joined a small choir called the Rollerson Singers, which was run by a bored maths teacher but really good musician, Brian Rollerson, whose wife Joan also had a lovely voice, which was more than you could say for the rest of us. The pianist was the chain-smoking Nancy Hartley who was very good on the ivories and was married to Conrad Hartley, who amongst other things wrote several North Country recitations, the general structure of which is that you subtly multiply the improbabilities. The very best of them all was written by Conrad and is entitled *Sam's Low Note* (see appendix). I used to recite this or one of the others I know in the concerts as an interlude. Each summer we did a concert performance of a light operetta, in Lyme Hall. Nancy had a terrible voice herself, but was an excellent teacher, and fed up with singing badly I went to her for some lessons which helped a bit.

Our sons were never very keen on the Rollerson singers, and deeply resented any coercion to come to our summer concert. They were, however keen on the idea of sailing so I bought an *Enterprise* dinghy, and for a time belonged to a sailing club based at Errwood reservoir, where I tended to come in last and we capsized with some regularity in the fickle winds. (This was good practice for a quarter of a century later, when I once crewed for my Rotarian friend Tom Sheppard, a former Hong Kong Olympic champion. We were well in the lead when, unable to respond lithely to the warning, 'Ready about!', I was projected open-mouthed into the bacterial sesspit that is Hong Kong's once-pristine harbour. The fleet passed us by as we righted the boat. I did better bacteriologically when that evening, after the first borborygmic-rumble, I started ciprofloxacin. I was never asked to crew again - but once again I have digressed)...

My brother Stuart had built himself a *Mirror* dinghy, which was more stable than an *Enterprise*, and which he left with us in the late 1970's, when he went off to do medical missionary work for a time in Zaire. In the summer of 1976 we took a holiday with Rupert, Jayne and their young family, in a place called Cour on the Kintyre peninsula, and we trailed the *Mirror* there with us. 'Let's sail over to Arran' I said. 'What a good idea', replied Rupert. We were becalmed and had to row on the way out, but on the way back we experienced storm-force winds. We compounded the error by heading for the wrong bay, but eventually got back to Cour somehow, just using the jib, and expecting an, 'Oh we were so worried, we thought you'd capsized, and we do so love you both', sort of reception. What we got instead was more like, 'You selfish inconsiderate bastards, we're never going to speak to you again, and you were supposed to be smoking the mackerel, you've ruined supper' one. No one seemed remotely relieved that we had survived, or was even impressed that on the way in we had rescued some poor swimmer who was being washed out to sea.

A TRIP TO JAPAN AND A LOVE OF JAPANESE ART

Jenny and I share tastes in art, and in 1983 we went to a bone meeting in Kobe, with Dr Isobel Braidman who had taken over the bone research from Stavros. I had just read *Shogun* and was jet-lagged when I awoke from a deep sleep at the end of a Japanese researcher's talk, to a startling announcement. 'And finally two Samurais!' he shouted. Rudely awakened I realised with relief that he was just announcing the end of his presentation. At the end, Isobel, her rabbinical husband, Jenny and I went for two days and a night to Nikko, burial place of Ieyasu, the famed first Shogun. I remember that the rabbi had the strange idea that the best way to communicate in Japan was to speak loudly in Italian. That trip to Nikko got me really interested in Japanese art, and we still have two *Ukiyo-e* prints we got on that trip, including a wonderful original *kakemomo-e* print of Hiroshige's *Monkey Bridge by Moonlight*. We paid 150,000 Yen (about £430) for it, shipped to Bramhall. The same print is one of two illustrated both in *Southeby's Art at Auction, 1983,* and in *Christie's Art at Auction, 1984,* auction price £24,000. Once I had touched up ours a little with water colours it actually looks better than either of the auctioned ones, as the colour and tone in all ten different blocks match perfectly in top and bottom halves (see illustrations). I shared Japanese lessons for a couple of years after that, with John Bu'lock, husband of Denise, the head of my steroid lab.

In 1988, when I took a year's part-time sabbatical to work on the molecular biology of Paget's disease, I went back to Japan for a further two meetings, and my little Japanese certainly came in useful in a remote *Onsen* where no English was spoken, and Jenny and I bathed discretely, towels concealing the naughty bits, in hot baths of steaming dilute sulphuric acid. I only gave up learning Japanese when it was clear that we were going to Hong Kong, when I changed to Cantonese, which is even more difficult. The 1988 trip was also my first visit to China, which was beginning to open up after the death of Mao Tse Dung. We went to Guilin, where I nearly learnt the hard way that Chinese buffaloes are not to be trusted, as I was sketching one across a pond by a paddy field; it spotted me and charged round, horns down. Only the lady in charge of the buffalo, shouting and waving her hat, stopped it tossing me into a paddy field full of human excreta.

Towards the end of the trip, Jenny went home from Japan, while I went to several scientific meetings. In Kyoto I booked myself and Kostos Mavroudis into a local downmarket *ryokan*, called a *minshuku*, which was at the lower end of creature comforts. The proprieter's elderly mother defecated in a little open toilet close to our room, much to Kostos' combined amusement and dismay! He even summoned me to witness this ritual. The *minshuku's* main advantage was its price, rather than its odour or its air conditioning. I wrote this in my diary of the first night there... 'Futons out, lights out, air conditioning on (v. hot). I wake up after two hours and switch it off. One hour later I wake again due to snoring Greek. 'Shut up, Kostos'...he shuts up. One hour later Kostos wakes up, too hot, and gets a drink of water. A half-hour later, I wake up sweltering and after another half-hour switch on the air conditioning, and the cycle starts again...'

MRS SUMIKO UEKI, NIIGATA'S PRIME GOLFING WOODBLOCK-PRINT ARTIST

The final meeting I went to in 1988 was In Niigata, which was memorable mainly because the organisers had offered the option of an evening being entertained in a real Japanese home. I wrote that I was learning Japanese, didn't need a translator, and asked if I might dine with Niigata's prime Japanese print artist, who had done the conference programme illustrations, and was obviously very accomplished. She was Mrs Sumiko Ueki, whose late husband had been a neurosurgeon, and whose two children were doctors. It was a very nice meal, and we spoke in a mixture of bad Japanese and bad English.

When she had got married her husband had said... 'I want be famous neurosurgeon', to which she replied, 'I want be famous woodblock-print artist'. 'No, not possible, you look after me, home, have children.' 'But I want learn to be woodblock-print artist.' 'No, you are my wife now'. 'When can I become woodblock-print artist then?' 'When you forty years old'... So there she was, patiently being a good wife and counting the days. Nineteen years passed quicker than her husband had expected ...'It my birthday, I now forty, you keep promise and I become Japanese woodblock-print artist'. So she got trained and became an excellent, if at times dangerous, (*vide infra*) woodblock-print artist. Her husband who had as I recall trained in Sweden, had died in his fifties, but had been a keen and respected member of Niigata Golf Club, so Mrs Ueki inherited his membership, and took to golf with great enthusiasm. I had a pleasant evening, and at the end she said she was going to come over to Sweden for two weeks in about six weeks time. I think there was an exhibition of her work somewhere. I foolishly said she should spend some time in England, and come and look us up. Maybe it was the *sake*, but it was certainly a mistake. Next day there was a message at the Conference desk from Mrs Ueki, asking if we could meet for lunch, which we did. 'I want take your advice come England after Sweden'. 'Oh that's nice, let me know when and maybe I can introduce you to some artists, and art galleries...' 'Oh no, I no want meet artists, I no want see galleries... I want play golf!' So now I've talked myself into organising a golf tour of Britain for Mrs Ueki.

When I got home Jenny was not pleased at the prospect of her staying, so we booked her in to Bramhall's Moat House Hotel, had her round for a couple of meals, and introduced her to the distinguished local artist Harold Riley. Harold was still recovering from the fact that his wife Ashraf had shared his bottle of *Chateau Mouton Rothschild 1943*, with her friend Helen Franks, in the mistaken belief that it was an old unlabelled bottle of worthless *Chateau Plonk*. This had been a gift of the Baron himself and the very recounting of it still, months or years later, made him apocalyptically apoplectic, especially as Ashraf had said it didn't taste too bad. Over the next two days Jenny and her ebullient Scottish playing partner Ina Aspinall took Mrs Ueki out on Bramhall Golf Course for two rounds of golf. Apart from losing her Seiko watch in a bunker, she had a great time, and went off north to Edinburgh, Gleneagles, and finally St Andrews. 'Thank God for that', we thought. Her watch turned up three months later and the Ladies' Committee refused to believe it could have lain in a bunker all that time, because it was still working. The watch was waterproof to a depth of fifty metres, but it took a great deal of persuasion to have it restored to its owner.

Now it so happened that the next weekend was the twenty-fifth anniversary of our qualifying as doctors, and our reunion was held in a posh hotel in Dunkeld. After the reunion, we decided to go home via St Andrews, and arrived there just before lunch. I had a pang of conscience about Mrs Ueki, who knew we might come to St Andrews and look her up, so we went to the Old Course Hotel to say 'hi'. She was out, so I wrote a message saying 'hi', and telling her not to forget that the following Wednesday she was due in Oxford to meet my Aunt Helen, a keen watercolour artist. We went to the bar in the hotel grounds, for a beer and a sandwich, and who was sitting there but Mrs Ueki, talking to Arnold Palmer's caddy. 'Oh, herrow, I want you meet Arnold Palmer caddy. He going to caddy for me too.' She had so far had the holiday of her life, because things had also gone swimmingly in Edinburgh and Gleneagles, where she had hijacked a golfer called Marge, who put her up for free. We said our fond farewells, first running over once again the arrangements to meet my elderly Aunt Helen the following Wednesday in Oxford.

David Coussmaker Anderson

THERE'S A CHINESE-LOOKING LADY FOR YOU IN RECEPTION, PROF.

Two days later at about 4 pm I was in the middle of a ward round at Hope Hospital, and got a call from the admissions desk...'Professor Anderson there's a very distressed Chinese-looking lady here asking for you. She says you know her and she has to see you urgently. She says it is an emergency'. I racked my brains as to who it might be, thinking through all possibilities from China and Japan as I went down; and there my worst fears were realised in the form of Mrs Sumiko Ueki. She was indeed distressed and had her hand placed in front of my mouth. 'Mrs Ueki, what the hell are you doing here, you are supposed to be on the train to Oxford to meet my aunt'. 'Oh no, doctor, I can't see your aunt now, I too embarrassing'. 'I know you're embarrassing, Mrs Ueki, but why are you here, and why have you got your hand in front of your mouth like that?' Well, it turned out that everything had gone fine until she bit into a British Rail sandwich to the north of Crewe, caught a concealed piece of bone, and broke her dentures. So, knowing I would come up with something, she got off the train at Crewe, took the next one to Manchester, and a taxi out to visit her tour-coordinator, who happened also to be Professor of Endocrinology at Salford's Hope Hospital. Desperate, I telephoned my dentist, explained the situation and sent her round by taxi, with instructions then to get her on to the next train to Oxford. He did a quick denture repair-job with Super-glue, charged her £25, and put her into another taxi to Manchester's Piccadilly Station, and so honour was saved.

The following morning my aunt met her at her hotel in Oxford. Mrs Ueki gave her a print (on my instructions, because she was quite tight and wanted to have one of Helen's watercolours). Aunt Helen drove her round to see the sites of Oxford and the Cotswolds. Mrs Ueki was a prolific photographer of reference material for her prints, and Helen said she would without any warning leap out of the car at traffic lights to take a picture she must have for her next, Oxford, print series. She survived and mid-morning they stopped in a teashop for a cup of tea and a piece of cake, and at first bite the Super-glue gave way and her dentures fell apart. But that was okay because they had now met. (She later complained about the dentist's bill). She had had such a good holiday organised by Ander-tours that she wanted to come and see Wales the following year, which she did, but this time with another, and professional, tour operator. Ander-tours, for obvious reasons, had gone bust.

MODERN ARTISTS

Over the years Jenny and I built up a sizeable art collection, initially of watercolours, then Japanese prints and woodblock-printed books. But it has been a real privilege to collect works of art by living artists, of whom I shall concentrate here on three in particular. The first is Carlos Nadal, a Catalan artist from Sitges, who in the late 1980's was being promoted by John Duncalfe in his gallery in Harrogate. We first met John at an exhibition of Harold Riley's work, which included two excellent dog drawings that I had bought from Harold, and we still have along with an excellent portrait of his first wife. Nadal's works are freely painted oils and acrylics, similar in style to Raoul Dufy, but in my opinion better. Eventually I got to know him and his wife Flore Joris, who was dying of metastatic breast cancer; we had been using pamidronate for bone metastases, and I got some for her, which greatly eased the last three months of her life. Carlos kindly gave us a fine oil painting as a generous thank-you gift. In 1988 when I was in Tokyo I found a gallery in the Ginza district where there was a Dufy landscape in the window. So I went in with some cards and catalogues of Nadal's work. The owner was very interested, and asked when he had died. I told them he was elderly but still alive. 'Oh no, in that case not interested - you see we only deal in dead artists.' 'But surely Picasso produced some of his best work when he was still alive?' I thought and moved on. Carlos did, of course, eventually die.

The second artist was Albert du Mesnildot, who had trained before the war in the *Beaux Arts* in Paris, fought in the resistance, and now lived in Aups in the Var area of southern France with his wife Claudine. They set up a pottery, where he threw the pots and she decorated them. He also did some very entertaining ceramic figures. My brother-in-law Rupert and family, while staying on holiday with friends, brought back some surreal watercolour drawings on display in the pottery. Albert always said he was an artist who just worked as a potter to earn money. I was immediately very enthusiastic, and thought that Duncalfe might be interested to promote him. Lika, a friend of Rupert's, selected ten for us, which we loved, and Jenny and I eventually also got to know Albert and Claudine on holiday visits. John Duncalfe was enthusiastic, and Jenny and I flew over one weekend in November with him and his partner Tony. The idea was to select works for an exhibition in Harrogate. John was bowled over by his work, and together we selected around 150, for which Albert was paid his asking price. The *Beaux Arts* in Paris could not believe that they had missed such an original and important living artist. Before releasing the work they even telephoned him to ask if he was still alive, and he said he was. The exhibition, in the summer of 1989 was a huge success, except that his daughter Veronique came, and when she saw the gallery's prices thought her father had not been paid enough. Rupert and I went over in 1990 to make a further selection for another exhibition. Then that autumn Lika, our initial go-between, committed suicide convincingly by jumping into the half-mile-deep *Gorges du Verdon*. Rupert and Jayne drove over for the funeral, and paid for and returned with the

Du Mesnildot ceramics, rather than the drawings. This was a mistake, because a short while afterwards Albert, whose health was poor anyway, died of a heart attack. Sad in its own right, it also meant that there was no possibility of Albert's achieving posthumous recognition, as his children refused to part with any more of his works; under French Napoleonic Law his widow had no say, which is surprising since a man chooses his wife and the children just happen.

Another and very special artist is the Mancunian artist Geoffrey Key, one of Britain's most original, inventive and industrious painters. We have collected his work since 1989, when we first met him and his life-partner Judith O'Leary, at an exhibition, and they since became close personal friends. When I went to Hong Kong I offered to take some drawings and see if I could interest an art gallery. I was not put off by the experience three years earlier in Tokyo over Nadal. Geoffrey was even more alive than Nadal, and his work has a sculptural quality, which is not surprising as he also trained as a sculptor. Trained in Manchester in the very dark *Northern School*, he had the strength of will to give up teaching, and for two years just to paint a single Derbyshire hill, the Nab, opposite his house. Eventually figures started to emerge, and these became progressively bolder and more authoritative, as he developed the ability to paint from his subconscious, exploring a range of constantly recurring themes. Initially he used muted tones, and then when he came to Hong Kong for an exhibition, as with Van Gogh moving to southern France, he suddenly and irrevocably discovered colour.

A WEEKEND IN MONTMARTRE, PARIS

I must admit that though Jenny and I share artistic tastes, I have been more of a driver in our collecting. So especially in the days when we had wall space to cover, and our lives still lay mostly ahead of us, she was reluctant to let me go into an antique shop or an art-gallery, and believed that it would be less dangerous if I had no money. And of course this would apply to trips away from home, for example to Harrogate, or Japan. So it was no surprise when, as we were about to go for a weekend to Paris and she had taken the money out of our joint account, she was reluctant to give me any of it. 'Look, it isn't reasonable to have all the money in one place, least of all in your handbag', I argued. 'You know perfectly well I shall be responsible, I always am'. But she was adamant, until we got onto the plane, and I insisted again. In fact I entered without permission one of most private places a woman has, as I took the sum of £300, half of the money, out of said handbag. 'It makes no sense to leave it all in one place'. So with tacit post-tantrum accord we went to our hotel, and then to Montmartre.

'Let's take a look in this gallery', I said, as I entered a covered walkway at the top of Montmartre, and in I went, turning left into this small gallery, and up some steps. Fifteen seconds later there was a familiar scream, and I rushed back to find Jenny in distress... 'a man in an anorak just stole my purse out of my handbag' she pined. 'Go get him!' Part vindicated and part angry, I rushed out and down the hill after the thief screaming in my best French, *'Voleur! Voleur! Arrêtez-le, il a pris le porte-monnaie de ma femme!* I kept up with him all the way to the bottom, when he vaporized into the crowd. In order to claim on the insurance we had to report the theft to the police, who were very relaxed, and said, *'Sans doute c'était un arabe'*, put us in a police car and drove us round to see if we could recognise him. But all either of us had seen was the back of a man in a hooded anorak. And yes, he probably was an Arab. On holiday ever since Jenny has always given me at least half the holiday cash.

CHAPTER 9

MEDICINE IN HONG KONG AND A SECOND CHINESE NIGHTMARE

AN INNOCENT TELEPHONE CALL

One afternoon in late 1990 I was working in the Paget's Disease Clinic which I ran with Sylvia Mercer, our excellent research nurse, and I got a call from Hilary Critchley, a young gynaecologist whose research I was supervising. 'Sorry to trouble you Prof, but do you remember me telling you that my brother, Julian, has taken up a post as Reader in Clinical Pharmacology at the Chinese University of Hong Kong? Well they are looking for a new Professor of Medicine and he has asked me to ask if you can suggest anyone'. I apologised, and said I was busy in the Clinic, but that I'd give it some thought and phone her back that evening. When I got home I said to Jenny... 'I had this phone call from Hilary in the clinic. There's a Chair of Medicine going in Hong Kong. She wants to know if I can suggest anyone, and I've been thinking about it on the way home. And I can't think of anyone except myself'. 'Why not?' Jenny replied, 'Go for it, we could do with a change!' 'You're serious?' Julian came over shortly afterwards, and we met rather furtively. I later learnt that everything about Julian was furtive. But I was coming up to my fiftieth birthday, and we had always intended to go abroad for the last ten years of our working lives. So Julian took the message back to Professor Tek Oh, Dean of Medicine, who seemed very interested in my applying. I sent a copy of my CV and an application. The more I thought about it, the more it appealed to me. The only downside, it seemed, was that I would not be able to continue to work on Paget's disease, for the simple reason that there is virtually none in China.

On my fiftieth birthday our youngest son, Neil, got married in Buckfast Abbey. Fortunately they chose that day, as a week later they would have been snowed-in. He and Mary Clare eventually had three lovely daughters, our first grandchildren. At the wedding, all four of our parents encouraged me to go for the Hong Kong job. Sadly, Jenny's (non-smoking) mother Elizabeth, who was expected to live to a hundred, was soon diagnosed with advanced lung cancer, and went downhill quite quickly. I went with Jenny to Hong Kong, where we stayed with my cousin Martyn, decided to apply formally and I was called for interview. It was shortly after that I discovered that my appointment was not likely to be welcomed by the Professor of Surgery, Arthur Li.

'CAN YOU SEE MY WINKING FINGAH?'

There was a neurosurgeon, Charles West, at Hope Hospital, with whom I got on well superficially, until we had a row over my attempts to put some improved structure into the ill-conceived 'snake' teaching-programme for the final year students. I asked him to do an extra teaching session every so often, and he refused. I was making a series of medical teaching films showing examination techniques, and before this falling-out I had asked Charles, who seemed keen, to demonstrate on film the examination of the cranial nerves. Having filmed him, Rob Mitchell and I decided that we just could not use the footage. For example when checking the visual fields to confrontation he would ask the patient, in a very upper-class tone of voice, 'Can you see my winking fingah?' So I quietly dropped Charles West and chose a neurologist from Manchester Royal Infirmary, Richard Metcalfe for the nervous system examination, with excellent results.

Well it so happened that Charles had gone as *locum* neurosurgeon to the Prince of Wales Hospital in Shatin, for six months, and was working in the Department of Surgery with his erstwhile Cambridge classmate Arthur Li. Julian Critchley warned me that there was 'trouble i't mill' as they say in Lancashire, in the form of Charles, who let it be known, or so I understood, that I was a man full of promises and no action. He appeared to have cited the uncompleted film I had recorded with him. In the end, forewarned, I brought a copy with me, and left it with Julian and so the dean. I met Charles there, and again back in Salford when I had been appointed, and he was very charming and congratulated me, but it was a long time before the appointment was confirmed. I know that all sorts of machinations went on behind the scenes, with phone calls to my colleague Professor Sir Miles Irving (a loud but eminent ano-rectal surgeon amicably nick-named Sir Piles Bleeding). I was the oldest of the five candidates. The best was undoubtedly Philip Johnson, who was probably seen as being too good, and maybe too young to get rid of if he turned out to be pushy. The move to Hong Kong was certainly a life-changing experience. I left Manchester University, where I had been made Reader in, then Professor of, Endocrinology, with considerable mixed feelings, not the least of which was the disconnection from my large Clinic of Paget's patients. Harold Cohen had long since retired, and been replaced with two young colleagues, so the team, which also included Dr Helen Buckler, was left in good hands. It was obviously disruptive for Jenny too, as she had set up a separate practice in Bramhall, just round the corner from our house. But she was game for it. Our sons, meanwhile had left home, although Neil, recently married, may especially have felt we were letting him down.

A FIRST TASTE OF INSTITUTIONAL DYSFUNCTION

I took up post on October 21st 1991, and Jenny joined me in the New Year. Long before her arrival I had discovered that the Faculty of Medicine at the Chinese University was, even by Manchester standards, extremely dysfunctional. The then-Dean, Tek Oh, Professor of Anaesthetics, was a good if at times irascible man, who had been very supportive of my appointment. Ethnically Chinese, he was Australian and didn't speak a Chinese language - so was colloquially labelled 'a banana'. It was very clear from the start that the power behind the Faculty throne was Professor Arthur Li, younger brother of David Li, the head of the Bank of East Asia. As soon as I arrived Arthur explained that we were at war with those 'f---ing bastards' in Hong Kong University (HKU), who will do anything and everything to destroy us! Partly as a result of this hatred, which did have a loose historical (as well as an obvious hysterical) basis, the Faculty of Medicine contained many foreigners like myself. There was a desire in the Faculty not to employ too many graduates from HKU, which was seen as the major and long-established rival. This, however, presented a problem, namely how to control free academic thinkers who (unlike local Chinese) were used to the reasoned expression of dissent. I soon discovered that although academic excellence was valued, it came a poor second to unquestioning obedience to the whim of one man.

NEW BOY ON THE BLOCK

I already knew John Gosling, the Professor of Anatomy, from his time at Manchester, when we were both on the Student

Selection Committee. He, Julian Critchley and I had decided we wanted to attract Philip Johnson. He had stood against me for the Chair of Medicine, but there was also the professorial post to be filled in Clinical Oncology; we persuaded him to apply, and his interview followed in early December 1991, when I had been in post for a mere six weeks. I was, of course, the new boy on the block, but I was put on the selection committee and was soon approached separately by three other members, Professors Arthur Li (Surgery), Alan Chang (Obstetrics and Gynaecology), and Joseph Lee (Pathology). All tried to persuade me to vote against Johnson, and appoint the alternative, internal, candidate, Dr Wesley Shiu, to a readership. Shiu would not be an academic threat, especially to the Department of Surgery. However he had done research and written his MD thesis in the Christie Hospital in Manchester, and I had done my homework. His erstwhile boss Professor Crowther, revealed that he had had problems completing his thesis.

When it came to the interviews I saw for the first time Chinese medical politics at work and it was not a pretty sight. The order of seating was, going round anti-clockwise, Andrew Wong (administrator); John Gosling; then a scientist who was external to the Faculty; then Professors Tek Oh (the Dean and Committee Chairman); Arthur Li; Alan Chang; Joseph Lee; and finally myself. Well there was basically no contest between the two candidates, in terms of academia, references and interviews. When the discussion started, opinions were sought counterclockwise. Gosling gave cogent reasons for Johnson and the chemist agreed on the basis of what he had seen. Then Arthur went into a blistering attack on Johnson, saying he would pinch all the kudos for his work on liver cancer; Chang and Lee followed suit each taking their cue from the leader. So the score was now three to two in favour of Johnson and it was my turn. I started by saying I found it hard to believe I had been on the same selection committee as some of my

David Coussmaker Anderson

colleagues. Shiu's English had been poor (and he'd lived in England for 16 years); I found his answers less than frank, and I presented the information I had got from his former boss, Professor Crowther. It was now three all, no one changed, and the Dean used his casting vote for Johnson, who was therefore appointed. After the interview the Dean was furious with his three colleagues and pleased I had not buckled under pressure. But I was now clearly a marked man. Philip Johnson was ultimately acknowledged to be the best appointment the Faculty had ever made.

HOME FOR CHRISTMAS, THEN BACK WITH JENNY

I went home for Christmas with Jenny and her family. Our Christmases were held in her brother O'Donel's house in Handsworth Wood in Birmingham, and were always splendid occasions. Jenny had a maternal Uncle, Joe, who was an eccentric bachelor GP and entertaining racconteur, who had been sunk twice while serving in the navy during the war. A measure of his eccentricity was that he spent the whole of that Christmas going through the London telephone directory, trying to discover his gardener's surname. He knew only his first name, address and telephone number. And I understand that he found him in Volume 4 several months later. It was never clear exactly why this information was needed. After the holiday Jenny accompanied me back to Hong Kong, where I had already appointed an excellent Thai maid called Guk.

On the recommendation of Julian Critchley I had bought his second car, a bright red twelve-year-old banger. When Jenny arrived in January, we also bought a new Mazda. We lived in Residence 2, flat 8A, one floor below Arthur Li and his very nice, English, wife Diana. Each flat brought with it a specific allocated car park space, but our predecessor in this flat had not had a car. Ours, which was right next to the entrance, was being used by Arthur for his Mercedes, registration plate AK1. Eventually, when it started to rain I asked Arthur for my car park space, so Jenny would not get wet. He grunted and she started to park the Mazda there. But she was working at the British Military Hospital, and when she got back Arthur's car would be back once again. So when she left I started to move the red banger there. One day Arthur said to Jenny, almost in tears as he came in from the rain, 'I'd rather like my car park space back!' His wife's car AK17 was kept in his allocated spot. License plates meant a lot to Chinese, and he explained to Philip Johnson that he had chosen 17, because upside down it read as 'Li'. He thought this was hilarious.

ON THE FAST TRACK OF FACULTY SCHEMINGS.

I was horrified in Faculty meetings to hear the cabal of its senior members openly insult the Vice-Chancellor, Professor Charles Kao, who was repeatedly referred to as *The Wimp*. Personally I have never seen why a University needs a Chancellor to run its vice, which always seems to run perfectly well on its own. But Kao was an honest, trusting and kindly man who was quite out of his depth fighting the psychopathic schemings of his most powerful Faculty. He did however single-handedly win the 2009 Nobel Prize in Physics for his earlier ground-breaking work in fiber-optic tele-communications. He was to be succeeded as Vice-Chancellor by Arthur K C Li.

I had made it clear at interview that my priority was medical education, any change in which was now fought tooth-and-nail. One problem is that teaching medical students brings departmental money for teaching staff and so power. Any suggestion that certain subjects, such as anatomy or surgery, might be receiving too much attention in the quest to produce rounded doctors, most of whom will enter General Practice, will be contested. Meanwhile I went ahead with my medical teaching film project, with the Faculty of Medicine of Manchester lending its name; but never that of the Chinese University. There was also a clear need to control a pretentious little upstart medical squit-professor who had shown himself quite unwilling to play the game. Within months of my arrival the elections for the post of dean were held. Tek Oh, fed up with Chinese medical politics, declined to stand again. Arthur was denying any interest, but it was clear from all that was going on behind the scenes that he wanted it, and was going to get it, which of course he did, protesting unconvincingly that it was against his will.

BEWARE OF AN ENEMY'S CONFIDENTIAL ADVICE

Within a very short time it became clear that the long knives were out for me. For example, the office I had been left by my New Zealander predecessor was a squalid shambles, and Arthur told me so and encouraged me to use the Departmental 'slush' fund to get it redecorated and refurbished. Julian Critchley thought it was a reasonable plan as well. However, when I started to have it decorated and order a new carpet and furniture it soon became clear that following Arthur's advice would cause an internal rebellion, which was just what my nemesis wanted. I had negotiated a good salary from the Vice Chancellor, and once the office was decorated Professor Oh called me to his office. I told him that I was paying for it out of my own pocket, which I did, but that Arthur had advised me to pay for it from the 'slush' fund. I was learning fast, but clearly not fast enough. Julian Critchley had become a friend, but that friendship was also a double-edged sword, because Faculty pressure was put on me to fuse the Departments of Medicine and Clinical Pharmacology, something he would resist. Within the Department my main *bête noire* was a Chinese nephrologist, who had been an internal candidate for my job, and was universally disliked and distrusted, but had been compensated with a personal chair after my appointment. He clearly felt he should have been appointed instead of me and seemed intent on undermining my position. Nevertheless once I had lost the Chairmanship, which took a year, that responsibility was in fact passed to Professor Jean Woo, a charming geriatrician, effective researcher and popular chairman. The nephrologist eventually moved to a Chair at Hong Kong University, to general relief all round.

LONG KNIVES OUT FOR MY PS

In the summer of 1992 I left the Department while on holiday in the charge of my deputy and fellow endocrinologist, Dr Clive Cockram. He contacted me to say there was a problem concerning my personal secretary, who was very efficient and who I had found invaluable. For example she had seen what was coming in good time over the decoration of my office. Well, doubtless with the help of those out to oust me, the other secretaries contrived to gang up on her. Her husband was a doctor in the Department of Pediatrics, and was in the process of setting himself up in private practice, and during her lunch break she had used my office to interview two candidates for his clinic. Arthur had interrogated her while I was away, and I was told to fire her. I told him I wasn't going to do so and if it was justified then he should be the one to fire her, which he promptly did. I objected, and a triumvirate committee of enquiry was set up under Professor Philip Johnson (under the Faculty's well-tried principle of passing the poisoned chalice to the new boy), with Joseph Lee and another judge. The purpose of this was to investigate my behaviour in supposedly going back on my word. I stood my ground, wrote a report and Johnson refused to censor me. But I lost the chairmanship of the Department. I remember Dr Joseph Sung saying he would vote for me, and 24 hours later saying he couldn't do so for fear of losing his job. (Joseph ultimately succeeded Arthur Li as Vice-Chancellor). I gave my professorial inaugural lecture, on metabolic bone disorders, and was followed shortly by Philip Johnson giving his, which Professor Li pointedly did not attend.

A SMALL MATTER OF BOVINE HEART VALVES

Looking back it is hard to believe just how surreal and unpleasant it was, especially for Jenny. Shortly after I had arrived I had appointed John Sanderson, who had a consultant cardiologist's post in the UK, to a Senior Lecturer post in Cardiology. He probably also came to see me as a trouble-maker, though we did quite a lot of amicable sailing together on the twenty-eight foot *Trapper* yacht Julian and I had bought from two colleagues. Arthur and the Department of Surgery were right that they had plenty of enemies, but one exceptionally foolish thing that he did was to let one of his senior lecturers, Jonathan Ho, who by all accounts was not a very good cardiac surgeon, start using bovine heart valves produced in India for valve-replacement. The results were catastrophic as patient after patient died. John Sanderson was given his poisoned chalice induction to carry out an enquiry into the results, and write a report, which he did sufficiently tactfully that it avoided the Department of Surgery being censored by the Hong Kong Medical Council.

At around the time of the Johnson enquiry I met Professor Alan Chang at a drinks party on campus, and he told me that to understand Arthur Li I should read the book Sun Tsu's *The Art of War*. 'That is his favourite book of all time - how to win wars by stealth, cunning and trickery without a shot being fired'. I bought and read a copy, and in what was by now a borderline paranoid state decided to apply the same principles to my defence. My cousin Martyn, a long-time Hong Kong businessman, gave me the name of a firm of investigators, and I met up with a quiet American called (as his boss also was, and as such men always are), Steve. I was seriously worried that living one floor below Arthur, my flat was bugged, and that everything we said would get back to him. I hadn't realised that spies have always been rife in China, and that authority is always venerated, which explains why there has never been any need for a KGB there. We had our flat swept for bugs, and needless to say found none. Anyway, from that time on I went everywhere wired up for sound. I had a tape recorder in my pocket, and a microphone behind my tie, now knowing that it was perfectly legal to secretly record someone if you thought you were being threatened. There is nothing like being told that on a specific date ... 'But you said, and I have a very good memory, Arthur - these were your very words'... and then to hear yourself quoted back verbatim.

I recall one official lunch in 1992, shortly after Chris Patten had lost his seat in parliament and been appointed Governor by the re-elected prime minister John Major. Julian and I were seated at a table with Arthur Li and the then Minister of Health, a very capable woman called Libby Wong. Chris Patten was for the first time pushing China for a degree of democracy in Hong Kong after the handover. 'It's ridiculous to talk to the Chinese about democracy', said Arthur, and then out of the blue added, 'I mean I could get triads to carry out a contract killing for a mere $20,000 if I chose to'. We wondered who this message was meant for - myself, Libby Wong, the new Governor, or all three! I had several good friends in the Department, who were often used to feed back messages to me from my nemesis. One such was the Department's rheumatologist Dr Edmund Li, who although born in Hong Kong, and member of an important Hong Kong family, had studied Medicine in Canada. As also applied to several others in the Faculty, this put him in a weak position relative to that of UK or Hong Kong graduates, since he was only allowed to practice in Hong Kong in a University teaching-hospital post. Edmund would frequently caution me not to stir up trouble, arguing that I should make my peace with the man in power. 'Edmund, let me ask you one thing. Of all the people you know in Hong Kong, if you were to predict in twenty years time who would be the first President of the break-away Republic of Southern China, who would you choose?' Without a second's hesitation he said 'Oh, Arthur of course'. 'So there is my answer, Edmund. QED.' As I often argued, all that is necessary for the triumph of evil is for good men to do nothing (*Burke*, also an Edmund).

GET AN ENEMY TO DO YOUR DIRTY WORK

Arthur Li was past-master at getting his enemies to do his dirty work. For example, also within the Department of Surgery was another politically-ambitious man, the ophthalmic surgeon and accomplished amateur violinist, Professor Patrick Ho. It was an open secret that he and Arthur were sworn rivals; for a time Patrick even had a notice on his office door, which was just down the corridor from Arthur's, which effectively told the Head of Department to keep out. It seemed, however, in 1993 that there was to be some kind of truce, as a plan was hatched for a unified academic Hong Kong Institute of Ophthalmology where the two Medical Schools would work together, and which would be set up and supported by a private charity, the Croucher Foundation. This would of course in reality be run by, and for the benefit of the Chinese University. I was on the Committee, and that was the gist of the plan. Patrick was charged with coming up with a proposal, on the clear understanding that he would head up the Institute, and it would be a joint Institution in little more than name. He wrote an excellent proposal, and after one meeting I remember warning him of the dangers of not getting everything signed, sealed and settled in advance. 'He'll put the knife in, Patrick, so take care'.

The proposal was approved by the Croucher, and the game plan was immediately changed. It was of course, to be a pure formality, but the post had to be advertised and Patrick Ho had to apply for the post. It went without saying that it was to be his, but equally predictably, he wasn't appointed. Instead the post was given to an ophthalmic pathologist from outside Hong Kong, Mark Tso. I understand that Patrick Ho was so angry, that he promptly resigned from his post at the University and went into full-time private ophthalmological practice. Already well-in with mainland China, in 2002 he joined the second post-handover Government under Tung Chee Wah and became Secretary of Home Affairs. (Cantonese is a tonal language and I sometimes wondered if it was really a coincidence that 'Tung, Chi, Wah', said in the wrong tones, could mean 'pain, shit, lies'). In Tung's government Ho was to work later alongside Arthur Li, who, after spending six years as Vice-Chancellor of the Chinese University, left and became a predictably controversial Minister of Manpower and Education. Patrick Ho left the Government in 2007, and continued his close ties with the Chinese mainland, working for CEFC, a Shanghai-based energy company. He has recently been detained in the USA accused of bribery charges in Africa, for which he is now on trial and has been refused $10 million in bail. Meanwhile, Arthur Li is currently a member of the Executive Council of the Hong Kong Special Administrative Region and, ironically Chairman of the Council of his old *bête noire*, Hong Kong University. Nothing is as it seems in Hong Kong, but at the time of writing Arthur Li appears to be doing rather better than his fellow ex-colleague, who should at least now have more time for violin practice.

David Coussmaker Anderson

THE SURREAL SAGA OF THE HONG KONG BRANCH OF THE BRITISH MEDICAL ASSOCIATION.

This story may seem small-fry compared with a meteoric career in Hong Kong politics, but as a man is in small things, so is he also in big things. Shortly after I arrived in Hong Kong I was made aware by Professor Li, of the importance he attached to the Hong Kong Branch of the British Medical Association. This had long been superseded in importance by the Hong Kong Medical Association, but it still had some constitutional relevance until the handover of Hong Kong to China, due in June 1997. Specifically, it had two nominees on the Hong Kong Medical Council, the organ responsible for disciplinary matters. This might be of considerable importance in connection with the Department of Surgery's problems over the bovine heart valves, already mentioned. I was obviously out of favour, but on the other hand I was sufficiently senior to be proposed by Professor Li as Treasurer of the Branch, and I was elected to this position in early 1992. The election of the officers and half the Council took place on alternate years. A surgeon called Michael Li was Hon Secretary, the President was Dr Robert Law, and I was Hon Treasurer.

So we move forward two years to the next elections. By then it was clear that I would not have been substantiated as Professor of Medicine even if I had asked, and would therefore be leaving the Faculty and, it was assumed, Hong Kong. Nominations were called for. I was proposed for the post of Treasurer by Robert Law, and seconded by a Dr Sung Wing Choon, while Professor Li proposed Clive Cockram, also from 'my' Department of Medicine, for the same post. The various other proposals included Dr Jake O'Donovan, an irascible surgeon in private practice, for the post of Hon Sec. When nominations had closed, Arthur Li fired his bombshell, pointing out that since Dr Sung had let his membership of the BMA in London lapse, the nominations of four of the people proposed or seconded by him were invalid. I was one of them, so was Robert Law, and so was Dr Lawrence Li, Arthur's half cousin by Ronald Li who had been notorious for a financial scandal in an official capacity as Head of the Hong Kong Stock Exchange. (I think it had been a small matter of insider dealing, which was frowned upon by the Independent Commission Against Corruption (ICAC), and for which he served time in prison.) My friend Robert Law said there was nothing to be done, but by then I had plenty of time on my hands. I was also very angry, because it was not as if the candidates themselves were no longer members in London. So I telephoned the headquarters of the BMA in Tavistock Square, and spoke to the Secretary, telling him what was afoot, and arguing that such subterfuge was bad for the name of his august Association. I was then told, 'Oh, that's interesting - some funny things have been happening in Hong Kong. We are very pleased, but a little perplexed, because we have had a sudden influx of new members'. 'Really?' I said. 'Yes, we have got fifty-three new members, all proposed by Professor Arther Li, and paid for over a period of ten days with four cheques on his personal London bank account.' Even by the very modest standards set by Hong Kong institutions this seemed suspicious. So as Hon Treasurer I asked for and was sent a list of all members of the BMA Hong Kong Branch.

MORE IRREGULARITIES IN THE BRITISH MEDICAL ASSOCIATION (HK BRANCH)

The list arrived a few days later, and I set to work on it. First, I found that the fifty-three new members consisted of thirty-nine doctors working in the Department of Surgery at the Prince of Wales Hospital, twelve from Department of Psychiatry and two odds and sods in private practice. Right enough, Dr Sung Wing Choon was no longer a member, but on close inspection

I found that Dr Jake O'Donovan (affectionately known in some circles as Joker Dollybrain) had also let his membership lapse, though he had now hastily renewed it. He was standing himself, and had seconded the proposal of Clive Cockram, with whom I had no quarrel except that he was standing against me for the post of Hon Treasurer. I told Robert Law, who was cock-a-hoop. I even found that Arthur's secretary, May, ever-loyal, had a pile of ballot papers kept under the table in her office, and was handing them out and telling the new members who to vote for. The Annual General Meeting was about to take place in the Victoria Room of the Hong Kong Club, a normally sleepy institution in a new building in the centre of Hong Kong. Things then moved into a gear that was even more surreal. Sue is the wife of Dr Peter Sullivan, a very good friend of mine who was working as Senior Lecturer in the Department of Paediatrics, who was also being persecuted by Arthur, along with his boss Professor Oppenheim. Sue was an ENT surgeon and had been working unpaid in the Department's ENT section, and although promised some income never received anything. In fact the only money she received in Hong Kong was from myself for working on the *MediVision* film series. She was by this time heavily pregnant with their second child. On the morning of the election she phoned me with some startling news. 'Listen to this, David - I have just been to a Surgery Department wives' coffee morning, and overheard Poon's wife ask another -' is your husband going to dinner tonight with Professor Li at the Shanghai Club?' 'Yes, is yours?', she said.

A SURREAL AGM

I spoke to Robert Law and he telephoned the Shanghai Club. 'Hello, I'm a member of Professor Li's Department at the Prince of Wales Hospital, and have an invitation to the dinner tonight, but unfortunately I seem to have lost my invitation. What time

Where Angels Fear to Tread

is the dinner and where will it be held?' 7.00 pm he was told. 'Is it a big party?' 'Oh yes, he has booked for forty people'. That evening the BMA dinner was booked for twenty members of the Hong Kong Branch of the BMA at the Hong Kong Club. This was just enough for a quorum. Julian Critchley said he'd be late - 'be sure you are there before nine, we are starting the AGM promptly' I said. (In fact it turned out he was a member in London, but not of the Hong Kong Branch, but I kept quiet about that.) So after an excellent dinner with many pleasantries around one long table in the Victoria Room, 9.05 pm arrives and we open the meeting and rush through the first two items on the agenda, which are the President's and the Treasurer's reports. 'The finances are fine, these are our incomings, these our outgoings, this is the balance... any questions?' Approved unanimously by ten past nine. 'Before we come to the election of Council members, I want to tell you that I have found certain irregularities. First, on the technicality that Dr Sung Wing Choon has let his BMA membership lapse, four people, including me, have been wiped off the ballot paper because they have been proposed or seconded by Dr Sung. I have been told by London that this is not within the spirit of the BMA. But anyway I have found looking through the London records that Jake O'Donovan has also let his membership lapse, and he is standing for Secretary and has proposed or seconded Clive Cockram for Treasurer, and Ronald Li who is standing as Council member. I therefore propose that the election be declared null and void, and a further ballot be held, with all proposals in order next time'. At that point in walked Arthur Li, and thirty-nine members of his staff who had just had an excellent meal at his expense at the nearby Shanghai Club! 'Good to see you Arthur, and to have such a good turnout, but I have found that Dr Jake O'Donovan has also let his membership lapse, so I am proposing that the election be declared null and void, and we have a re-election. I trust you will agree this is fair and right'.

'FACE' TO BE PRESERVED AT ALL COSTS

Of course 'face' is extremely important to the Chinese, and backing down would have involved enormous loss of it in front of his whole Department. (I remember John Gosling saying shortly after my arrival, 'Face is just as important to us as it is to the Chinese. It's just that we don't make such a fuss about it.') In the meeting all hell broke loose, and all round the table people were forced to take sides, and most went with Arthur. He phoned Jake, who said something non-committal, and eventually a vote was taken and of course with the sheepish crowds standing round the walls of the Victoria room, the election was declared valid. After the meeting Arthur's half-cousin Laurence Li said to me, 'If you think that was nasty you should come to one of our family meetings for the real thing.' I explained to the Hon Secretary in London, what had happened, and submitted a detailed report; and they declared the election null and void and ordered another to be held under the supervision of the Electoral Commission in the UK. I checked the legal situation with Peter Sullivan's brother, an eminent barrister, and had the greatest pleasure in sending out a letter to more 300 members marked, 'Strictly Confidential, for the eyes of members of the Hong Kong Branch of the British Medical Association ONLY', setting out what had happened including how the new members had been joined on four of Arthur's personal cheques. In the re-election Robert Law and I were comfortably voted in to our respective positions.

HONG KONG MEDICAL SPECIALISTS, AND WHEN IS A PROFESSOR NOT A PROFESSOR?

There is a small but entertaining post-script. When I left the Chinese University in October 1994 I moved into private practice to join a group called 'Hong Kong Medical Specialists' on the fifth floor of a small building in Central called Pacific

House. We included a dentist, Mike, a good golfer who had sold Rolls Royces, but was now into selling Australian wine. His room was painted a deep blue and looked more like a brothel than a dental office. There was an ENT surgeon called Ian Williams who had worked as an army surgeon in Iraq, written a sleezy novel, and later turned out not to be qualified as an ENT specialist; an elderly respiratory physician Sam Nariman, who seemed on the surface to be very normal, though I later had some doubts; an elderly non-operating neurosurgeon, Dr Fali Shroff (who had got me into HKMS). And there was myself, a troublesome failed Professor of Medicine. We all shared staff, and I made sure that they referred to me on the phone as plain Doctor Anderson. But I was still working hard on the *MediVision* films and wanted to be able to use the title Professor in the second series of eleven films. I contacted the Dean of Medicine in Manchester, Professor Steve Tomlinson, and asked if there was any chance of my being appointed as Honorary Visiting Professor in Manchester. I submitted my CV and this was considered, and approved on April 1st 1995. I was given the impressively long title of *Honorary Visiting Professor of Medicine and Clinical Endocrinology at the University of Manchester*. When I heard this news, which was very good for *MediVision*, I instructed my staff to start to answer the phone with; 'Good morning, Professor Anderson's office,... good afternoon, this is Professor Anderson's office...' In this way, knowing how Hong Kong worked, with spies everywhere, I set a trap. On May 16th we had a Council meeting of the Hong Kong Branch of the British Medical Association, and this was attended by Professor Li, who was clearly still angered by the election re-run. At the end, unable to contain himself any longer, he blurted out, 'And I understand that you are still calling yourself Professor Anderson, David'. 'But I am a Professor, Arthur, and I demand an apology'. 'Oh no you're not'... 'Oh yes I am'... 'Where are you a Professor?' 'In Manchester, Arthur and I demand an apology for a blatant slur on my character'. 'I don't believe you - you show me the evidence'... 'So you're calling me a liar... are you going to apologise or not?'

Well, there was no apology of course. Next I contacted a solicitor friend, Ashley Alder, and explained that I wanted a bit of fun at Arthur's expense. 'But I don't have much money, so I don't want to spend more than HK$5,000.' He put me on to a young colleague, Jeremy, who I met, and who sent out an official letter on Stevenson's headed notepaper to Professor Li, saying he had defamed me, an eminent colleague and demanding a retraction. Nothing happened, of course, and after a few more letters and phone calls, I got a bill for HK$20,000 from Stevenson's. I spoke to Ashley, and said I had made it clear I was not earning much, and that it was just a bit of fun. 'Explain to Jeremy, and ask him to help you wind it up, and say you'll settle for $10,000', he said. So I went to meet Jeremy who said, 'You mean you weren't really serious about taking him to Court?' I couldn't believe my ears - was he really thinking I wanted to take on the Bank of East Asia? We agreed to settle our bill for $10,000 and I drafted another letter, saying... 'Our client feels that you have besmirched his name, and that you owe him an apology. However, since the defamation you made on May 16th took place in front of the Council of the British Medical Association's Hong Kong Branch, and it is clear you both care about the good name of the British Medical Association in Hong Kong, he is prepared to drop the matter if you offer a retraction and apology to him at the next Council meeting'. And then I never turned up. I did, however, continue to use the title of Professor.

THE VALUE OF A PERFECT MEMORY

Towards the end of my three years as Professor of Medicine, and long after I had had the Chairmanship taken away from me, (though I was still using my nicely refurbished office), Arthur was attacking one Dr E K Yeoh. He was a Chinese Singaporean and Head of the Hospital Authority. Most disputes in Medicine centre around pay, and Arthur didn't like E K anyway, and wrote to the South China Morning Post (SCMP) complaining that we didn't know what his salary was. Well, as effectively second senior professor in the medical faculty I had negotiated my own salary directly with the Vice-Chancellor. I was well paid, but not quite as well as the Professor of Surgery (now Dean). So seeing this letter by Arthur, I submitted a letter by fax to the SCMP's Letters Editor Marianne Wong, pointing to a certain amount of hypocrisy because no one knew what the Dean earned either. I went off to a meeting, but half an hour later Arthur was on the phone to Jenny, saying that the Letters Editor had contacted him and I had to retract. Jenny claimed ignorance, and powerlessness, and said he should talk to me directly. So I heard about his when I got home, and next day went in wired for sound.

My ward round was interrupted by his loyal secretary May, saying Professor Li wanted to speak to me and would I come up urgently. I finished my ward round, went up to his (gigantic and tasteless) office, and switched on the tape recorder in my pocket. He started to harangue me about disloyalty to the Faculty, and how I couldn't even control my Department. I countered by pointing out that my position had been continually undermined by him. He said that if I didn't behave I would have the lump sum I was due on leaving the Faculty withdrawn. 'Are you threatening me, Arthur?' 'No I'm just giving you some facts of life'. Then he said - 'Look at Philip Johnson, and how well he runs his Department!' 'Oh, it's Philip Johnson is it? - I'd just like to remind you, Arthur why you have Philip Johnson here at all'. 'What do you mean?'...'Well, it is only because as new boy on the block at the Appointments Committee, I refused to follow your suit and vote against him, as Alan and Joe did, that he is here at all. So if you are going to throw Philip Johnson at me, I claim credit for his being here against your wishes, and for the success of his appointment'. 'What do you mean, David, we all voted for him in the end, didn't we?' At that point in came Alan Chang. 'Oh, hi Alan, good to see you; so where's Joe to complete the team? We were just talking about Philip Johnson and how good he is. Do you remember his appointment, and how you and Joe both followed Arthur and voted against his appointment? By the way why are you here?' 'I'm just here to make sure Arthur isn't misquoted'. 'Oh, don't worry about that Alan, let me assure you both that if I quote you, I shall be absolutely accurate'.

KNIVES OUT FOR A PARTING INTERNATIONAL WORKSHOP

Shortly before I left the Chinese University I had hatched a plan with Julian Critchley to organise an International Workshop on the Adrenal Glands, Vascular System and Hypertension, under the auspices of our two Departments, Professor Gavin Vinson, and the UK's Society for Endocrinology. Supported by several pharmaceutical companies we organised a number of eminent speakers from around the world, and when I decided to stay on in Hong Kong, rather than take a post in Trinidad or the Middle East, I wanted this to continue. So I worked on it both with Julian and Gavin. Finally, it was with considerable sadness mixed with anger, that I found Julian had decided to bow to Faculty pressure and boycott the meeting he had helped formulate, as did all members of my former Department. This did not create a good academic impression, but such was the power of one man. I put it on in Shatin Hospital, the local private Hospital, which was peopled mainly by doctors from the Prince of Wales. I signed a contract with the hospital's chief administrator before the authorities realised the ire that this would cause. Despite the Chinese University boycott it was a big success, and was well attended by academics from Hong Kong University as well as overseas. The proceedings were ultimately published by the Society for Endocrinology as a book. This took place in April 1995, and although I lost money over the meeting I am glad to say that the open rift with Julian Critchley was mended a year later, shortly before Julian, while holding his hood up to shield himself from torrential rain, was hit by a police car as he crossed the road in front of his young daughter. We attended his funeral, at which Arthur Li, by now Vice-Chancellor, gave a somewhat over-the-top eulogy, and was visibly in tears.

THE 'CARRIE OKAY' AFFAIR

Shortly after I left the Chinese University I was told that Professor Tek Oh was himself under investigation by the Faculty for misuse of his departmental slush fund. The fund amounted to more than a million Hong Kong dollars, and this was clearly seen as payback-time. Tek had a very loyal secretary called Carrie Lam, an exceptionally quiet girl who wouldn't say boo to a goose pimple. But still waters run deep, and apparently she had been having an affair with a doctor who was working in the Accident and Emergency Department. All requests for moneys, to go to conferences etc from the slush fund had to be signed by the Head of Department; but clearly an illegible 'T. Oh' was quite easy to forge, and no one would surely suspect the trusted Carrie. So the travel expenses of the Accident and Emergency doctor to several conferences were paid for from this other Department's fund, with which the sole connection was sweet besotted Carrie. It seems that with time they became bolder, but it was only spotted that something was wrong when Professor Oh's signature was put on an official Departmental order for two Persian rugs and a Karaoke set. The matter was exposed, and Professor Oh was humiliated. A crime had clearly been committed, but by whom? So the good doctor-lover, arguing his career would be ruined, persuaded the still love-struck Carrie to 'carry the can' and testify in court that he had known nothing about it. It had been entirely her doing and as her lover he had understood that it had come from her University Secretary's salary. So she was sent to prison for six months, and he was left free to continue to practice medicine.

There were two late addenda to this story. The first happened when I was well established in practice in Pacific House, and we were looking for a new Secretary. The practice manager was very excited to have an application from a highly qualified young Chinese girl with impeccable English. I met her, looked at the application, realised it was Carrie, checked her ID card with Dr John Low in the Chinese University's Anaesthetic Department and told my colleagues the story. 'I feel very sorry for her', I said, 'because she took the whole blame, the doctor got off Scot-free and I remember her as an excellent if rather timid secretary'. It was agreed that she be given a second chance. I would phone her, say that I had recognised her, but we had decided to offer her the job in the knowledge that we knew about her past, felt she had been very badly treated, but would let bygones be bygones. I phoned her. 'I haven't the slightest idea what you are talking about,' she replied, and rang off. Such is the importance to Chinese of face.

The second addendum came a few years later, when I spotted that the doctor, professional reputation unblemished, career untainted, and marriage presumably intact had been put up for Fellowship of the Royal College of Physicians of London, of which I was one of the Hong Kong assessors. I checked his identity carefully, and then exposed the story in a detailed report to the College, making it clear that in my opinion on grounds of character he should not be made a Fellow that year or indeed any year. The College expressed its appreciation.

CHAPTER 10

LIFE IN HONG KONG AFTER THE CHINESE UNIVERSITY

THE NEW TERRITORIES, GUK AND HER WORRIED FATHER

Obviously when we left the Chinese University we also lost our University flat on campus. I remember we looked at a property in the New Territories in Nai Chung with Geoffrey Key, when he was over for his exhibition of New Territories paintings. He only did one further New Territories-inspired oil when he got home, and this was of the sun low on the horizon from the roof of the flat we saw with him and went on to rent. We later bought that painting, as well as one of Ma On Shan, unsold from the exhibition, and together they magnificently sum up the splendour of Hong Kong's New Territories.

We rented the second and third floors of that property, which was a standard flat-roofed New Territories house. We took 1,400 square feet in all, with the added bonus of the roof and wonderful views, across sea to the Pat Sin mountain range on one side, and to Ma On Shan mountain on the other. The owner, Mr Wong, lived on the ground floor with his wife and children. Our Thai maid Guk came to join us, and seemed very happy. She had told us she had been raised by her father after her mother had committed suicide, and that he was very strict. It seemed that she had never told him she was working as a maid to an expatriate couple in Hong Kong. He thought she was working for very strict employers in Bangkok, who paid her well, but never let her have any time off. Anyway, in 1996 she decided to return home to see him for Christmas and New Year, maybe not knowing what would happen when Hong Kong was to be handed back to China the following summer. 'That's the last we'll see of Guk', said Jenny, with some prescience, as we left her at Kai Tak airport. On 2nd January I got a tearful phone call from Guk, saying her father had taken her passport, and believed she was a bad girl, living off prostitution in Hong Kong, and she was going to kill herself. I told her to bring her father to see for himself. 'That's the last we'll see of Guk', Jenny repeated, 'I told you so'.

But one week later I got another call. 'This Guk, I coming tomorrow, show my father. That okay?', she said, and right enough the next evening there she was on the doorstep with her bemused and subdued father, who must have been convinced that if his beloved daughter was working as a prostitute here she was not making much of a living. He stayed a week in the spare room on the second floor, Guk showed him round the sights of Hong Kong and that was the last we saw of either of them until he was dispatched home a week later. Apparently a cousin had been sent to pinch her passport from her bag, and saw the Hong Kong visa and that was how her father found out. She had locked herself in her room and threatened to commit suicide as her mother had done, so he knew it was for real, and they came to the compromise that he would come with her to Hong Kong.

We loved our time in Nai Chung, but it was changing fast and travel was difficult for Jenny who was now working in Central with the old expat practice Anderson and Partners. So after thee years we moved to a more convenient but small flat in Wanchai. Guk came with us at first, then told us her father had found her a wealthy Taiwanese husband, and she was going to get married. That really was the last we saw or heard of her; Nung, the Thai successor she found for us, likewise never heard from her again.

CLARE HOLLINGWORTH, WAR CORRESPONDENT, PATIENT, AND THE SCOOP OF THE CENTURY

Clare was, if I recall correctly, referred to Jenny for care by Dr John Simon, when she took over Maryse Badawy's practice in Princes Building. One could see why, because she was an extremely forceful old lady, who suffered neither fools nor waiting gladly. John was not a fool, but he was very busy. Clare was not entirely conducive to a smoothly run practice such as John Simon had. I think other patients in our waiting room soon came to understand her as a nuclear force to be reckoned with, and one best dealt with without delay.

For some reason Clare liked me, and I soon took her over, or rather it was the other way round. As Hong Kong's senior war correspondent, she was generally much-loved and revered in and by Hong Kong's Foreign Correspondents' Club, of which I am still an Associate member. There, accompanied by her Filippina maid at lunchtime she had a special place in the corner reserved for her, where she dined with others generally less eminent. When we first took her on as a patient she was already well into her nineties, forgetful of recent things, and intolerant of waiting for a nanosecond. But she could still be diverted into talking politics and especially of her past. Her first and most famous assignment was when as a new Daily Telegraph journalist in Warsaw, having just flown in, she was first to report the outbreak of World War Two. She had known

David Coussmaker Anderson

Poland well from working with Polish refugees... 'So I flew in on the last plane into Warsaw, and there was just myself and Hugh Carlton Green and all the other correspondents had left, and he said to me, 'I want you to go and find out what's happening old girl... everyone was called 'old girl' in those days... and let me know'. So I borrowed a flagged embassy car - they could still move freely across the border - and drove across into Germany, Union Jack flying on the bonnet, and I bought some food and things in the next town, and on my way back I took a minor road along a ridge, where I knew there was an unguarded crossing, and there was this tarpaulin fixed to posts along the side of the road, blocking the view into the valley below. I thought, 'That's a bit odd, old girl'; and as I drove past it was lifted up by a sudden GUST of wind, and in the valley below I saw hundreds if not thousands of tanks pointed towards Poland. So I drove on and back to Warsaw and went to see Hugh Carlton Green and said, 'I have something very important to tell you. I've just driven into Germany, and on the way back I took a minor road I know, and a gust of wind caught this tarpaulin and there are hundreds if not thousands of tanks about to cross the border. I want you to telephone London and say that war is about to start.' And he said, 'You're telling me that you've just driven across the border and into Germany?... I'm sorry, old girl, but I don't believe you'. 'Yes I have', I said, 'and if you don't believe me you can just go and look in the boot of the car and see all the food I bought there'. So Hugh telephoned the story to London, and that was how the outbreak of the war came to be announced to the world. It was later officially designated the Scoop of the Century.

COVERED FROM HEAD TO TOE WITH SPITTLE

I recall two other stories Clare told me. One was from 1948 when she was staying in the King David Hotel in Jerusalem with her journalist husband Geoffrey, and they were returning by foot when in the distance she saw the hotel blown up, and the roof sink slowly into the pile of rubble. She said there were guards on the roof, and she couldn't believe her eyes as the dust settled and she watched them walk off unscathed. When she told her mother what had happened she apparently struck her out of her will, because she regarded her daughter as totally irresponsible. Clare Hollingworth had the uncanny ability to be where things were about to happen. She spoke French and had got to know General de Gaulle during the war, and when he came to power she was there in Algeria when a hostile crowd was shouting at him, and banging on his car. De Gaulle, who she said was completely without fear, told the driver to stop the car, got out and walked into the jostling crowd and started to address them. Over half an hour of talking he turned the hostile crowd around completely, 'And in the end he had them eating out of his hand. When he got back to the car I saw that he was covered from head to toe with SPITTLE!'

When I left Hong Kong I handed Clare's care to another expat doctor, but still met her for lunch every three months in the FCC. 'Who are you?' she would ask over her spectacles. 'I'm David Anderson, your doctor', I'd reply. 'Oh are you? Well will you stay for some lunch?' Unfortunately Jenny and I missed her hundredth birthday celebrations, on October 11th 2011 (she was born on the very day of the founding of The Chinese Republic under Dr Sun Yat Sen). She died in 2017, at the age of 105. Her great nephew Patrick Garrett, who worked for Cathay Pacific, was a tremendous support to her, but she was vulnerable to smooth-talking men lurking round the FCC, including Ted Thomas who organised the publication of her memoir *Captain if Captured* and in the process talked her into parting with a lot of her savings. I was asked to be signatory to the document giving power of attorney to her great nephew and another long-term friend of Clare's, something that was contested by Ted, who was supported by a dubious psycho-geriatric medical opinion. But she was thereby entrusted to safe hands, and we thus succeeded in minimising her future financial damage. For many years, long after she had ceased to be a reliable correspondent, the Daily Telegraph, which I believe gave her a pension, maintained the ritual of a daily phone call from Clare to tell them the news from China.

THE MACLEHOSE TRAILWALKER

In 1995, while in Nai Chung, I decided to do my first Maclehose trail-walker, a spectacular 100 km annual charity walk across the New Territories that had been started by the Ghurkas, and still continues to this day. On that first occasion I went with Dr Lo Wing-Lok, an infectious diseases specialist, and his gynaecologist wife Anna, plus another medical friend of theirs. Wing-Lok, who died quite recently, was a nice man with medico-political ambitions, and later became medical representative in Hong Kong's parliament. We tried out the whole course in bits over the Summer and Autumn, in preparation for the real thing in late October. In all there are seven big and seventeen small climbs which take you the height of Everest up and down, of course all at near sea-level. It is not to be done with one's spouse, as the fourth in our group and I witnessed. We had to pour cold water on a spectacular example of verbal Chinese marital conflict, when we had all left poor Anna following behind; but all had been resolved when we got to the finishing post in just over twenty-eight hours. I was to do it again with different teams in 1998, and again in 2,000, which was the year of the Golden Dragon. Golden Dragons are very special people. Jenny, who is a little older than me is a rabbit, but doesn't behave like one. I am a 1940 Golden Dragon, and In 2,000 I felt I should therefore form a team of dragons. My niece, Sophie Dinkeldein, was a twenty-four-year old dragon's tail, and I had a practice nurse and a diabetic patient Edward who had done it with us in 1998, lined up as the other two, but they both pulled out, so in the end I had to settle for a Maclehose Trailwalker Golden Dragon sandwich, which included an unsuspecting rabbit and a golden rat.

The most dangerous thing when contemplating the Maclehose trailwalker is to have done a marathon and to imagine it is just a very long one. Sophie, who had done the London marathon said afterwards it was twice as hard. However Chris, our Golden Rat had done several marathons and had missed out on most of our team training-hikes. He seemed to be going well on sections One and Two, at the end of which there was a free food and water stop, before one of the big climbs up to near the top of Ma On Shan, by which time he was clearly wilting and definitely confused. 'What did you eat at the stop, Chris?' 'Nothing, I never eat on marathons!' We had to virtually drip feed him with sweet jelly the rest of the way, but I insisted he finish with us, and he did. We had hoped to do a good time, but finished at twenty.eight and a half hours. One of the main challenges was to finish as an intact team.The all-time record time is just over eleven hours. The second time I did it our team included Edward Wilson, an insulin-dependent diabetic, and he sleepwalked for part of the night. It takes you across parts of Hong Kong most people never get to see, and he didn't either.

MACAU AND GOLF

When I left Chinese University I sold my share of our boat, but continued as a member of the Royal Hong Kong Yacht Club. It is funny to think back how much Chinese Government second-guessing there was about the handover, with many Clubs feeling they had to drop the 'Royal' from the title, but the Yacht Club kept it, thanks largely to the insistence of a Canadian member, who was also a golfer. Of course the Chinese Government didn't mind. Jenny said she wanted to take up golf again, so I decided to join her. 'But I need some lessons, I'm fed up with playing badly' I said. In the Jockey Club building in Shatin there was an indoor golf range set up for non-race days, and I signed up with a Chinese pro called Johnny Wong. Jenny has an elegant natural swing, and I certainly don't, but she didn't want lessons. Johnny's swing was beautiful, but his teaching technique wasn't. He looked at a few of my practice swings, and recited six faults with the back-swing and six with the down-swing. It didn't matter much because he then turned round and started to teach Jenny, on the grounds I suppose that at least she had potential. I have had lessons from fourteen teachers since, and they have all said something different, but no one else has boiled it up to twelve separate faults.

First we joined the Yacht Club's Kellett Golf Society, with which we went on three or four day- or weekend-trips to China and Thailand. We were the only couple on these trips, and it was pretty obvious that for the unaccompanied men golf was only one of the attractions. I remember that once, after the good golfers had had a hard night out in Phuket, by some miracle I won the longest drive competition, which was mainly a measure of the weakness and waywardness of the others. That day 150 yards and straight was enough to win.

Jenny's aged and much loved father, Pard, died just before the handover to Chinese rule, which occasion she therefore missed as she went back home for his funeral. I stayed and went to the official ceremony with Jenny's friend Janet Kaye, as representative of the Hong Kong Branch of the British Medical Association, and we had two prime seats. Prince Charles came, and just as he started to speak the heavens opened and so did all our umbrellas. The Ghost of Queen Victoria was clearly distinctly pissed off. I still have my handover umbrella twenty.one years later. On the whole Chris Patten, the last Governor, did a good job, as evidenced by his being declared a 1,000-year enemy of China, for trying to prise out a teensy bit of democracy. I noticed it did not take very long for Chinese rhetoric to subside when he became European Union Commissioner. Jenny's father's will meant we had a little cash to invest, and we did so by buying a joint membership of the Macau Golf Club. Over the early years he and I had had a lot of fun playing golf together in Burford. We got membership at a bargain price and over eight years we would often go over to Macau on the high speed ferry, usually after work on Friday, and spend two nights and get in a couple of rounds of golf. I used to marshall for the Macau Open Championship, which always included one or two top notch golfers. We had first gone to Macau in 1992, when my first-cousin once removed, Jamie Napier, worked there for HSBC, and we visited him and Jackie. It was still sleepy, but was waking up and since has changed beyond all recognition and is now full of casinos. Twenty years ago there was just one, owned by Stanley Ho, a rich Hong Kong entrepreneur who basically ran Macau.

I WIN MY ONLY GOLF COMPETITION

One year I went in for a pairs better-ball knockout golf competition, and my partner was a local Macau Chinese called Winston Chan; in fact we went on to win it. In the third round we were competing against a Macanese called Roberto who was paired with a Japanese business man, and when we got to the ninth green Winston and I, after a dodgy start, had won the last two holes and were back to all square. Winston was very encouraging - 'All we need to do is get Roberto angry and his game will fall apart' he whispered. I drove off on the tenth, hitting a splendid and unaccustomedly long drive down the middle of the fairway. Winston followed with a slice into the sea.

'Shit' he expleted, 'it's over to you'. The Japanese did the same, and then Roberto hit his up the centre, but thirty yards short of mine. I was sizing my ball up from the side of the fairway when Roberto hooked his second shot into the rocks on the left, and promptly smashed his fairway wood into the ground and broke it. Winston gave a quiet chortle... 'He's getting angry David'. I hit a perfect nine iron, onto the green. One of the course's Filippino Marshalls then came over and said, 'Roberto, I think I can find your ball'. And there it was, in a difficult lie between two rocks, so Roberto took a nine iron to it. The ball moved two inches, and, now even more angry, he smashed and broke his nine iron on a rock. Two broken clubs on one hole and we were looking good. I two-putted, we won the hole and Winston was cock-a hoop. We won the next hole as well, and Roberto, who was now two down in both score and clubs, looked very dejected, so I went up to talk to him. 'By the way, Roberto', I said as we walked off the green together, 'I never properly introduced myself. I'm a doctor in practice in Hong Kong. What do you do for a living?' Roberto scowled at me and said; 'I'm Stanley Ho's bodyguard'. Fortunately the rules of golf only allow for fourteen clubs in the bag, so Macau triad members were always forced to leave their Kalashnikovs behind.

A FATAL ACCIDENT, A SUNKEN VESSEL AND A LAWYER FRIEND

One weekend in May 1998, just as the new airport, Chek Lap Kok, was about to open on Lantau, some friends were leaving, but we had already said our farewells and I had committed myself to help marshall at the Macau Open Championship. There was a fleet of Boeing-built jetfoils that went to Macau. Apparently Stanley Ho had taken possession of these vessels, which had originally been built to catch nuclear submarines. No longer needed for cold war purposes, they were bought by a Japanese firm, and then leased to Stanley Ho. On that day there was clearly something wrong with ours, as we limped out of dock, and the vessel then took an unusual and slow route round the North of Lantau island. Eventually the vessel got up to planing speed, and had been doing so for three minutes or so when WHAM! It hit something hard and came to an abrupt halt, tipping passengers all over the place. I got up to see if anyone had been injured, and found an old lady with a bad head injury on the upper deck, and another younger one who was hysterical and over-breathing. We didn't seem to be sinking, and eventually a helicopter arrived to take off the injured, principally the old lady. Shouts of 'keep calm' to people who by and large were already calm, came from agitated rescuers. The old lady was taken off by helicopter, and eventually died, so there had to be an inquest. The rest of us passengers were picked up by airport rescue boats, and taken to the (not-yet-opened) new Chek Lap Kok airport. Names and stories were taken and we were then bussed back to the starting point. I went home, and back to the golf tournament the next day.

It soon became apparent that there were all the makings of a classical Hong Kong cover-up. Various officials were quoted in the South China Morning Post, and along with others on board I was sure there had been something wrong with the jetfoil. I even phoned Boeing in Seattle, who were most helpful, and denied even having an employee whose name had been quoted in the SCMP. I put in a small bill to the owners, including for medical services, and inconvenience. Months later there was the old lady's inquest where it was revealed that we had struck a partly submerged vessel, the location of which was marked on the charts. There was much discussion as to whether the passengers had been told to wear seat belts. The Company representative said there had been an announcement, but the only other witness called, who had had to move because the engine was overheating and her seat was getting hot, testified categorically that there had not. 'Mrs Chang, I would like to respectfully suggest that you are mistaken, and that there was an announcement', said John Kerr, the barrister, who was also a Kellet golfing-friend. 'No there wasn't' said Mrs Chang. 'I would respectfully suggest you weren't listening and so you missed the announcement'. 'I always listen to safety announcements'. 'How can you be so sure that you listened on this occasion?' To which the reply came, 'My late husband was killed in an air crash ten years ago, and so I now ALWAYS listen to safety announcements'. All he could say was 'Oh...oh... oh well I suggest this was the exception!' I think compensation was paid to all those injured. I gave a wry smile, as he had earlier tried to unsettle me by suggesting I should not have submitted a bill for inconvenience and for professional help for injured passengers.

While on the subject of golf, when we bought our property in Italy I saw that there was space for at least one fairway and one green. I mentioned this to Jenny. 'Over my dead body' was her reply. However I was saved that summer when my sister Margaret and brother-in-law Richard (Roo) Dinkeldein came to stay and Roo thought it was a great idea and we set to work to make the first tee. 'You have to make it a USP - a Unique Selling Point', he said, so that is what it is. I now have a three green, four hole, five bunker, seven tee and 400 olive tree USP eco-golf course, and play with friends regularly every Sunday. Some people have even rented the property because someone in the family wanted to play golf. And so far we have seen no dead bodies.

CHAPTER 11

MEDICAL TEACHING FILMS AND THIRD WORLD HEALTH PROBLEMS

MEDIVISION AND A NEW APPROACH TO TEACHING CLINICAL MEDICINE

One of my professional reasons for staying on in Hong Kong was to continue with the *MediVision* project of showing good clinical practice on film - initially in VHS, then DVD, and finally by streaming on to central servers of Institutions. Much helped by Rob Mitchell, and by Alice Yip in the Chinese University, I completed the first series of fifteen films while still there, and we had a successful formal opening. I completed the second series of eleven films in 1996. Funded by sponsorship from pharmaceutical companies both these sets were published jointly in the names of the Department of Medicine of the Chinese University of Hong Kong and the Faculty of Medicine of the University of Manchester. Arthur Li would not allow his Faculty's name to be used, even though the series was published by Chinese University Press. I then formed a company called Medical Education Services Limited, bought out the Chinese University interest, and in 2001 was joined by our second son, Bruce, who had qualified in Medicine but decided not to practice as a doctor. I think we can claim that the sixty-film series was an educational success.

DOG BITES, RABIES PREVENTION AND THE WORLD HEALTH ORGANISATION

Amongst others, we made a series of twelve films on infectious diseases, which thanks to the Kadoorie Foundation were later distributed by a local charity free to third world medical schools. The one we made on Dog Bites and Rabies Prevention, led me into the quagmire of international medical politics, as practiced by the World Health Organisation (WHO).

While on holiday in 1998 in southern India I visited the Pasteur Institute in Coonoor and was horrified to find that the 1920 Semple-Pasteur sheep's brain vaccine my brother Antony had been given fifty years before, was still being widely used for post-bite rabies prevention. It is estimated that at least 55,000 people, mostly children and young men, die worldwide each year from rabies, which means that, as they are conscious to the end, they experience a truly horrific, and entirely preventable, death. On our way home after that Christmas holiday I met Dr B J Mahendra in Bangalore, and he put me in contact with other experts, as well as with Brad Jennings, Vaccine Development Manager in Chiron, a pharmaceutical company that makes a purified tissue-culture vaccine called *Rabipur*. Brad was involved with promoting its use intradermally (that is into the skin, rather than under it or into muscle), in order to simplify the procedure, reduce costs and eliminate the use of the outdated and dangerous Semple vaccine. So, with funding from Chiron, Bruce and I made several visits to India, Thailand and the Philippines to make a film on all aspects of Dog Bites and Rabies Prevention.

WITH THE DOG CATCHERS OF HYDERABAD

When I set out with Bruce to make a film on rabies prevention it was obviously important to have something on its prevention in dogs, so we interviewed several important Vets in Hyderabad. There were said to be around twenty-five million feral dogs in India, mostly in the towns and cities. The Government Vet was very helpful, we were shown and filmed some rabid dogs, and he organised for us early the next day to go out with the dog-catchers, to get some urban field-footage of their feral dog rabies-prevention programme. We waited at the appointed spot and at around 7 am the vehicle arrived. It was an open lorry with two rows of intercommunicating cages, and the team consisted of four men. One, the dog spotter-poker, sat precariously on top of the cages; the driver obviously drove, and the other two were the catchers, one of whom doubled as dog thrower. Bruce sat filming in the front, wedged between the driver and head catcher while I sat in the back with the second catcher, and took subsidiary footage. We drove surreptitiously round the back-streets Hyderabad, spreading havoc wherever we went, and not just with the dogs. The typical sequence was as follows. The man perched on the cages spots a lurking dog ideally in a side street and taps on the cab roof; we stop and the two catchers creep out furtively, hiding lassoos behind their backs. (The dogs are street-wise, and know about lassoos). The trainee catcher goes round the back way, and heads the dog towards the more expert lassooist... WHEEW! ... who expertly throws the lassoo round the frightened dog's neck, and said dog, which may be quite big, is hauled in and dragged to the back of the lorry, yelping furiously. The spotter-poker stands above one of the two last cages, ready to lift the gate. The lassooist, a muscular brute of a man, hauls the dog round several revolutions in ever faster circles, the lassoo tightens, the dog takes off and at a critical moment the cage man lifts the gate... WHEEEEE..! The lassooed dog is released, the dog flies cagewards, lands stunned inside, the gate is dropped, and spotter-poker-cage man uses his hooked pole to remove the lassoo, which is given back for next use. He then progressively pokes the dog from cage to cage, lifting each gate till our stunned feral Fido arrives terrified and exhausted at the last empty cage. Unfortunately about one go in three, timing of the dog throw was less than perfect, and the dog landed SPLAT on the unopened cage door, whereupon the process had to be repeated until success was achieved.

Of course, although these dogs were notionally feral, it was not really quite like that. They mostly had owners, and/or owned people, who paid them with scraps to guard their property. So children were running off with their pets in all directions, and I remember one elderly man in tears beseeching the team to release his dog, not being reassured that he would see his pet again. Once the lorry was full we went to the Veterinary Station, where they were poked out of the cages one by one, for castration and single dose immunisation (which may be better than none, but only if the dog has been through this before). I asked what happened at the end. Apparently once recovered they would be released in the general part of town they came from and told to find their own way home, which dogs do quite well. It is possible there might be a more efficient way, but that is what we saw in Hyderabad. Of course in our film we only used the humane footage. I noticed another time at a Hindu festival in Orissa, which is the second holiest place in India, that wise dogs there often sat themselves between holy cows for personal protection. Dogs aren't stupid.

A JOURNEY INTO THE WHO AND RABIES PREVENTION

Of course, we were bound to follow the guidelines of the World Health Organisation, but during the course of shooting the film I discovered their concealed soft underbelly. You need to understand a problem in order to solve it, so let's start with how after being bitten by a rabid animal, as my brother was in 1947, a previously unimmunised person can contract and die from rabies. In dogs the disease damages the central nervous system, generally making the animal aggressive, and the virus travels down the nerves to the salivary glands, ready to be passed on to you if you are bitten. Rabies can be prevented, but not cured once the virus has entered the peripheral nerves. After being bitten by a rabid dog, the virus replicates for a time in the tissues round the wound. It then enters the nerve endings and travels to the central nervous system by retrograde flow up the nerve axons. Once in a nerve, the victim's death warrant has been signed. Therefore the first urgent need is to wash the wound(s) thoroughly with soap and water, and pour in disinfectant or alcohol; that will reduce your chance of getting the disease by half. You also need to build up circulating antibodies, for which a modern tissue-culture vaccine like *Rabipur* is given; however this primarily removes the risk from any **subsequent** bite. Let us suppose that the washing has not cleared the virus. It starts to replicate locally in muscle cells, and it is now a race against time whether your own antibodies will be produced quickly enough to neutralise the virus locally before it can enter the nerves, where it is out of range of antibodies. So to be sure you are protected you ALSO need to be injected with **preformed rabies immunoglobulin** (antibody) into the wounds, in order immediately to neutralise the virus at the site of entry.

THE VITAL NEED FOR EQUINE RABIES IMMUNOGLOBULIN

The most cost-effective source of rabies immunoglobulin is the horse. Horses are big and cheap, and equine antibody can be purified so that it does not cause allergic reactions. When I tried to film good practice in the dog-bite clinic in Hyderabad, however, I found to my distress and ultimately great anger that only three percent of dog bite victims in India were getting local rabies immunoglobulin. In order to film the procedure we actually had to go out and buy **human** rabies immunoglobulin, at great cost, from the local pharmacy. The situation is no better in the rest of the third world. And the reason? The WHO Guidelines, which are treated with the greatest reverence all over the world, made no sense and were actively counterproductive. What they instructed was to calculate the dose to be injected based on the weight of the patient, not on the size or number of wounds, then to inject as much as the wounds will take locally, and to give any that was left over into a distant muscle, where there is no virus to inactivate. In a word, the guidelines were impractical nonsense. The WHO would surely be expected to advocate a practical approach that recognised the need for all at-risk victims to receive immunoglobulin injection into the wounds, at the minimum effective dose, and to facilitate its production and worldwide availability? Instead, I found there was not only no move by the WHO to address this obvious weakness; it was acting as if its own guidelines were set in stone.

I tried to argue this case with Dr François Meslin at a meeting in northern India when our film was launched, but to no avail, and in 2004-5 I was encouraged by a world authority on rabies, Professor Henry Wilde, to write a paper analysing the history of these guidelines. In doing so, I found they had grown up like Topsy, and I argued the case for their reform. This paper was well written, but was turned down by *The Lancet,* because third-world diseases are not given high priority in first-world journals. Eventually, in 2007 Henry Wilde accepted it for a new Journal, *Asian Biomedicine,* and in 2009 he also invited me to speak in October at a WHO rabies-prevention meeting in Annecy. I did so and the feedback revealed that the delegates liked my proposals individually but not collectively. Welcome to WHO politics, which does not like to make any change that might suggest it had previously been wrong. I argued for rational change in the guidelines so that they made sense, were affordable, and no longer counterproductive. Existing evidence dictated that the amount of immunoglobulin given could and should be reduced, given entirely where the virus had been deposited, and according to the size of the wound(s) and not the size of the patient. My arguments were rejected by people who should have known better and who did not want to upset the powerful WHO controller of rabies-prevention guidelines, and Annecy conference-convenor. I was told that in order to change illogical and obviously damaging guidelines, clinical trials were needed; yet there has never been a clinical trial of common sense, because to do one is obvious nonsense.

DON'T ROCK THE BOAT, OR IS IT THE GRAVY TRAIN?

I have always believed in calling a spade a spade, but experts, including Professor Wilde, urged caution, and ultimately insisted clinical trials were needed. We could not simply change the guidelines based on existing data, let alone the bleeding obvious. You will of course appreciate that I was an outsider with no business meddling in rabies prevention. I should go bark up my own tree. Seven years later, when I next visited the problem, nothing had changed. My efforts had not been entirely wasted, however, because a courageous doctor, Dr Omesh Bharti, in Shimla in northern India had read my paper, and it gave him the necessary moral, historical and scientific support to introduce the scheme I had proposed. Lo and behold, doing so he found evidence of a dramatic fall in rabies deaths. The approach even works in cows bitten by a rabid dog. Saving a cow that has been bitten is very important to a north India farmer. In August 2016 I presented a paper on my proposed changes to the guidelines, traveling at my own expense to the

APCRI Rabies Prevention meeting in Bangalore. One year and a half (and therefore 80,000 rabies deaths) later new guidelines have been drafted, that though still imperfect at least now make more sense. Alas, as we will see later, in a completely different area, the WHO is not the only global organisation where common sense is in short supply.

A ROTARY PROJECT TO HELP LEPROSY SUFFERERS

I have a friend called Nick Pirie, a barrister who had consulted me as a patient and who belongs to one of Hong Kong's many Rotary Clubs, that of Hong Kong South. For some time, due to Nick's unrelenting drive, the Club had been supporting a Catholic organisation based in Macau that was working on leprosy rehabilitation in Liangshan Prefecture in China's southern Sichuan Province. Now Nick is not someone you can easily brush away, and one day early in the new millennium I dangerously bumped into him as I was crossing Queen's Road Central to go to work. Opportunistically, and as it turned out opportunely, he started to tell me about this project, and how they needed some medical input, and was I interested? He is not an easy person to whom to say 'no', so I said I would think about it. The next time he went to Liangshan to visit several of the villages I went with him. We were also accompanied by Charlotte da Vita, a fiery young British woman dedicated to funding charitable third world projects that gave work to the disadvantaged. There was no doubt that China's central Government was embarrassed at the level of poverty in these remote parts of China, and there was a massive programme of road construction. The first time I went, travel was extremely difficult in the mountains especially, where there were regularly places where only one vehicle could pass. Nick, inspired by memories of his military father, would then leap out of our vehicle, and direct the traffic in English, which of course no one understood. In 2009 there was a massive earthquake in northern Sichuan, and on my next visit Dr Liang said that on one cliff road there were two vehicles going in opposite directions, whose drivers both refused to let the other pass where the road narrowed. Face, again. After an hour of wrangling there were two massive tail-backs when the earthquake struck and equitably settled the question as an estimated 500 people in two lines of vehicles and the two proud litigants, plunged to their deaths.

The predominant racial group in Liangshan is *Yi,* one of over fifty racial minorities in China. I reckon that in China there are five clear economic levels - the first, Hong Kong, Shanghai and the affluent east; the second - the central area; the third - rural western China; and the fourth - rural Chinese minorities such as the Yi and Tibetan peoples. The fifth economic level is represented by the Leprosy Rehabilitation Villages. One probably good thing that Chairman Mao did was in each district to set up a separate village for leprosy sufferers to work the land, and eke out some sort of existence with their families. At least this kept them away from the hatred of their fellows. I was told by one of our workers later that his parents told him of an uncle with leprosy in the 1950's who was killed, before his niece was allowed to marry. The standard method being to be buried alive. The Yi traditionally believed it was unsafe to travel for three days on the same road after a leper had passed. In Liangshan there were seventeen such 'rehabilitation villages', of which half were being looked after in some way by Catholic nuns, and for whom Nick's Rotary Club was doing some fund-raising to help.

A FEW WORDS ON LEPROSY THE DISEASE

I need here to make a small clinical diversion into Leprosy, which is a chronic disease caused by an intracellular bacterium *M.*

leprae related to *Mycobacterium tuberculosis*. It is essentially a disease of poverty, and contrary to popular belief is not highly contagious. In the wild it infects the armadillo, indeed many years ago my good zoologist friend Bill Lasley contracted it from an armadillo, of which he was studying the reproductive cycle, in San Diego zoo. The armadillo is a mammal with a low body temperature, which suits the *lepra bacillus*. This also probably accounts for its preference for the skin and peripheral nerves of Man. Nowadays the infection is easily eradicated with a regime of six to twelve months of triple antibiotics provided free by the WHO. But unfortunately once nerve damage has occurred it cannot easily be repaired. On average from onset it takes seven years for it to be diagnosed, and in China at least a third of people infected have nerve damage and deformities at the time of diagnosis.

THE ROTARY MODEL

When we first started to try to help fight leprosy in Sichuan we concentrated for obvious reasons on these 'leprosy-rehabilitation' villages, but it became clear that their need was not treatment of the active infection, but dealing with its long-term consequences. In fact, most of the cases of active infection were out in the general community, where the problem was often compounded by denial ... 'No child of mine can possibly have leprosy'. In these grossly disadvantaged remote villages the problem was mainly rehabilitation and education of people who had long since been cured of active infection. Charlotte da Vita put me in contact with two excellent Chinese doctors just across the border in Guangdong, Dr Yang Li-He and his young deputy Dr Michael Chen. Dr Yang had worked all his professional life in Leprosy, and was one of the nicest and most dedicated doctors I have ever met. Once retired he set up a charity called *Handa,* and it seemed obvious that to get anywhere we needed to work with them. When I got back after my first visit with Nick and some other rotarians, it was made clear to me that there were differences of opinion within Rotary, and some clear friction between Nick and certain others. Since it was a medical project, they asked me to join their Club, and to work alongside the project's driving force. So I did so, and have been a member of Rotary ever since.

By and large Rotarians are nice empathic people, who come from all professions and live up to the motto *'service before self'*. The philosophy is to combine conviviality with doing a bit of good. I was a little slow to appreciate the origin of many of the tensions, which in retrospect derived from a conflict between *Handa*, whose mission was to help the leprosy sufferers help themselves; and those with a more missionary motivation. That is to say, between helping the sufferers improve their own lot, by *Handa*-style empowerment; and helping therm for the glory of the Lord, or in our case Rotary, for whom there was the potential for Kudos. The precedent for the latter was the poliomyelitis-eradication campaign, in which Rotary has been the flagship charity.

WORKING WITH HANDA, CHINA'S LEPROSY REHABILITATION NGO

The authorities in China were basically interested in getting us to part with our money, and were delighted when we expressed interest in establishing a Centre in Xichang that would, we thought, serve as a place where leprosy rehabilitation could take place. We were offered the use of a large former technical school on the outskirts of Xichang, and during the course of the negotiations we visited it with Dr Yang. I also used the occasion to start a *MediVision* educational film on Leprosy, with him demonstrating the clinical features of some early cases attending the public health clinic. For this we had also filmed early cases of leprosy on our visit to Hyderabad. On this trip, on which we were accompanied by my wife, and son Bruce who did the filming, it became clear that my vision involved Rotary funding *Handa* to extend their programme which was working so well in Guangdong. There was definitely tension, and on one occasion I was told that Dr Yang had a hidden agenda. I failed to persuade all others that this trip was the perfect opportunity to strike up an arrangement in which we would work together for the benefit of all, but with *Handa* the force on the ground.

The essence of *Handa's* approach to leprosy rehabilitation was to concentrate on simple but effective education designed to reduce secondary damage caused by lack of sensation. The sensation of pain that we normally experience when we touch a hot object, or develop a wound, has a major protective effect. The individual with leprosy lacks this sensation in parts affected by the disease. Furthermore, the affected limbs are subjected to abnormal pressures leading to the build-up of hard skin (callus). Because of damage to the sympathetic nerves the skin is dry, with consequent cracking, entry of bacteria and infection. These people had to work in the fields to support themselves, often with appalling deformities. A feature of the programme was to provide simple materials such as plastic basins to soak the hard skin, simple files made with coarse emery paper stuck to wooden tongue depressors with impact adhesive, and natural oils to rub in. More difficult work involving use of a scalpel was done by 'barefoot doctors' often quite young, and some of whom were very good. An important element was the provision of footwear, often specially made. Some patients needed amputation, and eventually the hospitals in Xichang agreed to accept such patients. A particularly poignant case was a girl born with *spina bifida,* who eventually had successful neurosurgery done in Hong Kong.

FRIENDSHIP, PEOPLE'S FRIENDSHIP-COMMITTEE STYLE

Our local liaison person in the People's Friendship Committee, (better named the 'People's Committee for Ripping-off Gullible Foreigners'), was a middle-aged Yi woman called Jiwu Aying. Superficially affable, she was not to be trusted and clearly wanted to pull me into line, which rather to my naive surprise included the oldest one in the book. At a critical stage of negotiations on one trip on which Michael Chen was with us, I was sharing a room with a visiting ophthalmic surgeon from South Africa who Nick was trying to interest in doing cataract surgery. We had an early supper in a restaurant, at Friendship's expense and got into cars to go back to the hotel. Aying signalled to me and I wound the car window down... 'Anderson, you in White Swan Hotel, what room you in?' asked Aying. A bit puzzled I told her. Back in the hotel, my eye surgeon colleague and I were reading on our beds, and there was a knock on the door. Outside stood two young girls clearly offering more than just room-service. I sent them away, and told Michael Chen, who was in the next room. We agreed it must have been an attempt by Aying to compromise me. As we were talking, the phone rang, Michael answered it, and after some discussion thanked the receptionist and put the phone down, splitting his sides with laughter. 'That was about the two girls' he said. 'Reception wanted to know if you had sent them away because they weren't good enough.' On another occasion in another prefectural town I was in the same hotel as Sally Chun, our Programme Manager, and after supper there was some dancing, with the friendly local police. I heard later that one of them tried to interest Sally, who of course rebuffed him and went back to her room. I was asleep at about one-thirty, when there was a knock on the door, and two policemen were there wanting to see my passport. I suppose they thought they would also find Sally there!

David Coussmaker Anderson

'TOO MUCH MAO TSE DUNG, AND NOT ENOUGH DENG XIAO PING THOUGHT'

There is no point in going over the chronology of our experiences in China, but we did get into a position where at one meeting the local health chief flatly refused to let people come into our centre, on which a great deal of money had by now been spent, to be treated. The head of Community Medicine, a very nice man called Dr Liang, said to me in Chinese after that meeting: 'The trouble with the Liangshan Health Department is that there is a great deal too much Mao Tse Dung thought, and not enough Deng Xiaoping thought'. That was powerful criticism of his superiors. Eventually, after several years of trying to get the Centre to work, and with frustration by *Handa* over what was seen by Michael Chen as excessive ambition on the part of our Hong Kong-based Sally, *Handa* pulled out, and ultimately the team moved into a flat in Xichang, which had grown into a typical bustling Chinese first-world city. The model that was finally used was to have a traveling team of two locally-trained doctors, some nurses, and the odd barefoot doctor from one of the leprosy villages.

An interesting hark-back in history to the time of the crusades helped us secure funding for water to supply one of the villages. In the dark ages many of the crusaders came back to Europe with leprosy, and the Order of the Knights of St Lazarus of Jerusalem was founded to established *leprosaria* across Europe. My late friend, the controversial judge Miles Jackson-Lipkin - about whom more below - was a member of this organisation, which was short of ideas, but not of money. So I worked in 2007 to try and raise funds to create a multipurpose Centre in one of the remote villages. The bulk of the population in the leprosy Villages were in fact family members of the people afflicted by leprosy. They were of course stigmatised by proxy, something which is slowly changing due to the work of Rotary and *Handa*. I was by now spending two months in

Italy and one staying with son Bruce, continuing an endocrine practice in Hong Kong, and trying to help with the leprosy project. This included keeping the peace with Michael Chen who had taken over from the ailing Dr Yang LI-He. In one of the remotest of our nine villages, Jin Yang, with Sally's help we came up with a proposal to use part of the partially-derelict village school, which was a mile from this particular village, as a multipurpose rehabilitation centre. I submitted the request for funds to the Order, and three months later found that the Government had moved the school to the centre of the village, where they were building a new one! One reason was that getting the water supply from a mountain source to the old school was not practical. I insisted on going and looking for myself, so that I could revise the proposal I had written with Miles. The project was approved with the Order's leadership, and then it was up to the individual branches to come up with the funds, which they eventually did. Meanwhile the prices had gone up, but both Centre and water pipes were in the end finished, in part with local Government funds. I was told I had been made a Knight of the Order of St Lazarus of Jerusalem, but I was never dubbed because I am not a Christian. They could have turned a blind eye to that, I suppose, had I said I did at least believe in some sort of higher being.

Once I stopped working in medical practice in 2008 it was clearly impractical for me to continue to supervise the medical programme in Liangshan's leprosy villages, but I was able to hand over to a highly motivated and effective oncologist, Dr Theresia Liem, who has developed and still is working on the clinical and many other aspects of an ever more ambitious programme. My local Rotary Club in Todi supported this for nearly ten years, although the bulk of the funding was raised in Hong Kong, via an organisation separate from normal Rotary. Everyone can be justly proud of what has been achieved, even though along the way we made a lot of mistakes.

David Coussmaker Anderson

THE STRANGE CASE OF SEVERE ACUTE RESPIRATORY DISTRESS SYNDROME (SARS)

Viruses are simple parasites composed of RNA or DNA whose sole function is to invade and exploit more complex living beings so that they can reproduce themselves and spread havoc. Ever since the influenza pandemic at the end of the First World War, which killed more people than that horrific war itself, the world has been haunted by the spectre of this killer disease, which originates in China. By 2002 much was known about the interaction of bird and mammalian hosts in the evolution and spread of new strains of influenza in Hong Kong, a large modern city with its people increasingly squeezed into ever-taller high-rise buildings. It has a good public health service, which at that time was under the direction of a Dr Margaret Chan.

Hong Kong is essentially Chinese in its eating traditions and these include its so-called 'wet markets', where live chickens, mainly coming from China, are housed. Birds transmit influenza, and the backdrop to SARS was that a new strain of influenza was (as always) on the horizon. After a few cases and deaths were traced to chickens from China, there was a massive and justified cull of the birds, under Dr Chan's orders. Meanwhile rumours were rife that people were dying across the border from a new viral disease, thought to be spread from exotic animals, such as the civet cat, and the Chinese desire to eat them as a perceived delicacy. The first instinct in China is to suppress evidence, to pretend there is no problem, and to hope it will just go away. But some courageous doctors knew otherwise, including one respiratory physician who travelled to Hong Kong for a wedding, and stayed in a cheap hotel in Kowloon. He developed respiratory distress, was admitted to the Baptist Hospital, and warned the doctors that what he had contracted was highly virulent. Meanwhile the disease had passed from him to seven others in the lift and foyer of the Kowloon hotel; some were visiting from Canada (and later took it back with them).

The next step in this unfolding saga came when one of these seven people was admitted to my former teaching hospital, the Prince of Wales, in Shatin, in the heart of the New Territories. He was breathless, diagnosed with asthma and, as was the custom, was given nebulised anti-asthma drugs. With hindsight this ensured that a cloud of virus, encased in fine droplets of water, was spread around the ward. Now in fact SARS was not particularly infectious, but the patient in the next bed had an interesting heart murmur. Word soon got around among the medical students, and large numbers, armed with stethoscopes, arrived to hear his early diastolic murmur, and so became SARS-infected. One of them was also being taught on the renal ward next door, and in turn transmitted it to a renal patient who was on peritoneal dialysis. The index patient in Hong Kong, the physician from Guangdong, had meanwhile died and panic was spreading.

The next episode of note came when the renal dialysis patient went on weekend leave to visit his brother, who lived in Amoy Gardens, an old multi-story building in the New Territories which had, it turned out later, a cracked effluent down-pipe. Inhabitants on the eighth floor went down with SARS and Margaret Chan insisted on all occupants of Amoy Gardens being internally isolated. In the end excellent Public Health detective work revealed that a cracked sewage down-pipe had allowed infected dialysis-fluid to escape. It was exceptionally hot weather and air was being drawn upwards and into flats through water-free U-tube traps in the toilets of a stratum of flats above the offending crack, infecting the occupants who were using their air conditioners. A unique mix of disease, dysfunctional buildings, and simple physics.

During the epidemic there was near-panic in Hong Kong, with up to 30% of people on the streets clad in (often filthy) face masks. We had bought our Italian retirement house earlier that year, and Jenny was traveling a lot to Italy, to supervise work on the future rental property being built, and where she too was treated like an extra-terrestrial 'Sartian' from H G Wells' *War of the Worlds*. Virology tests at the University of Hong Kong were establishing that the disease was caused by a *coronavirus*. Eventually it was contained, after having been disseminated worldwide by air travel, and was tracked back to the civet cat, and certain restaurants across the border. China was very slow to respond, pretending at first that the problem didn't exist, before finally putting all cases into a newly-built 1000-bed infectious diseases hospital near Beijing. 800 people died, more than 200 of them in Hong Kong, where of course heads had to roll. The first to go was head of the Hospital Authority, Dr E K Yeoh, who was replaced by his deputy, a man who had actually managed to contract SARS by visiting the Prince of Wales Hospital in person, in a misguided effort to provide public reassurance.

THE IMPORTANCE OF JUMPING BEFORE ONE IS PUSHED

It was clear that, though she had got some things right, including helping Beijing minimise the spread of the disease further in China, Dr Margaret Chan would be next on the list, so she wisely jumped before she was pushed, and took up a post within the World Health Organisation in far-away Geneva. Two years later, following the sudden death of the Director-general, Dr Lee Jong-Wook, and with support from Beijing, she came to head this organisation, which she did from October 2006 to July 2017. I had been on good personal terms with Margaret Chan during and after my 'troubles', but when I wrote to her in 2009 and again 2016 urging a review of rabies-prevention guidelines, I regret to say I got no reply. A nasty disease with no person-to-person transmission, rabies is pretty low down on the list of WHO priorities, even if it was obvious that its hallowed guidelines are an integral part of the problem.

CHAPTER 12

WHERE SHALL WE RETIRE TO?

HOW WE CAME TO CHOOSE UMBRIA

Our last flat in Hong Kong was a former University of Hong Kong staff flat overlooking a Hall of Residence in Pok Fu Lam. We had been reasonably happy in what was a very small flat in Wanchai, which was convenient for our joint practice, but when after three years we came to renegotiate the rent, the owner became greedy, and increased it. He said, 'It's very convenient for you, so you won't want to move', to which I thought, 'Watch this space, mate'. More or less on impulse one Saturday I went over to look at an ex-University of Hong Kong staff flat, which was bigger, nicer and less expensive. We immediately decided to move. The owner of the Wanchai flat, when we told him said, 'Why didn't you negotiate?' Our new flat was also much better for our maid Nung, who no longer needed to live in a shoe-box. In the end we stayed there for nearly five years.

There was no way we would stay on in Hong Kong after retirement, so where were we to go? Jenny wanted to live somewhere with better weather than the UK, and having considered Spain, Portugal and France, new neighbours, Ray and Penelope Wacks, both lawyers, told us about their holiday home in Umbria, where they meant to retire. They had done up their main house and had also converted a pig stye into a rental property, so we decided to rent it the following summer (2002). Jenny said cryptically, 'Darling, I think you should enquire about getting a mortgage in Italy', which seemed a strange request so, as was my normal practice, I ignored it. Meanwhile she herself negotiated a potential one for 150,000 Euros with the Abbey National Building Society. So here we are with a hired car for two weeks holiday in an ex-pigsty in central Italy, and about to be joined by a son and some grand-daughters. I am looking forward to a day by the pool, and I innocently ask my wife what she is planning for the day. 'Don't say you have forgotten, you know that Penelope has arranged for us to see Guido at nine-thirty. 'Well I'm planning to stay by the pool and wind down. And who the hell is Guido?' 'I've told you five times, he's the estate agent'. So the euro starts to drop, as I think maybe if I'm going to live here for the rest of my life, I had better put the swimming pool off for a day.

Guido was very nice and we spent the next three days, viewing Umbrian properties starting at about 150,000 Euros. I remember one lovely ruin at the bottom of a steep drive, with turkeys living in the roofless kitchen. So we had inched up the price-bracket by Day Two, and by Day Three we have settled on a very sensible house with an acre of ground, and space to build a pool, going for 600,000 Euros. We are no longer thinking of a holiday home, because we really like Umbria, and Guido is persuasive, as are the Wacks'. We do not usually spend long deciding on houses. We were about to return with Guido to his office to sort out the paperwork, and he said to me (in Italian), 'David, there is one more house I want you to see - it's a bit more expensive but *bellissima!* It's something else altogether'. I was sitting in the front trying to converse in Italian, and I tell Jenny, who is in the back. 'No we're not seeing anywhere more expensive, we are way over budget already', she said.

Well, I was curious and didn't want to upset Guido, so I said, 'Darling Jenny, he's taking us there now, and my Italian isn't good enough to stop him.' We drove through the gate and both said, 'Wow'! The whole property was spectacular. We spent the rest of the holiday putting in an offer and negotiating. (I got to use the Wacks' swimming pool once). The owner, a banker, had to sell because he had bankrupted himself. 'Of course, it means we'll have to sell our London flat', Jenny said. 'Great, I replied, I never wanted to live in London'. We were fortunate all went smoothly, the tenant in Canary Wharf wanted to buy the flat, and over Chinese New Year of 2003 we completed, and took over the property, which included a second house on site where caretakers Danilo and Helena Poli lived with their son. They worked the land including 400 olive trees a small vineyard and vegetable patch, under what was in effect the tail end of the ancient *mezzadria* system. The previous owner had planning permission for a notional extension to their small house, to make a rental property, and we took this up. We paid off the mortgage, came for holidays twice a year, and planned to retire at the end of 2005. Surprisingly, not long afterwards, the Wacks' decided they had itchy feet, sold their nice house and adjacent pigsty rental-property, and moved to a much inferior one in Tuscany the other side of Voltarra, where we visited them in the spring of 2007 on the awful weekend when Madelaine McCann was abducted.

LIFE IN PRIVATE PRACTICE.

Many might think that someone with academic medical pretensions would find private medical practice mundane. But I can honestly say that I didn't. In 1997, by which time I had been out of the Chinese University for three years, Jenny took over the practice in Prince's Building of an Australian GP, and I decided to join her. This worked very well, and gave me some free medical education in General Practice. So I would call on her for the solution of simple problems that seemed complicated to me, and she would refer her complicated problems to me, where they usually still seemed complicated. We enjoyed working in the same practice, and both gained confidence from it. Jenny had at one time been employed to work in one of the longest established Hong Kong practices, Dr Anderson and Partners, but we thought better of my suggestion to call ourselves 'Dr Anderson and Partner'; the original Dr Anderson was long dead, after all. In the end it was plain 'Drs Jenny and David Anderson'. Following the handover there was a progressive fall in the number of expatriate doctors. When we arrived in Hong Kong anyone on the UK Medical Register was allowed to practice. This changed with the handover when everyone had to take a written and clinical examination to become a Licentiate to practice in Hong Kong. At the Chinese University I had made some effort to improve the multiple-choice part of the exam, whose running was given to the Faculties of Medicine of each of the two medical schools in turn. Dr E K Yeoh asked me to analyse the exam and I found many of the questions made no sense, and the same bad questions were being constantly rehashed. Once in private practice I continued for a time to give tutorials to candidates. I was delighted when one candidate, a Canadian-trained paediatrician, passed the clinical exam that included a case of mitral stenosis, which she diagnosed correctly by copying the good practice shown on one of the *MediVision* films on cardiac cases.

PART-TIME RETIREMENT, AND CAPTAIN JERKOFF

At the end of 2005, Jenny retired fully, I did partially, and we moved to Umbria. We came back via New Zealand and then Australia, where we spent a week with my second sister, Louise and her husband Andrew Child. For two and a half years I continued to go back to Hong Kong one month out of three, and continued with my endocrine practice. This was only possible because Bruce, who was renting a flat in Wanchai kindly found space for me in his spare room. Jenny had sold her patient list and records to a Canadian GP, who for a year-and-a-half provided sanctuary for me with an office etc. We came to an equitable financial arrangement, or so I thought, until her Australian husband, who was a Cathay Pilot and so had lots of time on his hands, and who I shall call Captain Jerkoff, tried to interfere. He was definitely an obsessive-compulsive and seemed to run the practice books. For example his wife had bought from me some equipment including a machine for use on diabetics, called an HbA1C monitor, which would provide immediate feedback on the last three months of glucose control, which was therefore a strong patient-motivator. I was the only one to use it. Anyway, on one return visit in 2007 it became clear that the practice owed me money, about $HK 5,000 in all, and this was being withheld. There was some unpleasantness, and so I left, and for my last year went and joined another local practice in Central as their physician, which proved much more suitable. I bought the HbA1C monitor back, and asked for the money I was owed. Nothing doing, I put in a claim to the Small Claims Court for just the HK$1,800 owed by the practice for the HbA1C measurements. When the case was eventually heard, as I had expected, Captain Jerkoff was there representing his wife, and we were seen by a small and bemused Chinese conciliator. He could not believe that two doctors were going to Court over such a trivial sum. 'I am here representing my wife, who has had to go to the Adventist hospital', Jerkoff said. 'Oh I'm sorry to hear that' I said - 'nothing serious, I hope'... 'It's to see one of her patients', was the angry riposte. I have noticed that Cathay pilots are not noted for their 'senses of humours'. He then tried to pull rank by boasting how much his wife's practice netted, an unwise brag which made both me and the arbitrator wonder why they wouldn't settle such a trivial sum. After about half an hour, the conciliator, very cool up to this point, finally warned us that, if we didn't settle it would go to full arbitration where we both stood to lose much more. Eventually the Cathay Captain put his hand in his pocket, pulled out his wallet, and offered $HK1,000 which, being more than half the amount I was owed, I accepted, and we shook hands. The affair gave me some harmless fun, and both of us a little practical experience of very-small-claims arbitration.

By October 2008 I felt I had done enough medicine and endocrine practice, and handed my patients and their records to Professor Clive Cockram, who had recently left the Chinese University. I feel it is such a privilege to be enjoying an already long retirement, which as I shall describe later, has led me into areas I never dreamt of entering.

THE HONG KONG CHAMBER MUSIC SOCIETY

One of the advantages of being self-employed and working with your wife is that you are answerable only to 'Sheehoomusbeobeyed', to whom you were answerable anyway. Jenny organised for us to go to a nice evening of classical chamber music in the Hong Kong Club. It later turned out that a committee member was leaving and would I be interested in helping them, in the short-term of course, out of an organisational tight spot? There seemed to be no harm, but it was not long before I was Hon Sec and then President of the Society. It made little difference because I was doing the work anyway, and as a result we got to hear and meet many excellent musicians from Hong Kong and all over the world, some of whom have since become good friends. These evenings were generally held in the Hong Kong Club or Kowloon's Pacific Club about once a month, the concert being followed by a dinner.

David Coussmaker Anderson

POINTLESS PERSECUTION OF MILES AND LUCILLE JACKSON-LIPKIN

I don't remember when I first met Miles and Lucille, but it was soon after I went into private practice. Miles was an elderly larger-than-life bearded figure, reminiscent of James Robertson Justice, and several people told me of his colourful past, when his supposed wartime naval exploits were in fact revealed as confabulation. He had however, by all accounts been a good barrister and a fair judge, but being driven around ostentatiously in a Rolls Royce in his heyday he had made plenty of local Chinese enemies. He resigned in 1987, when his economy with the truth over his war record was exposed. His wife, Lucille Fung was a barrister, and when we knew them she was definitely getting a bit scatty. But MIles especially was always entertaining, and they often joined us for Hong Kong Chamber Music Society concerts. Unfortunately through profligacy and I believe loss of his pension, they fell on hard times, and had to give up their flat. That was when, in around 2003, quite inappropriately they decided to move into a room in the China Coast Community. There they were persuaded to apply for help from the Government Community Fund, which was paid straight to the CCC. They clearly didn't realise they were under the watchful eye of enemies within The Law. Details were hard to come by, but Lucille claimed the cost owed to the China Coast Community from public funds, they were assessed, and she was found to qualify. However it later transpired that they had not declared a property worth US250,000 they apparently owned in Canada, but which was in fact an unrealisable asset. The amount of money concerned was not enormous, something like $US 6000, and they immediately offered to pay it back. But they were trapped, and after a trial which dragged on for more than a year the couple, now in their eighties, were found guilty of fraud and in 2007 sentenced to eleven months in prison. Lucille, by all accounts, had a great time in the female prison in the New Territories, but Miles was miserable. In fact he spent most of the time in a bed in Queen Mary Hospital, under prison guard and at enormous state expense.

When the Jackson-Lipkins were under investigation and being tried, we were almost the only people to keep in touch. After their release they moved into sheltered housing in London, and for several years till Miles died I used to visit them in their nice public flat near Baker Street station. When I was in practice I found on several occasions that his medico-legal opinion was very sound. His keenness on *la bella figura* had also led him to set up a Hong Kong Branch of the Knights of the Order of St Lazarus of Jerusalem, and he was very helpful in getting funding from them for the Jin Yang Leprosy Village water project. He died in February 2012 at the age of 87.

Miles once told me an interesting story about the infamous Treaty of Versailles at the end of the First World War, which also throws some light on the abuse for political purposes of talking in code. It is widely agreed that the punitive reparations imposed on Germany sowed the seeds for the rise of the Nazis, Adolf Hitler and so the Second World War. David Lloyd George, Britain's Prime Minister, was a native Welsh-language speaker, while Georges Clemenceau the French Prime Minister was a native of Britany and spoke the closely related celtic language *Breton*. So the two celtic linguists were able to thrash out between themselves the harsh conditions of the Treaty, without the knowledge of other parties.

CHAPTER 13

DISCOVERING HONGSHAN NEOLITHIC JADE

FALLING IN LOVE WITH HONGSHAN JADE

In early 2,000, as was my wont, I went one Saturday to Dandelion Fine Arts, in Cat Street, just off the Hollywood Road. It was an antique shop I frequented a lot, and I had got to know the owner, a Professor of Economics at Hong Kong University, who claimed to be a friend of Milton Friedman, but also did a sideline in antiques. I had never liked jade, but that day I became fascinated by a figurine about 8 inches tall, a squat pixie-like figure with on its head a shiny green ovoid bump between two crescentic bumps; the head, in contrast to the rest, was quite highly polished (see illustrations). It reminded me of something, but at first I couldn't say precisely what. He told me it was jade from the 5,000 year old Hongshan Culture, but that the locals were ignorant and didn't recognise a genuine piece of archaic jade. He quoted a price of $HK3,200 but added, 'You are a good customer, David, so you can have it for half price.' I parted with HK$1,600 (about US$200), and feeling rather guilty, took the bus home and showed Jenny. To my relief, far from being angry she was also fascinated. I put it on the coffee table. 'It somehow looks familiar', I said, and it was only later that it hit me. 'It's obstetrics', I said, as I suddenly saw it as the god of safe delivery and imagined all those pregnant Hongshan women paying the Shaman to touch the head of the baby being safely delivered through the oedematuos vulva. 'Please, Oh God, let it be a head, let it be the head'. 'Yes, Mrs Fung, just stroke the head and she will bring you a healthy child; that will be five shillings'. On my next visit I bought another extraordinary piece about the same size - a giant mask held aloft by a poor miserable human - which I saw as the weight of religion bearing down on the shoulders of Man. Next time my son Bruce came with me, and said, 'Have you seen the small pieces in the window, Dad', which to my shame I had walked straight past. These were wonderful for three reasons - mostly small pendants they were a fraction of the price; they had a highly diverse iconography; and they used the natural colours of the jade, which vary on quite a small scale, to great effect.

THERE ARE SKEPTICS EVERYWHERE, SO WHAT IS AN EXPERT?

Thus began an extraordinary saga, and an example of being in the right place at the right time, with eyes open. And, above all, when collecting unique artifacts, of following your gut feelings, rather than relying on the opinion of accepted experts. (I like the spoof origin of the word 'expert', that it comes from the Latin: - *Ex,* a has-been, and *spurt* a drip under pressure.) I belonged to the Oriental Ceramics Society (OCS), which also included such people as the Hong Kong solicitor and jade-authority Angus Forsyth. I showed him a few pieces, and he was not convinced, but he did later suggest I show some to Professor Guo Da Shun, the universally accepted Hongshan expert's expert, and to take my microscope, and some of my pieces when I went to China. I had bought an excellent binocular microscope from a local firm, *Atto Instruments*, on the recommendation of another member of the OCS. The next thing of note was when I showed Geoffrey Key some pieces. As well as being a great artist Geoffrey is also a prolific 'gut-feeling' collector, who really liked the Hongshan pieces. He suggested I go on to eBay and search under 'Hongshan Jade'. And he was right, because under the name of *Bron-From-Down-Under*, there were on sale some pieces labelled, 'from the collection of Tony Wilson'. I bought a few, contacted Tony Wilson, and met him when he was next passing through Hong Kong. His opinion was that my now considerable collection of maybe fifty pieces was authentic. He also recommended I join a jade web discussion forum, a blog called *www.Chicochai.com/jadeforum*. And he recommended my getting a copy of the only volume on authenticating archaic jade, the proceedings of a Taiwanese conference in *Acta Geologica Taiwanica*, which I also did.

EBAY, A HONGSHAN TREASURE TROVE

Once I got onto eBay I discovered Skylink Antiques in Kowloon, run by Kelvin Choi. He would deliver the pieces to my office in Central. Soon after that I took some of my first 'Dandelion' collection with me to London, and consulted the head of Oriental Art at the British Museum, Carol Michaelson. She was both gracious and helpful. 'I can't authenticate them you know', she said and I assured her I wasn't asking her to do so. She promised to give me the contact details of Professor Guo Da Shun. I remember asking her, 'Carol, if this piece had come from an authenticated 'dig' what do you think it would be worth?' - to which she replied, 'Oh quite beyond-price, you know, quite beyond-price'. So we left it there, but I did in time contact and ultimately meet Professor Guo. I had also got my neighbour and friend Dr James Griffith, interested, indeed before long also hooked. He was living with his radiologist and Chinese Malaysian wife Clara Ooi, and their two young daughters, in the same block of Hong Kong University flats as us in Pok Fu Lam. For a long time I would do most of the collecting of small pieces, and James and I would then have a Santa-Claus-style session where we divided them out, thus effectively collecting twice as many pieces between us as we could afford individually. I got selection of the first piece, but thereafter we alternated and it was amazing how rarely we set our hearts on the same one. James and Clara's collection, which is in Hong Kong, is now at least as good as mine, and the two collections are obviously complementary.

A TRIP TO NIUHELIANG, CHINA'S PRIME HONGSHAN BURIAL-SITE

I wrote to Professor Guo at the end of 2003, and proposed to him that China was losing an enormously important heritage. I suggested that China should consider a proper business model whereby the excavations would be done, under archeological supervision, by the erstwhile tomb robbers. Half the items would be sold at auction (thus commanding high prices), the rest kept for museums, and the former clandestine robbers and farmers would be paid from the proceeds. He wrote back that he thought this was a good idea. In the summer of 2004 Professor Guo took three of us (James Griffith, myself, and Kelvin Choi's friend John Liu), to Niuheliang in a car provided by a Mr Bao. The latter ran a business selling small arms and uniforms to the police, and was also a collector of Hongshan jade. We met them in Shenyang, and Prof Guo's son acted as translator. I asked the son if he was interested in Hongshan, or archeology, and he said, 'Good god no, we just encourage my father because it keeps him happy'. In Shenyang we were shown some supposedly authentic pieces that were to be the pride and joy of the museum that was being built. And I showed Professor Guo the seven small pieces I had brought with me, and the evidence culled from my microscope. 'These are all fake' he said. 'But how can you tell?' I asked.

Then by way of argument he said, 'Well, some farmers brought us some pieces like these and said they had found them in a river bed, but we told them, 'These are all fake''. It was a disappointing first response.

Traveling via Fuxin and Chifeng, we visited museums and met some Chinese jade collectors who were clearly interested, and also terrified of the police. We visited another Hongshan site, and then came to Niuheliang, where there are multiple graves as well as a singularly unimpressive 'Goddess Temple', where artifacts excavated included pottery and some figures in unbaked mud, one depicting a human head with jade eyes like buttons pressed into the eye sockets. But we preceded our tour of the recently-excavated sites with a visit to quite an impressive six-metre high virgin burial mound (number thirteen), which was surrounded by the remains of a limestone enclosure. This was in stark contrast to the other tombs we were shown in a book that had just been published to celebrate recognition by UNESCO of this as a site of special interest. One of the pictures in this book shows a skeleton, with the head of the femur articulating with the knee joint. 'Some rats must have moved it', Professor Guo said when I challenged him later. No, he insisted the tombs they had excavated had all been virgin, although the rest of the site had already been well worked-over. I asked him how he had discovered Niuheliang, and without a trace of irony he said - 'Oh a farmer brought me the piece you saw in Shenyang, and I asked him to bring me to the site'. It seemed the farmer argument could be used both ways.

TWO JADES SAVED AND A BURIAL MOUND ROBBED FOR THE OLYMPICS

Beijing was due to hold the Olympic games in 2008. I was amazed to hear Professor Guo say that a recently-excavated tomb had yielded two very exciting jade carvings, which would be announced in four years time to mark the Beijing Olympic Games. As for the 'Goddess Temple'; it was just a muddy hillside, with a large metal awning over it, funded by the World Bank for US$25,000. Before we left I asked how much money we would need to raise in order to fund an excavation of Burial Mound Thirteen. The considered reply was US$12,000, which I offered to raise in Hong Kong, provided it was properly supervised. I was told the archeologists would dig a long trench, because that is how archeologists work. They definitely have different interests and methods from those who make their living from objects the tombs conceal. And classical painstaking archeology was what we saw in a (1000-year-old) Liao site in a city on the way back to Shenyang. Professor Guo was excited at my proposal, but later he sent an email saying he had discussed it with others and they would like to spend the money protecting the sites that they had already excavated. I told him that was not the offer. In Shenyang we were shown Mr Bao's jade collection, which was interesting, and doubtless contains some genuine pieces, most of which were polished to extinction. Back in Hong Kong, when Professor Guo came for a meeting I showed him more of my collection in my office. These included a beautiful perched bird. 'This is wrong', he said, 'because the Hongshan people carved hawks that were flying, like that one, which is right', as if birds never perched in the Neolithic period. He is not unique among experts in preferring his own authority to internal evidence.

Four years later, the year of the Beijing Olympics, I went back to Niuheliang once again with Professor Guo and Mr Bao. I was accompanied by Josef Muller, and a Chinese friend, and we found that the site had deteriorated substantially. I urged Professor Guo to take us back to burial mound thirteen, which he did after we had visited the paltry 'museum' on site. Mr Bao was talking throughout to Professor Guo as they skirted round the burial mound, while I climbed onto the top, and thought, 'That's odd'... there was some subsidence on one side of the 5,000 year-old burial mound. I called Josef, and we went down to the base of the mound, and there was a line of subsidence leading to a deep hole, which had been partially blocked off. You could see where limestone rocks had recently been lifted from surrounding soil. There were recent sweet papers and wrappers on the ground. I called Professor Guo over, and he looked into the hole. He was distinctly unhappy, and phoned the so-called Security Guards, who apparently said, 'Oh, that's funny, we saw a hole there first two years ago, and wondered what it was'. I later suggested that as an archeologist he should go in and at least explore with a torch. But he said, 'Archeologists don't do it that way, and anyway they won't have taken anything, because to get through the limestone graves they would need power tools.' Josef told me not to disturb the site by removing food wrappers, because the police might need it as evidence. I think he must have forgotten for a moment that we were in China. But not for long.

A WARNING GIVEN, AND WE RETURN THE FOLLOWING YEAR

That night we drove twenty-five kilometres to a nearby town, where news had clearly already got to the police. They took our passports for examination, while I wandered off to explore the town. They were very concerned not to be able to find where the record of entry had been stamped in mine. That evening we were entertained by the locals and the police, and I had difficulty stopping Josef from taking photographs with his distinctly obtrusive camera. My gut feeling was that they were suspicious. The following day we headed back to Shenyang, stopping at another town for the night. After supper I said to Josef and the Chinese friend with us that we needed to talk to Professor Guo away from Mr Bao, so our friend phoned him in his room. I told him that he should know that I was extremely upset about burial mound thirteen, and that he needed to report that the tomb was being robbed, because I was definitely going to the press when I got back to Hong Kong, which I did. I didn't particularly want to get Professor Guo into trouble. The following week an article and my photographs were published in the South China Morning Post.

THE HONGSHAN JADE PLOT THICKENS - WITH AGATE AND NATURAL GLASS

I had found my first piece of Hongshan agate, a wonderful owl-disc pendant, in *Pian Jia Yuan* 'Old things' Market in Beijing in 2003, while at a medical meeting. However it was not until three years later that I found more pieces in Mr Wong's stall at the Hong Kong Jade Market, and then on eBay. Surprisingly I encountered a lot of skepticism about the authenticity of the agate carvings, on the *Chicochai* forum. However some pieces showed clear and often gross weathering, in which alternate bands in the agate were more weathered. With the help of friends at the Nanovision Centre at Queen Mary University of London, we did mineral analysis on the brown soil on several pieces, and found it was high in fluorine, and so concluded that the pieces had been buried in soil high in fluorine, and the agate etched by dilute hydrofluoric acid.

On a trip to Hong Kong in 2007 I found my first Hongshan carving in what is called '*shui jing*', (literally 'clear crystal'); when I wrote about this discovery on *Chicochai* jade forum, it aroused even more anger than the agate had done. Someone pointed out that there was a massive amount of this stuff to be bought on eBay, which I found was correct. So I started to collect it. The prices were for the most part ridiculously low. When I looked at the very first piece under my microscope, I found that in one of the recesses there were hundreds of tiny glistening microspheres, which we were later able to prove by two independent methods were impact microdiamonds. These are only formed when a large meteorite impacts on graphite or coal deposits. They look quite different from synthetic diamonds used nowadays. I shall return to the quest for an impact site below.

A MAN CALLED JONTY

I tend to browse in bookshops a lot, and on a trip to London in early 2009 I found an interesting book by Jonathan Tokeley, *Rescuing the Past - the Cultural Heritage Crusade*. This is a well-written account of his experience collecting, restoring, and smuggling dynastic carvings from Egypt, for which he was eventually prosecuted, convicted and imprisoned for three years *pour encourager les autres.* I was impressed with how much his experience with Egyptian artefacts, and the counter-productive effect of the do-gooder UNESCO-UNIDROIT conventions, resonated with what I had found in China, and especially Hongshan jade. So I wrote to him, and shortly thereafter Jenny and I visited him in his late mother's house in Devon. Now Jonty is a dealer and restorer, rather than a collector. He is very good at what he does, but it is always with an eye on making a living. There is nothing wrong with that, of course, but the 'pure' collector tends to seek things because he or she likes them, even sometimes in the face of overwhelming denial by acknowledged 'experts'.

We invited Jonty, and his erstwhile business partner Phil Baker, to visit us in Umbria, so that they could see my collection, and they soon had grandiose plans. While in Hong Kong at the height of my collecting, I had started to keep detailed notes of much of my collection, which included eight books of annotated pencil drawings, with notes on many of my microscopic findings. These books are now quite extensively further annotated in pencil, under the mistaken assumption that my failure to reply to an email implied permission. Though erasable, in the interests of science and posterity I have left these supplementary notes. At all events, in the summer of 2009, Jonty started to rent our villa, and remained on our property until October 2011, when he and I drove to the UK immediately after the release of Amanda Knox and Raffaele Sollecito. I say 'rent' but in fact we are still owed money which I am assured will come when his ship comes in. Ships of course do sometimes sink without trace, but we live in hope.

This experience, and our joint trip to China in October 2009 was instructive. We have different approaches to China and the Hongshan Culture in particular, but with much agreement over nephrite jade; however our paths diverge completely over *shui jing*. This actually worked to my advantage, because ultimately Jonty went in for gilded bronze-decorated later jades, for which there is a definite market. He did some excellent restoration, on one belt buckle in particular. But when visiting antique markets in China together I found he was rather less discrete than I was, as I saw dollar signs flashing up in the eyes of the vendors.

Jonty and I reported in person the pillaging of the site I had witnessed in 2008 to the UNESCO office in Beijing, where it aroused no interest. With Jenny we then met up with our friend and fellow collector Mr Bao, and had an amazing tour of his office next to Tiananmen Square, where he was selling just about every sort of police and military gear (short of tanks), in which he traded. Mr Bao then took us back to Niuheliang, where we have photos of him traipsing across the sacred ground that once held the 'Goddess Temple' and is protected by the rusting $25,000 World Bank awning from the elements, but not from the Bao's of this world.

Mr Bao was extremely helpful in taking us to the modern agate carving factory in Fuxin, which brought home to me how there was absolutely no interest in carving little Hongshan-style pieces. Not because of lack of skill, but because the market is already flooded with authentic pieces whose existence is being denied, and for which there is no Chinese market. On the same trip we met Professor Guo in Shenyang, and I gave him a *shui jing* flying hawk pendant, which he examined scornfully and probably threw away. Mr Bao was astonished that I should be interested in Hongshan *shui jing*, and happily took us to Beijing's *Shi Li He* market, which is where recently excavated pieces were flooding in. Otherwise I doubt if we would have found it. When I found and bought a cobalt blue cow-handled bowl, I left the bag in Jonty's safe keeping, which turned out to be a mistake, since he put it down and it vanished without trace. 'Don't worry, David, they are all fake anyway', he said, reassuringly. In the end I benefited from his official disinterest, because I ended up with some fabulous pieces, initially part of a proposed joint collection, which include a glass fish with an excased three millimetre glistening putative microdiamond, which he wanted no part of. When I wrote my *Hongshan Jade Treasures book* in 2011-12, Jonty was helpful with the jade and agate chapters, while advising that the glass should be excluded. Time will tell who was right, but many people are equally stunned by the glass.

WHAT IS THE EVIDENCE THAT SHUI JING GLASS IS OF IMPACT ORIGIN?

My evidence, accumulated over eight years can be summarised as follows. First, the composition of the clear areas of the glass is pure silicon dioxide, with a melting temperature in excess of 1,600C. It contains no additives or modifiers. It is very similar to Libyan Desert Glass, which was formed from a meteorite or cometary impact, under exceptionally high temperatures and pressures. To synthesise such glass is extremely costly. I have a collection of tubes of glass which contain holes which are undoubtedly natural. The red streaks seen in many of the glass carvings map to iron, aluminium, potassium and sodium. The biggest of these pieces is a metre high, and independent evidence points to the existence of massive red-streaked glass spheres (see illustrations). Some other carved pieces contain opalescent streaks, which map to titanium. Others contain streaks of cobalt colour. Many carvings and recently-cut pieces contain incorporated creamy-coloured material, consistent with melted soil and rock picked up from the ground by bouncing spheres of red-hot glass. Some carved pieces contain incorporated glistening clear crystals, strongly suggestive of impact diamonds; lonsdaleite impact diamonds have also been found in drill holes. It suggests the impact was on an area of desert, overlying coal deposits and was ejected in gaseous or liquid state, cooled, and formed during flight into spheres.

The evidence is also strong that it was carved in China from the neolithic period by the Hongshan carvers using impact diamonds as an abrasive. Furthermore it is still being mined, and carved into glass balls, or to look like quartz crystals, or cut into slices from spheres; while shard residue is crushed and used as a thirty percent filler for porcelain. Names on the bags in which the glass is shipped to Porcelain City strongly support the hypothesis that the mine or quarry is in Tong Liao province. To test this hypothesis, and identify the impact site, it is essential to find the glass mines.

CHAPTER 14

WHERE IS CHINA'S MISSING METEORITE-IMPACT CRATER?

A SEARCH ON GOOGLE EARTH

In late 2009 Jenny's niece Sarah and her husband, Fergus Wells came to visit us for a few days in Umbria. I told Fergus about my conclusions that the Hongshan-style carvings I was collecting, were in glass of meteoritic impact origin, and had been carved four to five thousand years ago using impact diamonds. I desperately wanted to find the impact site, and his very sensible advice was to look on *Google Earth* for a crater. So when they left I first looked on the *Earth Impact Database*, which is a record of all known impacts on Earth. What it better reflects is where geologists have been asking relevant questions. In the whole of China and Mongolia I found only one certified crater, named *Tabun-Khara-Obo*, which despite its nominative appeal to me as an oboist was clearly too small and much too old. There must be some mistake, so I went on to *Google Earth*, and within forty-five minutes of searching in and around Inner Mongolia I stumbled across an extraordinary pair of craters, at around 114.24E and 44.14N (see illustrations). The coordinates themselves even seemed symbolically memorable. I had already visited the Ries Crater Museum, in Nördlingen at the centre of one of Europe's largest impact craters. I had met the very helpful Director, Michael Schieber, and had shown him some carvings in my collection, including two with encased microdiamonds, during my first visit. His response to the twin craters was that the northern one looked much more typical of an impact crater than its southern twin. He educated me on what features to look for. It seemed obvious that the two were formed at the same event, but if they were indeed volcanic calderas, why would there be two so close together?

TWIN CRATERS: I DECIDE TO GO AND TAKE A LOOK

On one of my now less-frequent visits to Hong Kong I tried to interest the head of the China Exploration and Research Society, Wong How Man, that these were worthy of an expedition. I met him in his office in Hong Kong's Aberdeen, and he agreed they looked interesting, but politely declined, on the grounds that they didn't do purely geological expeditions. Meanwhile I was talking to my German China-photographing friend Josef Muller. With no official support we just decided to go and have a look; I agreed to cover his expenses. The year before I had met Rebecca Middleton's driver Louis, a very independent-minded Chinese, and on request he found us an ethnic Mongolian driver who agreed to take us there in his (non-Mongolian) four wheel drive vehicle.

So late in May 2010 I took the Cathay flight from Hong Kong to Beijing, and for some reason it was held up for two hours on the runway. Seated beside me was a young Chinese girl student with a massive Teddy bear on her knee; while parked on the runway we engaged in some polite conversation. It transpired she was an only child (no surprise there), her parents were divorced, she was studying in Chicago, and was on her way to visit her father for a week in Beijing before going on to spend the rest of the summer with her mother. She had no idea how she was going to occupy a whole week with her father. 'So why are you going to Beijing?' she asked. I told her about the twin craters. 'That sounds interesting' she said. 'Then why don't you come and bring your father too? I'll cover hotel and travel expenses' I said, thinking that a couple of Chinese in the party would provide useful cover.

MY FIRST VISIT TO THE TWIN CRATERS, ESIGE WULE AND CHULE WULE

Once we had landed, with baggage in hand, we were met by her father, and he kindly gave me a lift to the Middleton's very up-market estate. 'Yolanda, we leave for Abag Qi at eight tomorrow morning, when Josef and the driver arrive - let me know what you and your Dad decide' I said, and left her my mobile phone number. Later that evening Yolanda phoned and said, 'My Dad thinks it's a good idea; and he and I can share a room'. So the following morning, once Josef had arrived late, we departed for Abag Qi. I didn't have a detailed local map, but our Mongolian-Chinese driver seemed to know where it was. I reckoned it was a journey of about six hours. Three hours later we arrived there. 'Where are we?' I asked in my best Chinese. *'Zhè shi Abaga Qi'* ('This is Abag Qi)' he said. 'It can't be' I said, we haven't even got half way to Xilinhot; and we went to buy a map in Chinese of Inner Mongolia. I showed him. 'Oh', he said, 'you told me to go to Abag Qi, that is Abaga Qi!!'. As a result of our Chinese drivers maplessness, and my imperfect tones in Mandarin we had taken a forty-mile detour, and arrived in the wrong Abag Qi but four hours ahead of schedule. Every expedition should have a name, of course, and taking the initials of the four participants I called this one the Jymdaft Expedition, and the driver Jim. We drove on, and eventually got to the right town, and found the White Horse Hotel which was reserved for Chinese, but courtesy of our newly acquired Chinese cover, they let us all stay there. I asked an old man about the twin craters, called locally Chule Wule and Esige Wule, and what people thought had caused them. 'A giant meteor' he said 'that's what people say, but we don't know for sure'.

After the usual breakfast of noodles and dumplings in a roadside café the following morning we got under way, heading first along a main road west, past massive open-cast coal mines, and then took off north for the town of Bogd Ul. It was well-named as it consisted of a dozen or so mud huts and one shop. An Umbrian friend Chris Redfern had lent me a GPS, and that is where I finally decided it was useless in Inner Mongolia and stopped trying to use it. Following local instructions we went past an impressive volcanic mesa, across the open plateau towards the northern crater. The plan was to explore both on foot, and the first day we spent mostly at the northern one, and the north side of the southern one. Since by now I was heavily involved in fighting for justice in Perugia, and I saw these craters as falsely accused of being volcanic, I poetically named the more beautiful northern one, *Amanda*, and the southern one *Raffaele*. Yolanda was as enthusiastic as her father was bored, and she came with us to explore the centre of the *Amanda* crater, while her father sat on a rock under an umbrella gazing blankly, and doubtless thinking what a pain his week with his daughter and two mad *sai yan* was going to be, and what were these idiots doing here anyway? I got enthusiastic finding possible suevite and what I saw as shatter cones on ejected rocks. But I was clearly out of my geological depth. The north crater has multiple concentric outer ridges, and finally rises to a main ridge which falls down into a two kilometre-wide plain, with a couple of peaks in the middle.

David Coussmaker Anderson

THE SOUTHERN CRATER HAS A BIT MISSING

After we had taken a brief look at the confusing northern rim of the southern (*Raffaele*) crater we headed back to Abag Qi. The following day we drove back and started by climbing the volcanic ridge (leaving Yolanda's father in the four wheel drive) to the east of the southern crater, baptised it *Yolanda ridge*, and then continued to circumnavigate the *Raffaele* crater, which has steeper sides, and most of the top of which is relatively flat, without the subsidiary ridges seen on *Amanda*. We found a place where they were mining volcanic rock (for road metal), where there were some huts, and finally got round to where we had explored the day before, just beyond a projection I named *Rocket Peak*. It was there that Josef, with consummate insight said, 'David there's a bit missing', and right enough there was a smaller hemi-crater, a bit missing about one kilometre across, which I have therefore named after Josef.

We returned to our hotel, and the next day went back to Beijing, stopping on the way at the large town of Xilinhot. There we asked where the antique shops were, and were directed to the local race course, where Yolanda got a ride on a tourist pony, and Josef and I explored the shops, one of which was interesting. There was quite a lot of *shui jing* glass. including what looked for all the world like a quartz crystal in the same red-streaked material, for which the owner was asking 2,000 RMB (about $US 250). On closer examination, and with some relief, I noticed that the opposite faces were not parallel, so it was clearly a piece of glass that had been inexpertly carved to look like a quartz crystal. 'Where did this *shui jing* come from?' I asked, and he said he could take me to the mine, which was a few hours drive away in an area called Tong Liao. I took his phone number and said, 'Maybe next year'. We drove on back to Beijing after an evening meal, and came upon a massive queue just north of the Great Wall at Badeling. Our Jymdaft driver Jim was constantly leaping out of the vehicle, and asking for information. In the end we drove back eight or so miles the wrong way up the hard shoulder of the motorway into the oncoming traffic, lights blazing and flashing and horn blasting, to a petrol station. There we found a service road under the motorway and our fearless driver took another route home.

FINDING A TAME EXPEDITION GEOLOGIST

Let me fast forward ten months to the spring of 2011, when I was preoccupied with Amanda Knox and Raffaele Sollecito's appeal against their conviction, in the bowels of Perugia's Appeal Court (see Chapter 15). One evening, over a beer in Perugia's Hotel Brufani, I fell into conversation with some of Amanda's defence team, including their lovely Italian-American translator Giulia Alagni. I told her about the twin craters and how I felt sure they had been falsely accused of being volcanic, and how I had mischievously named the more beautiful one *Amanda* and the more complex one *Raffaele*. I wanted to go back there in the summer with a real geologist, both to take a more expert look at the craters, and to visit the glass mine, which I had been told was in Tong Liao. Unexpectedly she said that her brother Keegan was a qualified geologist, out of work at the moment, and that she would mention it to him. Shortly afterwards he got in touch, so I explained what I wanted to do. I said if he could get himself to Beijing I would cover all his other costs. This time I wanted to concentrate on the Red Hot Balls of Fire (RedhotBOF) glass mines which I had been told were in Tong Liao, which is the name of a large geographic area as well as a city. He agreed, so to get him up to speed on Impact Craters I took him over a long weekend by car to Nördlingen, to visit the Ries crater museum, meet Michael Schieber; and then to go to Vienna to meet the famous impact geologist Christian Kőeberl, who Michael warned me might be a bit difficult. Not to worry, I had experienced difficult people before. I took a number of pieces of *shui jing* with me. Michael was very helpful, and brought Keegan up to speed quickly on what to look for. We spent the rest of the day exploring the Ries Crater, and then drove towards Vienna, stopping overnight just short of the Austrian border.

Next morning we looked round the Natural History Museum's collection of meteorites, and then met Kŏeberl's very helpful assistant Ludovic Ferriere, who listened patiently, and said the Professor would give us ten minutes of his precious time. It sounded like we were being given an audience with the Pope. And the encounter, which in fact lasted half an hour, mainly consisted of him talking about his most recent paper and giving a long harangue as to how ours could not possibly be impact craters. I was clearly a fool to think *shui jing* could be an impact glass, and he was implicitly asking, 'Why are you wasting my extremely important time'? At the end, I asked him if he was always that rude to guests. He was clearly taken aback by this, but Ludovic was most apologetic, and agreed to test the samples I had brought back, just once, as long as I would not bother him again. Interestingly, Kŏeberl has since been very courteous in correspondence, and has even referred some people to me for further information. I do have some sympathy because those in the impact field are constantly being bombarded by amateurs who think they have found something special. Parenthetically, I remember on our 2005 trip to New Zealand, picking up what I thought might be a piece of green jade in a river bed near Hokitika, and showing it to one of the carvers, who earlier that day had been very helpful and friendly. He studied it and then looked at me ...'David, this is a piece of Levitrite'... 'Levitrite?' I asked, puzzled. 'Yes, Levitrite where it was!' It was a commonplace bit of serpentine.

OUR SECOND (REDHOTBOF) EXPEDITION AND ETHNIC RIOTS CHINA-STYLE

A month later we all met in Beijing - my son Bruce, Josef, Keegan and me; and the long-suffering Middleton's Louis had found another driver. He had also phoned the man in Xilinhot who the previous year had offered to take us to the *shui jing* mine in Tong Liao. It seemed he had delegated this to the mine's manager. Unfortunately three weeks before the planned trip a Han Chinese coal lorry driver had run over and killed an ethnic Mongolian worker, and this had led to race riots in Abag Qi. When we got to Xilinhot, and met the manager of the mine in his shop, it was explained that because of the riots we could not go to the mine without special permission, and agreement of the workers, which would take several days. The mine workers, we were told, were all ethnic Mongolians. In the shop they had two red-streaked *shui jing* glass balls, that had been carved in a ball-carving factory in Shandung. I photographed these and bought one of them for US$40. So reluctantly we decided to visit the twin craters first, for Keegan to do a bit of field geology, and then to return and hope to visit the glass mine. The following morning before leaving we met with Billy the manager, and his 'minder' Danny; unfortunately Josef was as usual late getting up. This is because he always works long into the night on something else on such trips, and so is constantly sleep-deprived. His Mandarin is much better than mine, and it might have gone differently had he been conducting the conversation. The gist of the story was that the mine had originally, like all else, been owned by the Government who knew *shui jIng* was special, with its very high melting temperature, and wanted to use it for making spacecraft windows. But they found it was too inconsistent, so they had passed it on for private commercial exploitation in the late 1970's. Foolishly, I think I said too much about why we were interested.

TO THE CRATERS AGAIN, WITH A FRIENDLY POLICE ESCORT

After breakfast we drove to Abag Qi, which had changed beyond recognition, as happens fast in China. By some miracle we did manage to find the hotel we had stayed in the year before, and were greeted like long lost friends. We checked in, and twenty minutes later the police arrived to look at our documents and talk to us. They told us we could not stay in that hotel, which was reserved for Chinese (which had also been the case the year before). Josef explained what we wanted to do, that I was a harmless crackpot retired doctor who was very interested in geology, and he detailed the important special roles each of the others in our party had. The police chief was very reasonable, let us stay in this hotel as an exception, and said we could go to the twin craters provided we had a police escort, which he would provide free of charge. The escort joined us the following morning. We retraced our tracks from the year before, going straight to the north (*Amanda*) crater. One of the policemen had brought his daughter for the outing. We stopped at a Yurt, where they spoke to the Mongolian farmers, and where we later had lunch for which I paid very little. On this occasion we walked right across the north crater, climbing the main central peak on the way; it was clearly volcanic. Our police escort mostly just sat in their car and smoked health-free cigarettes. They were clearly puzzled by us, but seemed convinced of our innocence.

That evening we drove back to Abag Qi, to return with our tame police to the craters the following day. We revisited all the previous year's sites, including the quarry for road metal, which was now closed. Keegan's conclusion was that all the evidence on the surface was of volcanism. But as you will realise that may not be the whole story, since absence of evidence is not evidence of absence (*Carl Sagan*). After our second day there we were uniquely treated to an evening meal in Abag Qi by our police escort, and returned to Xilinhot, where we again checked in to the main hotel, and made contact with the mine manager. We were very hopeful we would complete the main purpose of our trip the following morning, when the story suddenly changed.

A CHANGING OFFICIAL STORY, AND SOME HARD NEW EVIDENCE

We were taken to the manager's office and given tea; and we were shown several large crystals of quartz. It was explained that we had got it all wrong. They were mining quartz, shipping it down to Donghai where it was crushed, melted in a furnace and copper was added to give the red streaks. I knew this was nonsense, but the others seemed to swallow it. By now it was raining hard, and they still had not got the permit. Before we left I asked Billy to mark precisely on my map where the *shui jing* mine was. Remember, *'shui jing'* refers to both quartz and to the tektite silica glass. He put a precise mark on the map. Disappointed, we returned to Beijing, stopping on the way in the antique quarter of Chifeng. Once back in Beijing, I introduced Keegan to Professor Yang Xiao Ping at the Institute of Geology. Then Bruce and Keegan went home, Josef and I stayed once again with the Middletons where we shared a double bed! The next day we went to a cheap hotel, where I met my friend Cody Wei, who gave me a twelve kilogram 'splat' of recently-mined *shui jing*, with large circular saw marks, for nothing but the price of packing and shipping it to Italy, where I still have it (see illustrations). I went back to the shop that the year before had had on display the *shui jing* glass slice, but it had closed. After further visits to Shi Li He market I flew home to Italy and back to the Amanda Knox appeal.

I wasn't sure how convinced Josef was of my impact story, and I was heavily involved in completing my book on jade, plus the never-ending saga to secure the release of Amanda and Raffaele, but I kept in touch with both Josef and Keegan. In the summer of 2012 I completed the publication of my book *Hongshan Jade Treasures - the art, iconography and authentication of carvings from China's finest Neolithic Culture.* In early 2013 I gave two lectures in Hong Kong, one to the Foreign Correspondents' Club, and one to the Royal Geographical Society, on the impact theory and China's unique natural glass, and I also sold copies of my book.

From 2012 I was also involved each year in running a music festival starring my cousin Libby Wallfisch. Then in late 2014, Josef found what promised to be an important lead. He travels all over China doing promotional and industrial photography, (which means traveling with him is slow, as he constantly stops the vehicle to leap out to take pictures!) He had been visiting a factory in Porcelain City, which is 550km inland from Shanghai, and found there a big pile of hessian bags containing shards of the same clear and red-streaked glass. The bags were clearly meant for shipping glutamate, which is called *wei jing* in Chinese, and characters printed on them referred to a factory on the edge of the town of Tong Liao. On one of my visits to Bruce in Hong Kong, I met up with Josef, and he gave me a couple of shards of this glass. Josef said that the glass was being crushed and added as a 30% bulking agent to porcelain; he had also seen a TV programme in China where a factory claimed to have found a method of making pink porcelain, something they boasted that no one before had achieved.

2015 AND ANOTHER EXPEDITION IN SEARCH OF THE SHUI JING GLASS MINE(S).

So this was further evidence that the *shui jing* mine was also in Tong Liao province, near where the hessian bag factory was, and that the mined material was being shipped to Porcelain City in bags made for shipping *wei jing* (sodium glutamate). Since there were many such bags, it appeared probable that a bulk side-order of labelled bags was made for the glass mine, as they would obviously need to ship the shards somehow. A lorry full of bags labelled 'glutamate' would not arouse suspicion at check-points, and they could always have a couple of bags of the real stuff to show any curious transport inspector. This discovery by Josef was my main incentive to mount another expedition in 2015 to Inner Mongolia, starting this time in Tong Liao City and Province. I felt, and still feel, that locating the glass mine or quarry would point back to the impact site, thereby testing my twin craters impact hypothesis.

In April 2015, Jenny and I drove via Prague and Dresden, to Colditz castle in Germany, for the celebrations of the seventieth anniversary of its liberation, and a concert and tour organised by my brother Stuart. Dad had after all been a prominent - if discrete - inhabitant there over the first four years of my life. We returned via Luxembourg and finally met up with Josef and his family at their home in Bavaria, visited Nördlingen, and planned our next trip, this time to Shenyang and the *Wei Jing* factory in Tong Liao.

Once in China we were picked up by our new driver in Shenyang. He had never driven outside town before. Selected by a friend of Josef, he had a two-wheel-drive vehicle, and some idea that we would not average more than 200 km a day. We first explored Tong Liao city and its antique markets, and met the man who ran its mediocre museum. Actually, to call it mediocre is an insult to genuinely mediocre museums in China such as the one in Shenyang. Apocalyptic would be a better description. There was a whole floor dedicated to enormous 'muriels' to the glorification of the tyrant Genghis Khan. The next day we tried our luck at the biggest biological toxic-food-production facility in China, and therefore probably the world, the Tong Liao *Wei Jing* plant, whose address was written clearly on the bags full of *shui jing* in Jingdezhen (Porcelain City). Basically, no one important was there, but we did have a chat with the man at the gate, who said they must have got some bags (like maybe thirty or forty) second-hand because they are very fond of monosodium glutamate all over China and maybe especially in porcelain factories.

AT LAST A 'SHUI JING' MINE, AND A NESTING WILD GOOSE TO CHASE

It seemed we were at an impasse, and as I was paying for the driver by the day, and was basically skint, we had to look to the best use of our time. Albert was the research fellow entrusted to us by Professor Yang Xiao Ping, of the Institute of Geological Sciences in Beijing. So we decided to go to places I had marked on the infamous map four and five years before. This involved some definitely off piste driving, along brand new stretches of road that then defaulted into dirt. But fortunately a major storm only started just after we had left the dirt road. Once we had arrived at the relevant town we went to try and find the *shui jing* mine indicated by Billy on the map four years before, and became very excited when Albert found '*shui Jjng* mine' marked on a Google map. We checked in to the hotel, and then took an incredibly circuitous route, and were finally accompanied on the last bit by a Mongolian with his wife and a live lamb for supper, sitting meekly on her knee. From above, the mine was nothing to look at, and as it was almost dark we retraced our steps. Back at the hotel we looked on Google Earth, and the following morning took a direct route back past a new reservoir, and parked the car within hiking distance. Google Earth showed air vents for the same mine we had visited the night before. And what was it? A long-disused quartz mine, with a wild goose poetically making its nest deep within! We left the eggs, and drove north through a landscape wrecked by strip-mining for the world's near-total complement of rare earth metals. This time we were on better roads, and had settled our differences with the driver who, now back *on piste,* was gaining in confidence. We stayed overnight in a really polluted northern town, and next day headed south to Tong Liao and finally Shenyang, whence we took the train to Beijing the following morning. So all we had achieved was to unscramble the lie and get further evidence of the confusion that resides in the name '*shui jing*'.

2016, AND ONE MORE TRY

The next year, using the same driver, Josef and I went back once more, this time with my cousin Libby Wallfisch's protegé Lamin Ceesay, a tall handsome African from the Gambia who was studying Chinese in Nanjing. In many places where we went it was clear they had never seen a black man before. This time we tried a different approach, which involved going to Fuxin, where we found the agate factory we had visited in 2009 with Jonty; they had no information about *shui jing*, and they were not carving it there. Then on to Chifeng, where at least in the indoor market I found the most fabulous Liao dynasty egg-shaped pendant in opalescent *shui jing*, for Jenny, for a very modest price of US$120. This was much better than a piece we had seen on offer the year before for twenty times the price. We went to somewhere I had identified on Google Earth, having gone as far as Ba Lin Zuo Qi, the town where we stayed last year, before tracing our way back and round to a bifurcation in the river which marks the 'tongue' of Tong Liao province, which is right on my postulated twin craters glass ejection line. The whole of that part of Inner Mongolia is being built on and taken over by Han Chinese. We were fortunate to meet someone

David Coussmaker Anderson

with a four-wheel-drive vehicle who actually took us to the river bed. I collected some sand from low down where water had been swirling in the last flood - hoping maybe to hit a stratum of impact diamonds, but back home my Spanish collaborator Ignacio Hernandez found only quartz. There must be a simpler way to locate the elusive glass mine, but I have yet to find it.

CHAPTER 15

ON IMPACTS AND CLIMATE CHANGE, PAST AND PRESENT

CHINA'S MYSTERIOUS METEORITE IMPACT - A 2018 UPDATE

If you are working outside your own narrow professional field, minding other people's business as I tend to do, important matters can easily pass you by. To help counteract this, I never miss an opportunity to talk about the Hongshan Culture, and especially about the glass and my impact theory. In September 2015 I put together an exhibition of Hongshan carvings from my collection, in Todi's *Palazzo del Vignola,* where the glass pieces especially aroused great interest. Then later that year and in early 2016, introduced by my musician friend Radu Pantea, I gave two lectures at the *Cercle Munster Club* in Luxembourg. The one on the glass was recorded by Radu's father Ionel, (a world famous baritone), and can be viewed on *youtube*. I marshaled many of my more cogent arguments, and presented the latest version of my theory on the elusive glass mines.

Then last summer, 2017, Bruce's friend Andy Byrne spent a week with his family in our rental villa in Italy, and in a sober quiescent period, I outlined for him the essence of my impact theory. He looked at my *youtube* lecture and effused with enthusiasm. He asked whether I had read any of the writings of the world-renowned and controversial catastrophist, Graham Hancock, and I hadn't. 'You should read '*Magicians of the Gods*,' he said, emphatically. Now please appreciate that I am on the old side, somewhere between fuddy and duddy, and so I would normally avoid a book with that sort of glitzy title. It was therefore with both surprise and pleasure that several months later a copy arrived in the post from Amazon, gifted to me by Andy. On reading it I realised the importance of what he had been talking about. A geologically-recent global catastrophe, in which my personal postulated impact might just hold centre-stage.

HOW IS GRAHAM HANCOCK'S 'MAGICIANS OF THE GODS' RELEVANT?

The central message of this fascinating book, is that contrary to what most archeologists tell us, mankind has been 'civilised' before, towards the end of the last ice age, when global civilisation was destroyed by a catastrophic impact event and associated flood. He presents strong evidence that many of the massive man-made wonders of the world are much older than current archeological dogma allows. He postulates, but with no direct evidence, a comet hitting the massive three kilometre-thick North American (Laurentide) ice sheet. Such an event about 12,800 years ago dramatically changed the Earth's then-warming climate, was followed by the 1,200 year Younger Dryas cooling period, and then catastrophic melting of the ice sheet and a rise of sea levels of up to 400 feet. I started to contribute to Graham's blogsite, www.grahamhancock.com, and this is what I posted on December 11th 2017...

I mentioned when I opened the speculative thread on natural gas balloons, that I might start another on the Hongshan Culture and its carvings. ...As described in my book (Hongshan Jade Treasures) thanks to colleagues at Queen Mary College University of London's Nanovision Centre, I have direct evidence that they used impact diamonds (lonsdaleite) 'magic sand' at least to carve shui Jing natural glass... Our direct studies on the glass in London and by colleagues at Johnson Matthey led to the conclusion that shui jing is similar to LIbyan Desert Glass, with no network stabilisers or additives, and a melting temperature in excess of 1,600 C. It is almost pure silica glass. If anyone on this forum is interested I suggest you view the second of my two lectures on Youtube - Data is presented there also on the nature of the red streaks, as well as opalescence on sacrificial fragments of Hongshan-style carvings. Two pieces in my collection contain what appear to be impact diamonds actually encased in the glass, and there is great variability in the nature and amount of encased detritus. The relevance to this particular forum is strong evidence that the glass was ejected at an oblique angle and landed far away as spheres of up to 1 metre in diameter. This speaks of a unique solid impactor, with some of the liquid silica ejected into the lower troposphere so as to form into large spheres, some of which retained their shape as they cooled and bounced across ground. Doing so they picked up surface minerals which partially melted and often became encased in the glass. Furthermore this glass is still being mined, and wasted (on glass balls, executive toys, carved pseudo-crystals, and crushed as filler for porcelain), in western China.

I discuss the evidence, albeit circumstantial, that the mine is in or near Tong Liao County: and my theory that the impactor was a 600 X 250 metre dumbell-shaped bolide that struck relatively recently and produced the twin craters you can find on Google Earth at 44.14N, 114.24E. (see [www.google.it]). I believe there is a strong probability that these are in fact impact in origin, although the direct evidence we found on the ground is of volcanism. I speculate in the presentation that because of the nature of volcanism in this part of China (which is caused by the Earth being pulled apart) it is possible that such a relatively small dumbell-shaped impactor would crack through into a surface volcanic chamber and reactivate local volcanism within and near the craters. Working from the diameters of the twin craters, and an assumed entry speed of 20 km/second, I estimate an explosive force of around 300,000 megatons of TNT, or 10 million times that of the Hiroshima atom-bomb. This is much less than Graham has suggested for his postulated comet hitting the North American Ice Sheet. But of course volcanic ash would augment greatly the effect of the impactor, and might therefore have had a devastating effect on world climate. The 'missing corner' of the southern crater suggests a small waist piece fifty metres in diameter, slowed by the shock wave, might have arrived a second later and bounced off the exploding surface dragging silica gas and liquid behind it.

At all events I have proposed a testable hypothesis, the first element of which is to locate the glass mines, which I know are now in private hands. Wherever they and other elements of the splash field are will point back to the impact site. I have tried to interest the Institute of Geology in Beijing, but unfortunately the nature of academia everywhere is such that there are few brownie points to be had from pursuing studies outside the individual's (or an Institution's) academic comfort zone! I hope someone on this forum with relevant contacts will see its importance, and put pressure on China by at least pointing to its potential for geo-tourism. It should be easy for those in power to locate the shui jing glass mines, which were doubtless originally in Government hands. Incidentally, on my first visit to the craters in June 2010, I asked a local what he thought had caused the twin craters Chule Wule and Esige Wule, and he replied 'a giant meteorite'.

HOW MIGHT A GIANT IMPACT IN CHINA HAVE LED TO A GLOBAL DISASTER?

My suggestion is that at a time when it is known from ice sheet data that global temperatures were rising, 12,800 years ago, 'my' meteorite struck in Northern China (where, despite its latitude there was no ice sheet), caused abrupt global cooling, and triggered off local volcanism, which kept the global cooling going. I suggest that until this event the North American Laurentide ice sheet (which was up to three kilometres-thick) had been melting, maybe as a result of human activity and greenhouse gas (methane) emissions from agriculture, and was therefore on the surface a porous though still solid lattice of ice with lakes of water at ground level. With the reactivation of atmospheric cooling induced by the impact, the Earth was plunged back into a temporary extension of the ice age. Ice would have built up again on top of, and at the advancing southern edges of this and other ice sheets, which below at ground level were now dangerously unstable. The 'Younger Dryas' period lasted for 1,200 years, which is fifty human generations, plenty of time to colonise mainly land close to sea level. It ended abruptly with a sudden rise in global temperatures, melting of the ice sheets, the catastrophic flood so well documented by the Scablands of North America, and a massive rise in sea levels, with catastrophic destruction of an advanced civilisation and of many animal species.

An important question is what caused this sudden temperature rise 11,600 years ago, which has continued more or less ever since. Was it, perhaps, collective human activity in the form of agriculture, with its increased levels of atmospheric methane?

Did the civilisation even learn how to farm methane biogas, for lighting and heating purposes, as happens in the third world today, from anaerobic partial degradation of organic waste? Is it even possible, as I have suggested, that the massive stones used to make the pyramids of Egypt and the temples of Goebekli Tepe, intended to ward off disaster by appeasing the wrath of the gods, were lifted by harvesting methane from biological or even ground sources, to create massive methane balloons? The density of methane is roughly half that of air and it can easily be produced biologically. Albert Einstein said 'If at first an idea is not absurd, then there is no hope for it'. Those stones certainly weren't lifted by magic.

FAST-FORWARD TO THE PRESENT, AND JET STREAMS AND CURRENT CLIMATE-CHANGE

I once sat in the first class lounge at Hong Kong airport, invited by friends, and spotted ex-Vice President Al Gore (author of *'An Inconvenient Truth'*) not far away. I should have gone up and asked him the simple inconvenient question. 'If as is clear from your excellent lecture, a rise in global temperature has historically *preceded* a rise in CO2 levels how can you blame the first on the second?' But I didn't. It must be more than ten years since I asked a further very simple inconvenient question about the jet streams, in the *South China Morning Post,* and I still think it is a deserves an answer. It is very clear that over the past several decades global weather patterns have become more extreme and more unpredictable. The question is why?

Wherever possible, passenger jets flying from West to East in the northern hemisphere increase their ground speed by hitching a lift in the North Polar Jet Stream. The jet streams are four important high speed tunnels of air that run from west to east, located at the tropopause, the level at which the troposphere below (where air temperature decreases with altitude) interfaces the stratosphere above, (where air temperature increases with altitude). The two polar ones (at around 60 degrees north and south) are the most important drivers of world weather, and of these the North Polar Jet Stream covers the major land masses and world populations. Of course under natural conditions their position changes with the seasons, and so does the weather below. But they do not naturally have massive aerodynamic chunks of metal (ie aircraft) gaining ground speed and maintaining altitude at their expense. They do this by forcing the air they are flying in downwards, as each plane gains lift from the forward thrust of the engines and the aerodynamic shape of its wings. *'Primum non nocere'* (first do no harm) is a medical dictum, and I believe we are being irresponsible in assuming without strong evidence that interfering with the jet stream(s) by flying in them whenever possible is harmless. At present the adage, in Google latin, seems to be *'Primum, non crescere cibus consummatio'* (first do not increase fuel consumption).

This is what meteorologist Jeff Masters had to say on August 10th 2014 in an interview on *The Real News,* on how the jet streams affect weather patterns.......

(see [www.therealnews.com])

.... I was talking about the jet stream, which is that upper-level river of air that tends to control our weather. And the reason it controls our weather is because it acts as the boundary between cold air to the polar side and then warmer subtropical air on the other side. And normally the jet stream flows straight, West to East over our latitudes, which means you don't have a big sort of variation in the weather patterns. But when that jet stream starts to take these big bows, these big excursions like a meandering river, that's when we tend to get really major

extreme weather events. In particular, this past winter over the Eastern US and Midwest, this so-called polar vortex episode happened, and that was (due to) a big bulge in the jet stream. It went way far to the south, allowing cold air to spill out of Canada, down much farther south than usual. And on the converse side, over in California you have a compensating ridge, kind of a U-shaped bulge in the jet stream going far to the north, which allowed very warm air from Mexico in the south to bring California its warmest and driest winter on record. So when you get one of these major jet stream undulations, it tends to bring extreme weather of both kinds, both the hot extreme and the cold extreme, and wet and dry extremes. And there's evidence that these sorts of unusual jet stream undulations are increasing in frequency. In fact, they've doubled over the past 11 years compared to the previous 22 years. So that's a big concern. And we don't even know what's causing this jet stream behavior, but it makes sense that something to do with climate change might be involved. When you put the level of heat and moisture into the atmosphere that we've done over the past few decades, something has to give. Weather patterns have to shift. And one of the culprits we're looking at right now is the fact that the sea ice in the Arctic is about a factor of 2 less than it was 40 years ago, and that could be affecting global weather patterns and the jet stream.'

ARE CLIMATE SCIENTISTS IGNORING AERONAUTICAL JET STREAM ABUSE?

So here we have an eminent meteorologist expressing concern, and elsewhere all he talks about is CO2 and reducing the burning of fossil fuels, while studiously ignoring the fact that the northern jet stream is being systematically used in a way never tried before. Also, incidentally ignoring the obvious fact that there is enough heat at the equator to melt all the sea ice (and doubtless much more) if the atmosphere were to be churned up enough.

These high speed tunnels of air flow mainly from west to east, are driven by solar heat, the Coriolis effect, and the rotation and axis of the earth, and they themselves drive the weather below. Until sixty years ago, though doubtless variable, they were at least relatively undisturbed natural phenomena. Then we started to insert aircraft into them and this has continued increasingly as bigger, more numerous and faster commercial aircraft systematically hunt them while flying with and studiously avoid them while flying against. Newton would surely have agreed that since the jet streams are being used to change the flight of aircraft, there must be an equal and opposite effect of the aircraft on the flight of the jet streams. Is it commercially too inconvenient to ask for the answer to a simple scientific question; what effect are aircraft having on the jet streams, and if it is significant how might it be mitigated?

If dispassionate scientists were involved, and especially if there was potential in it for profits and publications, then simple controlled experiments would be done to actually address this important question. As aircraft get bigger the effect is likely to increase. Of course ninety to ninety-five percent of the backwards thrust of the engines is diverted into lift, to oppose gravity, rather than drag from air resistance. It follows that each plane is causing a downward and deepening effect on the jet stream it is flying through. An A380 at lift off weighs 550 tonnes, and if we assume the average weight of a transatlantic aircraft to be 250 tonnes, with 2,500 crossing the Atlantic each way each day, it amounts to over 60,000 tonnes net downward force each day along the length of the stream being abused. A further 30,000 commercial flights criss-cross the USA each day, doing the same thing. It should not just be assumed that the effect is negligible. It is time, surely, for some real data?

Forcing the commercially exploitable sections of the jet streams downwards, from their normal place in the tropopause, into the upper troposphere, along with other distorting effects, might surely be important factors in recent climate instability and the devastating epidemic of disasters seen of late especially in the USA & Caribbean? In Medicine when something new is introduced we look for side-effects, having learnt lessons from, for example, the Thalidomide Disaster. Here it has just been assumed the jet streams are there in order to economise on airline fuel costs. In writing on this subject recently on Graham Hancocks blog I wrote ....

*I am assuming that the weather satellites and other, local, measurements made provide the capacity to monitor and measure changes in position, direction, width, depth and temperature of jet streams, as well as weather changes below. So a start would be to have (control) jet-free days, where all planes flying from West to East are made to fly at a ceiling below the tropopause; and to compare them with 'normal' days. A variation would be to have say 2000-mile stretches of jet streams that are jet free, alternating with 2000-mile stretches where planes hunt the jet streams as at present. The **opposing hypotheses** to be tested are **flying in the jet streams significantly alters them,** and **flying in the jet streams does not significantly alter them.** Obviously, the conditions need to be randomised and analysis done by observers double blind. Once there is data on whether or not there is a significant effect, more sophisticated questions can be asked, specifically on whether, when and how flying in them as at present has a damaging effect on weather particularly at ground (and sea) level.*

I have read recently that the cost of climatic disasters in the USA over the past year (fires, floods and hurricanes) is estimated at $306 billion. So it would seem reasonable for the

US Government to fund, say, one thousandth of this amount ($300 million) on research to explore prospectively what is happening, and what effect systematic jet stream (ab)use by jet aircraft is having on said streams. Okay, let's be more modest, and settle for a paltry $30 million (one ten thousandth of the cost of the disasters), spread out, say over ten years. That should cover ten well-paid researchers to set up and execute experiments along the lines I have suggested. The airlines can pay out of profits the cost of extra time spent flying at lower altitudes, and if they wish pass it on to us passengers. It just could be a no-brainer.

Sooner or later, I believe events will force such genuinely inconvenient questions to be answered. Let us just hope it is not too late for humanity, and this unique and lonely planet we are so intent on abusing. Or are we just going to wait and hope that jet stream misbehaviour doesn't cause the collapse of the world's remaining ice sheets and so a further rise in sea levels of more than sixty metres? After all that is what happened 11,600 years ago when unexplained climate change caused the then-massive ice sheets to undergo a sudden catastrophic collapse. And at a more mundane local level, let us hope such questions are asked and answered before London airport (a comforting twenty-five metres above sea level), at enormous financial and environmental cost, is given a third runway. After all, Miami's airport lies only three, San Francisco's four, New York's and Rome's five, and Hong Kong's eight metres above sea level. So in the event of a real *'Jetshit'*, where will the extra planes, so expensively catered for in London, fly to and from? For further argument see www.youtube.com/watch?v=q7hOgPs5aao&t (youtube film by the author)

CHAPTER 16

BEHIND THE SCENES IN ITALY'S AND OTHER INJUSTICE SYSTEMS

WORKING FOR THE RELEASE AND VINDICATION OF AMANDA KNOX AND RAFFAELE SOLLECITO

I have already written extensively about the Kercher murder and subsequent police and judicial charade, in my book on the psychopathology of unjust prosecutions, written with Nigel Scott. Here I want to touch on some things not covered there.

I awoke to the obvious injustice of this case in late 2009, when I saw images from the Court in Perugia and contrasted the bombastic and pretentious Public Prosecutor with the pleas of an obviously innocent girl. I remember discussing the case at a Todi Rotary evening, and realising that at the centre of Italy's criminal injustice system lay the unbridled power of the *Publico Ministero* (Public Prosecutor). When Amanda Knox and Raffaele Sollecito were declared guilty after the long-drawn out first trial, I decided not to waste my years of retirement just playing golf and studying jade, as it came to me slowly that maybe I had a special responsibility. Most people are only paid if they work, but with a pension one is paid regardless, and the main requirement thereafter it is to live the right side of actuarial line, as others on the same starting-line progressively fall away on the wrong side. And here I was living in Italy and a mere thirty miles away from the scene of Meredith Kercher's murder, and the police and courts paid to find and punish those responsible.

Almost immediately I was shocked to find how many people had swallowed the prosecution lies, which were then turned by press, blog sites and social media into a modern-day witch-hunt. I found especially that demonisation of beautiful young women comes easily to some other beautiful, but now older, women. Of course the worst of these were the two journalists, Barbie Nadeau and Andrea Vogt, both of whom I have met and conversed with on several occasions. Once a preposterous *hocus pocus* story has been fed to and propagated by the press with conviction, and swallowed *holus bolus* by a gullible public we tend selectively to seek out anything that supports the case into which we have been suckered. This is to do with how our brains have evolved to respond to unexpected threats. Paradoxically the more ridiculous the story, the more firmly it becomes embedded. I have since met Amanda Knox and Raffaele Sollecito, and they are both very nice and normal young people, and I can count them and their close family members as friends. So why would friends and/or close relatives dear to me, who have never met them, still buy into what was anyway a preposterous story, let alone continue now that the Courts have definitively declared them to be innocent?

One friend said, 'I could see it in her eyes, David. She looked as guilty as hell'. This reminded me of my mother, who was a great believer in *first impressions*. A close relative, after reading my book, said that I write very well, which is nice to know. 'But I still think she was involved in some way'. Then there is Nadine, who is a physically small, but in all other ways larger-than-life elderly American lady with a house in Umbria, who we first met back in 2008, in a hardware store in Todi. We are still good friends, but she was convinced of Amanda's guilt; at least she heard me through in the presence of a young friend of hers who was dying of breast cancer (and who immediately told me she appreciated the strength of my case). Her consistent attitude has been, 'You know, the thing I admire about you David, is you are prepared to fight for what you believe in. But I still think she had something to do with it. If not, why did she keep on changing her story?' 'Sorry, who says that?' Answer, Mignini, the main source of tainted stories fed to the press. Nadine says she admires that I fight for what I believe in; but actually, I mainly try to fight for scientific evidence. And then there is Judy, who also has a copy of the book which she has been reading for six months now. I await her considered opinion, but it doesn't look good, because by the time she gets to the end she will have forgotten the beginning. All this is in contrast with Roland, a male and German friend who read my book starting at the end, ('But David, I always read books starting at the end'), and only realised what the message was going to be when by this tortuous route he finally arrived at the first chapter. He is convinced by the evidence, and says the book reads just as well backwards as it does forwards.

I want to touch here only on what I had occasion to do that was different from the many others who also fought for the reversal of this obvious injustice. I was almost unique in being both English, as was Meredith Kercher, living in Umbria a stone's throw from Perugia, and being free to choose what to do with my time. I have mentioned in my other book many of my interactions with journalists good and bad. Furthermore, after the appeal was over I also met both of the Appeal Court judges (see below). I was present for all but one of the twenty hearings in the Hellmann-Zanetti appeal; the only one I missed was when I was in China in 2011. I was with Myriam Spezi, mingling with the crowd, late on October 3rd 2011 when the appeal verdict was announced to angry shouts of *'vergogna!*

vergogna!' (shame! shame!). I did not conceal my joy just to placate those around me. And the following morning, before I was interviewed on a British breakfast-radio programme, on my way to the square in Perugia, I met the journalist John Follain, who came up with the prophetic statement, 'We'll see, David, we'll see'. I wished later that I had gone to the press conference organised by Francesco Maresca for the Kercher family - you would think they too would have been pleased to see two innocent people released, but they weren't. I didn't do so because I was about to start the journey to England that day.

After the two were freed I felt an overwhelming sense of relief. I only realised how much it had affected me when on my way by car with Jonathan Tokeley, who was finally going home with his stuff to Devon, we stopped at the spectacular top of the Brenner pass. I went for a short walk on my own, and suddenly felt a unique mixture of joy, sadness and relief, and sat down and wept. Later, on the way home coming off the night ferry at Portsmouth I had the bright idea of going to visit Meredith's grave in Croydon Cemetery, to see if what a journalist had told me was correct. I phoned, then called in on my lovely violinist cousin Libby Wallfisch, who never had any doubts and supported me consistently. She gave us breakfast and found a nice postcard of breaking waves; and she also gave me what seemed a poignant and symbolic white orchid which had one branch still covered in flowers and a second denuded. Jonty and I eventually found the cemetery. They were helpful at reception, and showed us where to go in this massive monument to the dead. (It would have made my grandfather Arder mad - he thought cemeteries were such a waste of land). We found it - a simple grave marked by faded plastic flowers, which I was astonished to confirm, now four years after Meredith's horrific murder, still had only a temporary marker and no headstone. I placed the orchid there and left a simple message 'with love from Amanda, written by a friend', and we left.

David Coussmaker Anderson

AN APOLOGY OF A BOOK BY FRANCESCO MARESCA, THE KERCHERS' LAWYER

One of the most disquieting things about the Italian system of criminal justice is that the civil case, ostensibly on behalf of the victim's family, is run both in Court and outside as an extra arm of the criminal prosecution. Understandable sympathy for the family of the deceased is tapped, and used as an emotional smokescreen to support the prosecution. Such emotional abuse was flagrant in the case against Amanda and Raffaele. The Kercher's smooth-talking lawyer Francesco Maresca, was suggested to the Kercher family at the height of their shock, and became one of the Prosecution's most powerful weapons.

In late 2016 Maresca wrote a book (more of a pamphlet really, but on sale for twelve Euros) defending his role in the case, and essentially arguing that **IN**justice had been served by the final decision of the Supreme Court to release two innocent young people he still sees as guilty. I bought a copy and translated it while convalescing over Christmas of 2016. During the appeal that led to the first acquittal, I had made a point of always sitting behind the prosecutorial team in Court, and I was delighted to read in this booklet that I had succeeded in getting under Maresca's skin. I had, incidentally, annoyed him by asking why, as lawyer for the civil case he was slavishly following the Prosecution, rather than acting solely for the Kerchers. I did not get an answer. Nor did I get an answer from Serena Perna, his junior assistant, when I asked why they had not insisted on a DNA profile being done on the semen stains left by the murderer. This is what Maresca says about me in his book....
in addition to Mario Spezi, there was also present at all the hearings an American retired doctor, resident in Perugia, who seeing how he observed me in court, probably loathed me, as I suppose he also did Mignini, retaining it as scandalous that an American was detained for four years awaiting trial. This

character also followed the hearings in Florence, becoming a spectator whose presence annoyed me greatly, because it was looming and biased... Obviously I am delighted to have been mentioned in the same paragraph as Mario Spezi, but deeply hurt that he describes me as a retired *American* doctor living in Perugia. It is, however flattering to be described as looming, *'ingombrente'*, a pejorative term usually reserved for witches.

An extraordinary feature of this booklet is that he manages to get almost every name and date wrong. British Consul Mrs Moira Mc Farlane becomes Mv Pharlen; the American reporter Anne Brennan, becomes Anne Bremnan (twice); The ridiculous witness Hekuran Kokomani, becomes Antonio; another witness Antonella Monarchia, Allessandra, while Nara Capezzali transmutes to Nadia. Even three declared journalist friends are spelt wrong - Tom Kington becomes Kingdom; John Follain becomes Follaine; and Andrea Vogt, Vought. He even indicates that 'Hellmann Pratillo', not Allessandro Nencini, was judge in the Florentine retrial. Claudio Pratillo Hellmann had of course presided over the earlier appeal in Perugia. Maresca repeatedly confuses the pro-guilt newspaper *Giornale dell'Umbria,* with the more balanced *Corriere dell'Umbria*. He writes June 2010, when he means October 2011, and marks the end of the first trial as December 4th and 5th 2010, instead of 2009; and the start of the appeal, attended by Stefanie and Lyle Kercher, as 15th December 2011, instead of the same day in 2010. The inconsistencies are so consistent that I began to suspect some ulterior motive; maybe it is that you cannot be sued by a misprint. On the other hand the fact that he gets Rudy Guede's date of birth wrong (1985 when in fact it is 26 December 1986) may point to simple sloppiness.

He writes that ...*The Kerchers 'chose the elegance of silence', maintaining complete silence concerning their real feelings, waiting solely for justice to take its course.* In fact what they have consistently shown, reinforced by him, is a belief in guilt which continues to this day, for example on the *True Justice for Meredith Kercher* blogsite, and of course in the writings of *Harry Rag*, alias *The Machine*. Maresca says without apology... *I worked beside the PM (Prosecutor), almost as a private investigator, with my consultants at my side. I was approached almost continuously by the police force, and many times I have replaced him to see for myself the results of scientific findings and the evolution of the investigation.* Here he hints at maybe a trace of guilt... *(it) did not always suit my personality or my method of working, such that, as had been taught by the old masters of penal rights, a good defense lawyer should never take on (the defense of) a civil party, since the accusatory approach, exclusive prerogative of the Public Minister (prosecutor), conflicted with the training of the barrister.*

Maresca makes the following extraordinary statement, which shows disdain for hard evidence as opposed to hearsay from dubious witnesses collected by the prosecutor to support his case... *The roots of the verdict came from the witnesses, such that it is true that my harangue at the end of the first trial, which lasted several hours, developed on the analysis of all the evidence concerning the accused except the scientific; in my opinion, in fact, the witnesses of whom I have spoken, and the breakdown of alibis'* (ie those of Amanda and Raffaele, in statements collected illegally under duress and without a lawyer present) *were more than sufficient to condemn them.'* If there is any doubt about the blurring of roles allowed under Italian law, here is another astonishing statement ...*The prosecutors were not able to release interviews, so I in fact found myself often speaking on behalf in the interests the prosecutor of Perugia, as I tried to report these facts. Thus I defended to the hilt the work of that Office dragging behind me the lines of journalists and criminologists who challenged it with no half measures.*

Finally these are the considered thoughts of this self-justifying lawyer, on Sollecito.... *Raffaele was a young man, according to others who lived with him at ONAOSI college during the first years at University, who was very timid, to the point of misogyny, who had never had any important rapport with the other sex, who was dedicated to masturbation* (like more than ninety percent of adult males, according to Kinsey you legalistic arch-wankaphobe!) *and spasmodic reading of manga comics... Obviously I wasn't there, but what I think is that Amanda intervened with Rudy, while I have strong doubts as to the presence of Sollecito in that house, not so much because of what the trials* (or the DNA evidence?) *told me, as from an evaluation of his character type;* (so here you are expressing reasonable doubt); *effectively the picture his defense had always made, namely of a young man detached from reality and certainly not capable of undertaking such a heinous crime,* (no different here from Amanda)... *and to then support its consequences, to be honest this could somehow represent the truth... It is certain, and this is more sentimental, that his whole characteristics in relation to Amanda made me wonder if he went to the house just the morning after to help his girlfriend clean up the crime scene...* So how was such a cretin allowed through Law School, I ask? If in the future some able, honest and determined Italian politicians decide to revisit the separation of the careers of Public Prosecutors and Judges, as well as indeed the whole Italian accusatorial process, they need look no further that Francesco Maresca's apology of a book for evidence that the civil case must not be allowed to contaminate the criminal trial, and thus strengthen an already biased prosecution.

David Coussmaker Anderson

THE JUDICIAL SPIDER CONTINUES TO SPIN ITS WEB ROUND THE INNOCENT FLIES

Frank Sfarzo and I both realised, and advised, that the successful Appeal was not the end of the matter, and that the two freed youngsters needed to go onto the offensive. We repeatedly argued that the only safe form of defense was attack, something Amanda was in a much stronger position to do than Raffaele. Clearly this was not the advice she was getting from her lawyers, in whom she expressed inordinate trust, or from her family. Yet the judicial spider was still alive and biding its time before casting a new web around two flies that were still well within range. In November 2011, two months after the release of Amanda and Raffaele, Giuliano Mignini himself and Michele Giutari, his police assistant in the Monster of Florence case, had their own appeal hearing in the old court in Florence, and I went along. It was heard before three female judges, who ruled that since some of the twenty-one people the two had accused in the so-called Narducci case came from Florence, the appeal case should have been held elsewhere. They chose Turin, which conveniently allowed enough time for time to run out. (The whole Italian judicial system runs according to Einstein's Law of Judicial Relativity). On my way out of court Michele Giutari struck me deliberately and firmly on the shoulder from behind, something witnessed by Myriam Spezi. 'You need to watch out, David, that was a *mafia* sign to say you are a marked man', she said.

A CELEBRATORY TRIP TO SEATTLE

In 2012 I was working hard on my book on Hongshan Neolithic Jade, and also organising the first Elizabeth Wallfisch Masterclass Festival In Monte Castello di Vibio which took place that July. We were invited over to Seattle for a party

Where Angels Fear to Tread

to celebrate Amanda's release, organised by her family and supporters, and this was scheduled for immediately after the Masterclass Festival. We flew out to Seattle, and Amanda's mother and stepfather generously put us up, as well as Steve and Michelle Moore, and Frank Sfarzo (who slept on the sofa). We had a very pleasant few days, and met many of the others who had worked for their release, including Nigel Scott, who was to become my co-author. I went to two Rotary talks given by retired judge Mike Heavey, and I myself spoke at the second on the psychopathology of injustice. We went to a party on Vashon Island, organised by Karen Pruett, which Amanda attended. There were strict instructions not to give photographs to anyone, but I thought it would be safe to let Frank download mine. It was not, because ultimately his computer was hacked into, my photos were taken by a guilter who had befriended him; they were then put onto the pro-guilt *True Justice for Meredith Kercher* website. It seemed Frank was not very careful with his friends. Chris Mellas and his good friend Joe Starr (now sadly deceased) took us on a boat trip in the bay with Frank, and the Moores. Jenny and I then went on a three-day drive to the west Coast, where we visited Mount St Helens volcano and stayed in the Heavey's shared holiday home. We then flew to New York, where we stayed with Tom and Elaine Holoboff, friends from Hong Kong days. Elaine had been a patient and is a jade-collecting friend.

PUTTING A SPANNER IN THE SPOKES OF ITALY'S GROSSLY UNFAIR JUSTICE SYSTEM

You would think that if two judges and a jury had found on appeal that a couple convicted of a murder were innocent beyond any reasonable doubt, then that would be the end of the matter. But not in Italy, where the prosecution has the right to appeal such a result to the Supreme Court. It becomes a battle between reasonable doubt and unreasonable certainty, with the dice progressively loaded towards the latter. This is what happened in early 2013, completely wrong-footing the Defense, when the First Section of the Supreme Court sent the case for reconsideration in Florence. The same Court turned down the Defense's appeal against the conviction for calumny by Amanda on her former boss Patrick Lumumba. I had been urging Amanda's family to be much more pro-active, and eventually that summer got clearance from her stepfather Chris Mellas to approach Judges Hellmann and Zanetti on her behalf. My brief was specifically to ask whether or not she should immediately bring the case to the European Court of Human Rights, on the grounds that the final judgement of guilt over the Lumumba '*calunnia*' would preclude a fair second appeal. 'No psychobabble', I was instructed. Lumumba, incidentally, still openly blames Amanda for his brief incarceration, and clearly believes she was wrongfully exonerated. Her calumny conviction is still being considered by the snail-speeding European Court of Human Rights.

The Supreme Court of Cassation had in effect instructed the new Court to find them guilty. With Frank Sfarzo's help I met Zanetti first, in his office in the Court in Terni. He said it was *importantissimo* - extremely important - to appeal to the ECHR without delay. He put me in contact with Judge Hellmann, who I met with a fellow-lawyer friend of his in the café in Terni station; we then moved to the foyer of a nearby Hotel. He said it was *urgentissimo* - extremely urgent. At the same time Mario Spezi introduced me to Alfredo Brizioli, the lawyer who had represented twenty-one people (including Mario) accused by Mignini of conspiracy in the Monster of Florence Case. Brizioli saw it as extremely important to link the illegal behaviour by the prosecutor in the Kercher case, and that of the so-called *Caso Narducci*. His view was that the Defense needed a further line of attack, outside Court, namely over illegal and corrupt actions by Mignini.

ANOTHER TRIP TO SEATTLE

So armed with this information and these proposals, and at my own expense, I flew to Seattle, and to my surprise found Judge Heavey and Chris Mellas each thought the other was taking care of me. Chris saved the situation by coming to pick me up at the airport, and I spent four days with them, but in the end got nowhere. It seemed that Amanda just didn't want to upset her lawyers. I understood that Amanda, who had received a generous payment from her publisher for her excellent and moving book *Waiting to be Heard,* had spent most of it paying back her father, and her lawyers to whom she was exceptionally attached. Brizioli was offering to help with an independent supplementary line of attack, and to work completely *pro bono*. I found later that he had himself been defended in Court by Amanda's Perugia-based lawyer, Luciano Ghirga who is an ex-mayor of Perugia, and that he counted him a friend. Ultimately I went back to Italy and Brizioli empty-handed, having left a draft appeal to the European Court of Human Rights, which Edda Mellas said she felt was a good plan. They gave me a barbeque my last night, when I again spoke to Amanda, who posed some questions for Alfredo Brizioli. If she had listened to the advice of the two judges, and had been willing to hear what Brizioli was proposing as a supplementary out-of-Court strategy at no financial cost or risk, I believe she might have saved nearly two more years of heartache and uncertainty. In the end all I could do with Brizioli was introduce him to Raffaele's father Francesco Sollecito and his uncle Giuseppe. This was indeed of some help as he successfully defended Raffaele in yet another ludicrous case of *calunnia* brought by Mignini over Raffaele's equally excellent and moving book *Honor Bound*. I got members of the AKRS Facebook page to help fund the purchase of 20 copies each of Amanda and Raffaele's two books, for Brizioli to use as he felt fit.

RAFFAELE'S INTERVIEW BY STEPHEN SACKUR, AND A HARRY RAG SPINOFF

The Appeal in favour of the Appeal against the Appeal, began in Florence in late Autumn of 2013, under the presidency of Judge Nencini in the new, grandiose, austere and spiky-looking Court on the northern outskirts of Florence, and it did what it had been instructed to do. In early February 2014, while we were away on holiday on a tour of northern Ethiopia, it restored the original conviction. Now the previous September (2013), Raffaele had appeared on Stephen Sackur's BBC programme *Hard Talk,* where he had withstood a withering 'sackurfull' of groundfire, and had confirmed he would be attending the appeal in person. He was true to his word, and early in the proceedings in Court he made his own personal plea of innocence on behalf of himself and Amanda. I felt, as did Alfredo Brizioli, that Amanda should also have come and spoken in person, provided he and Amanda's lawyers could secure from the Court the cast-iron guarantee of a safe passage back home, that Brizioli thought possible. This would have given Nencini a great deal of 'face'. Instead Amanda gave a written statement of her innocence, which achieved nothing except to irritate Nencini, the Court and the Italian press.

There was an interesting spin-off from the Hardtalk interview. The convener, Ross Fitzpatrick, who with the help of my co-author Nigel Scott had set up Raffaele's interview, was now completely convinced of Raffaele's innocence. Afterwards he engaged in a twitter storm with *Harry Rag*, the most notorious of the anonymous anti-Amanda, pro-guilt bloggers and twitterers. *Harry* also blogged on the *True Justice for Meredith Kercher (TJMK)* anti-Amanda blogsite under another strangely chosen name, *The Machine*. Michelle Moore was obsessively following *Harry Rag* on Twitter, and noticed that Fitzpatrick started to address him by what he believed was his real first name. Fitzpatrick thus revealed and later directly confirmed to me, that he believed this persona to be an emotionally-charged man employed by the BBC, and at the heart of the murdered girl's family. I referred this directly to the BBC Trust, which set up an internal enquiry, that effectively came to nothing. However I obtained further support for my hypothesis over his identity when, following the verdict, *Harry Rag*, was exultantly tweeting journalists with his assertions of Amanda's guilt. He then wrote an article full of his usual strong pro-prosecution lies on another aggressive pro-guilt blogsite. I promptly taunted him on the site's discussion page over the suggestive choice of his second pseudonym, TMJK being an anagram of TJMK. Did the clink of money had anything to do with it, or was it just an unfortunate slip of the *nom de plume,* I asked? Seeing this, *Harry Rag*, now angry, asserted on the blogsite that I had alleged he was a member of the family, forgetting there was only one direct way he could have got this information. The entry was immediately deleted, but not before I had made a copy. It is always wise, when hiding behind cover, to remember exactly who you are, especially if an adversary has just managed to get under your skin.

Of course, the matter didn't end there, and more than a year later the final Appeal against an Appeal in favour of an Appeal against an Appeal against the original Trial Verdict, was once again heard in what I sometimes called the 'Court of Castration' (*la Corte di Cassazione*, or Supreme Court). This was held in an austere Mussolinic building in Rome, on the shores of the Tiber. I had missed the earlier Appeal to the power 2, but was not going to miss the one to the power 3. In the meantime, I had not been idle.

FRANCESCO MURA, ROMINA AND 'CRIMES AND MYSTERIES'

Raffaele's father Francesco, with whom I was in touch from time to time, pointed out an article in a crime and justice magazine

Delitti e Misteri, by a judge, Angelo Matteo Socci, that was very critical of the Italian criminal justice system. Incidentally, since then Socci has been appointed to the Supreme Court. Francesco Mura was the director and editor of *Delitti e Misteri,* and lived not far away from us in Giano del Umbria with his girlfriend Romina Demori. He introduced me to Socci, who, however, did not like my suggestion that any Public Prosecutor might actually be a psychopath. Over time Mura and I became friends, working together to try and fight for final justice for Amanda and Raffaele. The most significant thing we did together was that early in 2015 I arranged for him to interview the famous forensic geneticist Professor Peter Gill, in his home in Colchester, an interview that was shown on Mura's *Delitti e Misteri* TV channel. Gill had written a book on over-reliance on and suspect-centric use of DNA profiling, which included a whole chapter on the Kercher case. Francesco Mura had never been to England before, came with Romina, and we stayed in a hotel near Stansted in the lovely town of Thaxted. He just could not believe the beauty of English suburbia, which contrasts so starkly with the monotonous suburbs below the hilltowns of Italy. After the interview I drove them in our hired car to visit Meredith's grave, which at last had a headstone.

THE SECOND SUPREME COURT HEARING

Eventually, at the end of March 2015, came the final Supreme Court hearing, and I went to Rome and stayed with Frank Sfarzo. The hearing had been scheduled for the smallest court, which was predictably so overcrowded that it had to be moved to the largest chamber, a massive hall. The most effective advocate was Raffaele's lawyer Giulia Bongiorno, but we really have no idea what swung the panel of five judges. During the endless waiting in Court I spoke to Luciano Ghirga, Amanda's lawyer, and asked what he thought would happen; he said the best he hoped for was another retrial. Instead the Fifth Session of the Supreme Court ruled the couple innocent, effectively saying, *'Basta!'*, enough! Fortunately common sense finally prevailed, although their 'motivation report' published three months later is in many ways confused and illogical.

A ROLE FOR ROTARY IN JUSTICE REFORM

In June 2016 (the day after the disastrous Brexit vote) I became President of the Rotary Club di Todi, and decided to make judicial reform a priority theme. This more or less coincided with the publication of my book, *Three False Convictions, Many Lessons - the Psychopathology of Unjust Prosecutions*. Two years before, we had had a meeting in Todi on the *Caso Meredith* and the Monster of Florence cases, at which Mario Spezi talked of his experience at the hands of Mignini in 2006. As Rotary President I planned four more meetings in Todi on four cases for reform of Italian Justice, with Francesco Mura and a fellow-journalist Giangavino Sulas. Unfortunately the first meeting was dominated by an exceptionally verbose criminologist, a man past his prime but greatly revered by Mura, who Italian-style exerted no control over his speaker. There was a clash of cultures, although we patched it up for the next meeting in October, which went better. Then for no apparent reason Mura withdraw his further support, although we were clearly committed to at least one final meeting. In December 2016 I was admitted to hospital in Hong Kong, with an embolic stroke, which further messed up this project. We did finally have an excellent concluding meeting on April 8th 2017, organised under the *Rotary Club di Todi* in memory of Mario Spezi, which included a courageous ex-magistrate and author Piero Tony, and the lawyer for one of our cases, Claudio Salvagni. As I write I am still working with these two, who I can now count as firm friends, to try and get the false conviction of Massimo Bossetti overturned by the Supreme Court.

David Coussmaker Anderson

MARIO SPEZI, JOURNALIST, CHARICATURIST, FRIEND AND FIGHTER FOR JUSTICE

The reader will have gathered that retirement in Italy has been a rich source of encounters with many exceptional people, and these include Mario Spezi and his wife Myriam. Mario, who was a lifelong heavy smoker, spent much of his life as a crime journalist and political cartoonist for the daily paper *La Nazione*. I came to know him after reading his book *The Monster of Florence,* written in 2009 with Douglas Preston, which contains an afterword on the Amanda Knox case. In 2006, Perugia's controversial Public Prosecutor, Giuliano Mignini had actually arrested, charged and imprisoned Mario for twenty-three days, with the preposterous accusation that he was the Monster of Florence himself. Fortunately his fellow journalists sprang to his support, Preston extended the outcry, and Spezi was released from prison. As I write Myriam is still awaiting a final decision by a Court in Perugia of his final (and posthumous) compensation. Jenny and I first met them late in 2010 with UK journalist Peter Popham, in a restaurant in Grassina, near Florence. We became firm friends and I soon appreciated his extraordinary talents. When working for *La Nazione* the editor recognised his brilliance as a caricaturist, and every day for many years he used to provide the paper with an article, and also a topical political cartoon. *La Nazione*, however, notably failed to support Mario when he was falsely imprisoned; indeed through pressure on the editor he was then fired.

One day in 2013 I was visiting the Spezis and noticed some entertaining cartoons on the walls of their flat. He then showed me his copy of a book of cartoons, *Ritratti Distratti* (Distracted Portraits), that was published in 1988 for an exhibition in Florence, in which he represented thirty-seven distinguished local, national and one or two international figures in the style of world-famous artists. I asked him to let me know if he ever became aware of a copy for sale; several months later, on my next visit, Myriam had found Mario's late mother's copy among her things, and Mario gave me his own copy signed *'per David, Con amicizie mai distratte'*. As someone who likes to doodle and sketch, I was astonished at his talent to encapsulate with great wit the essence of an individual, often just based on a photograph. He also had exhibitions of portrait-caricatures, and on the occasion of Jenny's and my Golden Wedding in July 2014, he gave us a typically humorous portrait of me looking self-satisfied, with Jenny simply represented by a female hand patting me on the head to keep me under control (see illustrations). Sadly Mario died in September 2016, after a long illness, from emphysema and respiratory failure. I had hoped that he would join Nigel Scott and me as co-author of our book, but in the end bad health meant that he decided not to do so.

INJUSTICE IN THE UK AND USA

When writing our book on the psychopathology of unjust prosecutions, which started with the Perugia case, we didn't want to pick on Italy for problems that equally affect other jurisdictions. So we included the Kiszko case from the UK, and the Routier case from the USA. These seemed symbolically right, bearing in mind that the murdered girl Meredith Kercher was English and Amanda Knox was a US citizen. When considering cases from the USA we were literally spoilt for choice, since there are so many patently innocent people in prison. We decided to select one that was still active and I quickly settled on the most improbable and evil of all murder convictions, that of then twenty-six year-old Darlie Routier, who has been on Death Row in Texas for more than twenty years. She was convicted of stabbing to death her two oldest sons, Devon and Damien in her home in Rowlett, Texas on the night of June 6th 1996. She was herself assaulted and stabbed in the attack, and was only saved from immediate death because the tip of the assailant's knife was caught in the neck chain she was wearing, and stopped two millimetres short of her right carotid artery. This immediately struck me as one of the most emotionally, biologically and physically impossible convictions of all time - a straight contest between the light of common sense and the darkness of a giant judicial black hole.

Most people are not aware that they have ever met a psychopathic serial killer, but I am. Such a person must have a severe dysfunction of the amygdala, a primitive part of the brain's empathy circuit that is necessary for socialisation. As a result of this inherited defect they lack a normal aggression-inhibition mechanism and any conscience, since they never feel the distress of another as if it is their own. Such a defect, which produces constitutional negative empathy (CNE), is a necessary, though not a sufficient pre-requisite for becoming a full-blown psychopath. But in any case, most such people have a propensity to engage in 'targeted aggression', often within their sphere of specialist expertise. I recall once giving a GP lecture in a nearby town of Hyde on Paget's disease of bone and its treatment. There was an undiagnosed serial killer in the audience who asked me a curious question about whether Paget's disease ever led to the death of the patient; my answer was that it doesn't. The questioner was a local GP, Dr Harold Shipman, who several years later was found to have murdered hundreds of his elderly patients over many years, by administering fatal doses of opiates. His patients and friends thought he was a lovely, kind man, and many literally loved him to death. His is an example of the dangers of someone born with this innate predisposition, working in an area where they are given unbridled power. As was seen with Jimmy Saville, the violence perpetrated by a psychopath (or sociopath if you prefer) does not necessarily involve killing, but always a lack of conscience and the abuse of power.

THE ROUTIER MURDERS AND AMERICA'S MOST PROLIFIC SERIAL-KILLER

The *modus operandi* of the Routier boys' killer was obviously different from Dr Shipman's. It was when researching the Routier case that I first came across the work of the Cold Case Detective John A Cameron, who has exposed the role of America's most prolific serial killer. Edward Wayne Edwards was a violent psychopathic satanic killer who by his own admission on his eponymous blog may have killed more than 500 people across the USA in a murderous career that lasted between the ages of twelve and seventy-six. He was finally exposed in 2009 by his daughter April, when she heard a radio programme on a cold case killing of two lovers Timothy Hack and Kelly Drew in Wisconsin twenty-nine years before. She remembered her father, as they hastily packed up and left the area, saying to her brother and her, 'They are going to find bodies in that wood'. So twenty-nine years later, on seeing the programme, she went to the police. The murderer had raped the girl victim, and the semen left in the victim's body was found to match Edwards' DNA profile. Edwards fulfilled all the criteria of an exceptionally intelligent CNE, whose dysfunctional amygdala had left him with no capacity for emotional empathy. In Edwards' case, both his parents were convicted criminals, and he probably shot his mother who then died, when he was aged five. Critically, he was then abused in a Catholic orphanage where his destiny as a full-blown psychopathic killer, for which he had inherited one essential brain component, was sealed; reacting to the abuse and love-less discipline, plus religious indoctrination, he thereafter cast himself as the devil's disciple. As part of his *modus operandi,* Edwards favoured special dates on the Christian calendar. And he was bound to have killed on the date of the 'Number of the Beast' (666), revealed in the Book of Revelations, and taken by satanists as the 'devil's number'. The Routier boys were murdered on the night of June 6th 1996.

Edwards, convicted of only five of hundreds of murders, died rather conveniently on Death Row in Ohio, just before Cameron was due to interview him.

THE COLD CASE DETECTIVE AND THE DOCTOR AGREE

When I contacted John Cameron he agreed that the Routier killings, of which he had been loosely aware, must have been the work of Edwards, and that the original secondary victim he meant to set up was the boys' father, Darlie's husband Darin. He also agreed that it may have been Edwards who killed Angie Dodge one week later and 1,300 miles away in Idaho Falls, one of his favourite hunting grounds. This was a murder for which another innocent man, Chris Tapp, was convicted, based on a false confession. Tapp has been freed recently thanks to the work of Judge Mike Heavey and his organisation 'Judges4Justice'. That is critical, because the assailant masturbated on Angie's body, and his DNA CODIS profile is known - in fact I even have a copy of it, which I passed on to Cameron, who at the time of writing so far has not obtained Edwards' profile for comparison. Such is the fear of exposing the truth of how Edwards single-handedly tied the FBI and the US state and federal justice systems in knots as he played his private game of Psychopathic Killer v Cops.

Part of Edwards' game-plan was then to get the system to use the Death Penalty to kill again for him. He was undoubtedly the Zodiac killer, and other famous murders and secondary victims he set up, in diminishing order of certainty include; Teresa Hallbach and the framing of Stephen Avery and Brendan Dassey (Halloween, 2015); Jimmy Hoffa; the six year old beauty pageant queen Jon-Benet Ramsay, and attempted framing of her parents (Christmas 1996); the MacDonald family killings (1975) and framing and conviction of Dr Jeffrey

MacDonald. I suggest possibly even the killing in June 1994 of O J Simpson's estranged wife Nicole and her friend Ron Goodman (for which the footballer and actor O J Simpson was tried and exonerated in the 1996 so-called *Trial of the Century*). When I mentioned the latter to John Cameron he wisely said 'I don't want to go there'. But certainly Edwards made a habit of targeting the rich and famous, and wrapping the justice system in knots. In the Routier case he probably helped set up an insurance scam involving Darin, who had been involved in one before. He may then have coopted the criminal son of a police officer into providing the getaway car for what he made out would be a simple robbery. On Cameron's website (*www.coldcasecameron.com*) you can download for free the horrific autobiographical book *Metamorphosis of a Criminal,* that Edwards wrote in 1977 as a story of supposed conversion from criminal to counsellor. He then used this story as cover to carry on killing and framing the innocent. It should be compulsory reading for all trainee criminal psychologists. I have just watched the first three of a series of films made by Paramount on this monstrous killer, which hopefully will bring Darlie and the many others framed for killings he did, closer to being freed.

WHAT MAKES A SERIAL KILLER?

In *Metamorphosis of a Criminal* Edwards claimed to have reformed, but describes how he committed every crime of violence 'short of murder'. He proudly tells how for two years he was on 'America's Ten Most Wanted' list (including as a suspect in a lovers-lane double-killing), but had reformed. Psychopaths, however, don't reform, they just learn to simulate better. Even without the admission of the killings he was perpetrating, which John Cameron has later tracked, his book is a monstrous account by someone with absolutely no conscience. He used the book to butter up gullible and lazy police as he travelled the country with his third wife and family, who he used as cover. He talked to church groups, and made TV talk-show appearances, all the while targeting more of the young and gullible, and killing and planting evidence to direct the police and courts to convict others. All his crimes were 'for recognition', and part of a game to show he was the best of them all. And all the while he continued to serve time in prison for arson and theft, yet people still believed he had reformed.

What had made Edwards a serial killer? First, he was born with exceptionally high intelligence but no capacity for emotional empathy, no conscience, and no aggression-inhibition mechanism. With strong **cognitive** empathy and using superficial charm, he became expert at reading others, and at simulating emotion. Then he had a very disturbed childhood, including six years in a Catholic orphanage where he was punished and humiliated by nuns and others for bed-wetting and lying. He was sexually-abused there, and fed Christian myths about a Devil, who he vowed to serve when, at the age of eleven and already sexually mature, he escaped. Thereafter he refined his satanic *MO* in reformatories and prisons, studying cults and the *Egyptian Book of the Dead*, and using the excuse of serving the devil and killing for slaves in the afterlife. Even now, seven years after his death, and twenty-two years after the 'devil's date' on which he slew the Routier boys and attacked their mother, the truth is still being actively suppressed. So just as he planned, even in death he has had the last satanic laugh, as the system continues to incarcerate and kill innocent people like Darlie, and protect officials who are very well-paid **not to** mind their own business.

CHAPTER 17

SOME PERSONAL LIFE HEALTH-LESSONS

Both Jenny and I have been blessed with generally good health. I have already mentioned my narrow escape from death by drowning in the summer of 1960, when I experienced the perils of over-breathing before swimming underwater. Carbon dioxide is the main driving force for the brain's Respiratory Centre, and boys and their parents forget that at their peril. I have also recounted how as a young doctor, feeling under pressure to study for postgraduate exams as fast as possible when on holiday, I managed to induce a severe anxiety state and then a profound depression. Four years later, almost the same sequence occurred when I took part in a research study the anti-oestrogen drug clomiphene. These experiences, and my recovery, has definitely made me more sympathetic to mental illness, and willing myself to take an anti-anxiety drug such as Xanax if stressed enough to have really anxious dreams. I have not hesitated to tell my patients, where it seemed relevant, of these experiences.

I have also touched from personal experience on the dangers of a doctor looking after relatives, instead of leaving him in the hands of a competent and respected colleague, while of course maintaining an active and intelligent interest. Treatment of family members should definitely be an area where all doctors, especially surgeons (for whom the stakes are inevitably much higher), should fear to tread.

BEWARE OF A FRIEND'S MUCH-BELOVED DOG

For Jenny's part, she has experienced a different kind of medical lesson, with a nasty scar on her right leg, from when medical then- (but I fear no longer-) friends invited us to dinner. A short while earlier they had entertained us to a generous and pleasant week in the Philippines. The weak point of the second invitation was that they had one of those dangerous small yappity and aggressive dogs, beloved of their female owners, which was yapping on our arrival and so was shut away to yap off in the kitchen. This dog was especially keen to defend the very friendly Filippina cook we had got to know and like during our week with them in the Philippines (while the dog had been left at home). There is a saying in Medicine that the most powerful of all diagnostic instruments is the retrospectoscope. So what happened was in retrospect predictable but in prospect had not been predicted. We had an excellent and friendly dinner chatting with them and their important ambassadorial friends, and just as we were leaving, and obviously unaware of the hidden danger, Jenny went into the kitchen to thank and embrace her friend the cook. The instantly-jealous dog, which was lurking under the kitchen table, rewarded her with a deep bite just above the ankle through her right stocking. We left with protestations of 'not to worry' and I won't pretend we thereafter managed the medical aspects of the wound to perfection, but eventually amid notable silence from our friends, and some infections and sloughs later, Jenny needed a skin graft. She has a large deep scar to prove it.

What, however, was especially revealed, was the singular lack of any expressed concern that the couple showed. An immediate screen was erected by the doctor especially, in which the entire blame was by legalistic degrees deflected onto Jenny, with the final accusation that the kitchen of a friend's house should be held out of bounds on the grounds that she had not been invited there to embrace the cook. One of their other friends who had been with us on the Philippine trip recommended to Jenny that they should be sued, which was tempting because we felt their whole reaction was even more hostile than the dog's had been. It was a lesson to me, as if I needed one, that there are different kinds of good doctor, and there is not necessarily any connection between reading the New England Journal of Medicine from cover to cover every week, and empathy. In the end we let both the matter and the friendship drop. But I sometimes wonder what if any lesson was learnt by the other couple involved.

HOW TO GET, AND TREAT OSTEOARTHRITIS OF THE HIP

Okay - another medical problem. While at medical school I was fooling around one day, and suffered from a self-inflicted slipped right femoral epiphysis, as I deliberately fell sideways onto a hard floor. The pain gradually settled, but I was clearly developing osteoarthritis there, and twenty years later found the hip was painful when I played squash or when I did a hard day's skiing. I went to see Jonathan Noble, our hospital's keen young orthopaedic surgeon, and he told me to give up squash and skiing. So I took half his advice and gave up squash. That was at the age of forty, and over the next decade we continued to share some excellent culinary skiing holidays in France with our former West Acton neighbours and friends Clara and Martin Lowy, and sometimes with family members including John Hunt of the Stavros' experiment-destruction story. Obviously the problem was not going to settle, and after ten more years the pain was getting worse, and making my bad golf swing deteriorate further. So in 2004 I consulted another orthopaedic friend, Jason Brockwell, who recommended a Birmingham hip resurfacing, which he said I should still just about qualify for on age grounds. I had it done, and made a good recovery from the immediate operation, but both Jason and I made the mistake of assuming that doctors look after themselves as well as they do their patients. He never referred me to a physiotherapist once I left the hospital, assuming I knew what to do. So I continued to push myself as I have always done. It had been my habit to go for a run from our Pok Fu Lam flat up the Hong Kong Peak and then back, and I think the first time I did this post-operatively, as a fast walk with one crutch, was on about day seven. Stupid I know, but most doctors are human beings too, and I was only acting true to form. Well, no harm was done, and I went on with extreme exercise, until after about a month it was clear that I really needed some physiotherapy; so I went to see a nice physio, who told me off and started a series of Pilates exercises, and after two weeks I was back to where I should have been a month earlier. And I must say that now that I have started some appropriate morning kneezy-bends, thirteen years later the hip has even stopped clicking, and it now never jams. Of course I always set off the alarm in airport security, but I rate the Birmingham hip resurfacing as a big success. But it doesn't mean my brain was resurfaced.

ATRIAL FIBRILLATION; IGNORE IT AT YOUR PERIL

One more medical story against myself, and health confessions are nearly over. I have long been subject to intermittent atrial fibrillation. The first attack was in my early fifties when I had a walking pneumonia while on holiday with the family in Portugal and suddenly noticed that I had a fast and irregular heart rate.

'Atrial fibrillation', I thought out loud. I consulted a doctor in London's *Harley Strasse*, having already put myself on the old-fashioned remedy digoxin, and after a few days I reverted spontaneously to sinus rhythm. You will realise, if you have been paying attention, that I tend to ignore advice and treat myself. Over the course of subsequent attacks I worked out that my irregularity was triggered by certain other stimuli, notably any form of alcoholic drink that had been stewing in oak casks or chips. I like the odd drop of alcohol. but in this case it was cask-specific. It included whisky, rum, cheap oak-chipped New Zealand white wine, expensive oak-casked Italian red *Sagrantino di Montefalco,* and even beer that had lain inadvertently in oaked casks. So I came to avoid them all. Much more recently I found that it was also triggered by garlic. During one longish attack I visited an Italian Rotary cardiologist friend, who treated me like an arrogant and tempus-expirato retired medical cardio-ignoramus, which is a partial description of what I am. He was right, but it didn't necessarily help being more emphatic than empathic, especially because you will have gathered that there are now things in my life that seem more important than Medicine. These include Hongshan jade, *shui jing,* impact craters, geology, golf, olive oil and fighting injustice, none of which he cared much about. So I felt it unreasonable to chastise me like a medical boy-child just for being a touch out of touch with the frontiers of other people's specialties. Whatever his advice was, I therefore chose for a time to ignore it. Silly old me.

When I returned from the Summer 2016 trip to India to tell them about rabies prevention, I was in the kitchen with our middle son Bruce, when I had what can only be termed an, 'Are you sure you're all right Dad?' type of funny turn. I remembered this later but put it down to jet lag. Then over Christmas 2016 Jenny and I flew Scrub Class to Hong Kong. In fact we were upgraded to Super-Scrub, because I asked the girl at the Cathay desk 'are you upgrading?' I had once been told by Julia Sanderson, John's GP wife and a Cathay Pacific employee, that this is worth doing because if you have paid full fare they are obliged then to bump any Cathay employee on a ten percent fare back to Scrub, and you up a notch. We got to Hong Kong, and my left leg was a bit swollen, and the next day I went up a hill for a walk, and felt a bit dizzy, then two days later I was trying to sketch my grand daughter, and I had a stroke. Just like that - speech slurred, left hand numb and paralysed, and mind a bit 'disentoriated' - Jenny told the maid to call the ambulance. I refused, and my four year old trilingual granddaughter Skye was impressed. That evening she told her father, 'Daddy, do you know what Yeh-yeh said? He said 'no, no, NO!! I'm NOT going to hospital!'. But when it came to push, shove and trundle, the ambulance men arrived and I set a good example. Fortunately the hospital was close by, and it turned out to be between Monday and Friday, and between 9 am and 5 pm, because those were the times when they had the equipment, staff and treatment all available; and since it was a thrombotic stroke I got thrombolytic therapy. So wasn't that lucky? I made a full recovery, (which had actually started before they put the drip up). And ever since then I have been on one twenty milligram tablet of rivaroxiban, a perfectly harmless 'it's-non-rat-poison' type of anticoagulant, and I shall take one every day from now until death me doth part. Finally, in the face of incontrovertible evidence, and several other consultations, all are agreed that I should continue to do the right thing, and also exactly what that is. But then that was always the problem in Medicine, getting a strong-willed patient to follow medical advice.

DICING WITH DEATH IN A TREE HOUSE

I almost forgot this story against myself, which happened nearly five years ago to the day. As well as several habitable properties on site we also have a house up a tree near the vineyard, that Danilo had made for his son twenty-one years ago and is still visitable and occasionally visited by visitors. Expecting a family of guests with children of a tree house sort of age, and remembering Kenneth had mentioned he thought there was a wasp's nest there three months earlier, I went to inspect. What I hadn't expected was two bloody big wasps nests - the bloody big wasp in question being the European hornet, *Vespa crabro,* known in Italy as the *Calabrone.* They are not normally aggressive, and were harmlessly going in and out of their nests. That was until my superior size, a broom handle, and a case of acute dementia praecox struck, whereupon natural selection kicked in and so did the hornets. Fighting them off, I exited as fast as I could, and scuttled down the steep ramped steps, lost my specs, and ran like hell, pursued by a swarm of exceptionally angry and armed mega-wasps. Fortunately, thinking I too could fly, they flew after me at tree-house height, while I was now down on the ground and had gone back to look for my glasses. I sustained no less than nine stings on my head, face and arms, which immediately swelled up and were extremely painful. I dosed myself with antihistamines, multiple doses of a steroid spray, pain killers, a dip in the pool, ice packs and sat it out. Danilo pronounced that four *Calabrone* stings would kill a horse, which means I am pretty tough. He dealt safely with the poor hornets later with smoke and insecticide. There didn't seem much point in my going to Casualty, so I didn't, but I painfully watched Wimbledon on TV instead. Interestingly four days later, now in Scotland, and after the swelling and pain had mostly gone, I started to get an itchy rash round the sting sites, so I decided to take ciprofloxacin, which seemed to clear it up. I reasoned that as well as acetylcholine and all sorts of poisons, maybe they had injected some bacteria as well.

David Coussmaker Anderson

A POLITICALLY-INCORRECT HOLIDAY HEALTH RISK; BOLLOCK-NAKED BARE-BACK BULL-RUNNING.

Jenny and I have had the privilege and pleasure of some really great holidays, and up there with the all-time greats are two winter ones in Ethiopia. The first of these (2013) was the pagan one to visit some commercially marketable sexual tribes in the Omo valley down south of Addis Ababa. The second (2014) was the more underground church-type primitive Christian holiday up north, where we witnessed a mass-baptism in a 400-year old swimming pool and saw some underground churches carved out of the rock. Both tours were organised by the enterprising Diana Williams of the Friends of the Chinese University of Hong Kong's Art Museum. The first was a kind of four-dimensional existential time-warp. We visited tribes with customs that varied from the fairly to the extremely whacky. Without doubt the whackiest was the bollock-naked bare-back bull-running ceremony, that is conducted as some sort of induction into manhood by the extremely flagellophilic Hamer tribe. We were extremely fortunate, I understand, first to see the willful flagellation of previously nice-looking women, all clamouring to be whipped and so cut and scarred with branches of some kind of whipping plant, by tall, handsome and rather languidly unscarred young men. And the flagellatees seeming to enjoy it more than the flagellaters. The men looked bored, but the women were whipped up into excitement - none of them burst into tears, and many came back for more, though we didn't stay for the prize-giving ceremony at the end. This part of the afternoon took place in a dried river-bed, and then we all, tourists and participants, sauntered up to a flat bit of open ground nearby for part two.

Once there the women herded together a dozen bulls, setting them up side-by-side in a row, half the women holding the tails, half holding the horns. All the while the men were preparing the bollockee for initiation. He was now obscured from the crowd of trippers and tribe's-women by a male circle for a ceremony which, if all went well, was going to entitle him, I presume, to at least one virgin of his choice. 'On your marks, get set, GO!' The circle opened and the lad set off, leapt with assistance onto the back of the first bull, ran along the row, and jumped off at the end. He turned round (still bollock-naked of course), leapt up onto the last bull, ran back almost the whole way, where he fell off and almost impaled himself on a horn of the first one in the line. He went back and ran again, this time along the full length of the bulls'-backs, jumped off to general applause, and that was it. Two completed lengths of bull-backs bollock-naked. Not much, you may say, but I wouldn't do it in my present or any other state I can tell you. Re-armed with clothes to cover his previous nakedness, he was declared initiated, and presumably received his naked prize, later, hopefully none the worse for flagellation. Altogether a jolly good piece of harmless pre-marital fun, we thought, yet we heard that the Ethiopian Tourism Board was thinking of banning it as being too primitive a custom, even though the tourists and the punters love it. 'What is primitive political correctness coming to?' you may ask.

CHAPTER 18

RETIREMENT IN UMBRIA, ITALY

WHY ITALY?

As I have already said, we ended in Umbria more or less by chance. But then that applies to much of our lives, or anyone's come to that. I want to say a few words about what has been special about our Umbrian experience.

First, on the **negative** side, we live away from our roots and our immediate family; but since they too are spread across the world, and as already discussed, air travel has been invented, that is not specific to us living abroad. Then we are disenfranchised, and subject to taxation without representation both in Britain and in Italy. We can, however, still vote for our MEP, whoever he is, and for the Mayor of Monte Castello di Vibio who is very nice; so that's something. Due to the arrogant stupidity of the UK's ex-prime minister David Cameron in running two consecutive referenda - Scotland and Europe - that excluded citizens that happen to live 'abroad', we have no vote in the UK or its referenda. The important question of Brexit was settled 51.9 percent for to 48.1 against, a mere public hair's breadth for such an irrevocable decision. Yet any Brit who had lived outside the UK for more than fifteen years was not allowed

Where Angels Fear to Tread

to vote. In my case that is one-fifth of a lifetime, and I still pay tax on two pensions, and have a British passport. How can he have allowed himself to exclude those with most to gain both from living in and contributing to Greater Europe? So we can lay that mother of all cock-ups squarely at the door of the mother of all Parliaments.

Then there are the frustrations of Italy's institutionalised disorganisation, which most here just seem to accept. You can wait for hours in hospital for the doctor to turn up, or in the bank for the teller to look up, and yet no one complains. There is total lack of control by the chairman in meetings, where everyone feels obliged talk at once, and the faster and louder the better. I would also cite the drabness of suburbia, (as opposed to the hill towns), which struck Francesco Mura in reverse when he saw England for the first time. And the apocalyptically bad justice system, already discussed here and elsewhere, which I am still working to help change. The taxation system is actually quite fair to us foreign pensioners, except that the normal *commercialista* has no understanding of international treaty rules. This is not yet a nanny state, so in the face of widespread tax evasion, why should the tax authorities help you not to pay tax if you want to? It is not against the law to be stupid. We recently discovered this to our cost, but then in a country with institutionalised non-government why should one be surprised to hear it is the your responsibility to govern yourself? This sounds like an impressive list, you may say, and I haven't even mentioned the nightmare of Italian electric plugs and wall sockets, which deserves a chapter all to itself. Or scary high speed taxi rides in Rome with no hands on the steering wheel, one being needed to hold the phone, and the other to wave around while speaking.

On the other hand there have been many **positive** things to moving to Italy, in addition to the better weather. First, the

Italians as individuals are among the nicest Europeans, who show absolutely no resentment towards fellow Europeans, especially anglo-saxons. Unfortunately this is unlikely to apply to anglophone African immigrants. Enormous numbers were driven north out of Nigeria by Boko Haram, and then from Libya into Italy by the elimination of Gaddafi after the so-called Arab Spring. I see no offer of help from Nigeria's ex-colonial masters. Once here we have made considerable efforts to learn Italian, and to not shut ourselves away in an anglo-saxon ghetto. Our local Rotary Club has been a great help in providing us with a nucleus of friends from the good and the great of Todi. Next, there is the privilege we have of owning a stunning property, with plenty of land and splendid views, and of having an extremely loyal and capable Italian family of our very own in the form of Danilo, Helena and their son Antony. The deal is that they live in a smaller house on site, semi-detached from the rental property we built in 2003-4. We pay their rates and heating bills, they look after the olives, vineyard and vegetable garden, and much else, and we share the produce. They are also known to everyone, and provide our security and look after our dog Ah Choi and now Pinky the cat when we go away. And Helena, for a modest remuneration, helps Jenny with the housework, which is also a boon to me as I hate housework. Mentioning the rental property reminds me to give an example of how Italy's dysfunctional system actually works.

TWO EXAMPLES OF THE POSITIVE SIDE OF ITALIAN DYSFUNCTION

When we went to Hong Kong it was easy to get a local driving licence if you had one from the UK, which my wife and I both did. Jenny can on occasion be hyper-efficient and when the old ones had run out, wanting new fancy plasticised UK/EU licences, she had the bright idea of sending the old ones with the relevant forms to the licensing authority in Swansea. But we weren't living in Britain, and were told to wait till we returned, which in the end we never did. By 2008 we have moved to Italy and can't continue for ever to drive on our Hong Kong licences, since now being part of China, it has no mutual licensing agreement with Italy. Obviously we could take the test in Italian, but we are seeking an easier solution. So I pay ten pounds each to get a piece of paper from Swansea to the effect that we both qualify for a UK license. This is shown to the police and a month later we are told by big friendly David in the Todi licensing office that it does not satisfy them. By now I know him quite well and he definitely wants to help. 'Ascolta, listen', he says, 'what you have to do is to make a *denuncio* to the *carabinieri* in Monte Castello saying you have lost your licenses while moving. Then the letters you have from Swansea will work'. So at 8 am one day we present ourselves to the *Marescallo* in our local *carabinieri* office, and certify that we must have lost our old licences in our luggage in the process of moving all our stuff from Hong Kong. The *Marescallo* is grumpy, chain-smoking and not a fast typist (he still has an old typewriter), but this is the most exciting near-crime to come his way that day, and after several torn up versions we have our *denuncios*, sworn before a bureaucratic Almighty God, and the paper work is complete. In a sense it was true, we did lose them in transit, by inadvertently posting them to Swansea, but we couldn't say that. Upon payment of another two fees for a cursory eye test and a mythical medical examination, we finally got our Italian driving licences.

I don't want to get our *geometra* in trouble, as he is both very nice and efficient, so I'll call him Carlo. A *geometra*, by the way, is a cross between an architect and a quantity surveyor. When we bought our house our predecessor, who was not very nice to Danilo and Helena (so they love us) had planning-permission for a notional extension to their house. It is set in a rocky hillside, which had to be carved into. Our Estate Agent, Guido, recommended - 'listen, I shall only say this once' - that we change *geometra*. No explanation was asked for or given, but Danilo agreed and recommended Carlo, who was just out of geometry school. So in 2003, when the plans have been modified to our taste, and the building work starts, in comes the man with a big digger, to dig out the space for the *cantina* under the new house, which is to consist above of two bedrooms, bathroom, dining-room-living-room and patio. He asks if we would like him to dig further into the hillside, and create an extra downstairs space behind the notional *cantina,* (which has a flight of stars for access from above). This seems a good idea, and the plans are changed to show two large 'just-in-case' spaces behind a dividing wall, to be filled with rubble. Well, Italian-style, with a convenient slip of the memory the said space was not in fact wasted, but was turned into an underground bedroom with a stained glass window obscuring a grilled skylight, a small utility room full of pipes and controls that looks like a submarine's engine room, and a superb toilet, with bath, shower and bidet. Nine years later, in a depressed mood, we start to think of eventually selling part or all of the property. Carlo, realises there is a slight problem. How can you sell a house with real rooms that only exist in theory? Now I have a strong suspicion that with an analogous state of affairs back in Blighty we might be in a spot of trouble, as indeed, on paper we are here. But the difference is that in Italy, given time, good will, and contacts, as long as no one has died, a sensible solution can always be found to any problem. The one he found is win-win-win. It makes Monte Castello's *Comune* and its *geometra,* (who happens to be Carlo's classmate) happy because they get money up front, and a bit more on tax on a second home. It makes Carlo happy because he gets a fee for his work. And it makes us happy, because for only 5,000 Euros we magic from a void full of rubble, a legal sleeping, storing and superloo underground extension. Okay, so it takes time to get the planning permission, but once that comes through a miracle happens overnight. But then we do live in a country of *Madoninas* and miracles.

THE EXPATRIATE COMMUNITY

I'll mention one further thing on the positive side, and that is the expatriate community. Inevitably we do much of our socialising with fellow anglophones, who come from the UK, USA, Australia, Canada, New Zealand and South Africa. Nobody, ourselves included, has come to live here because they are normal. Some of us of course are, but we certainly didn't decide to retire in Italy for that reason. Just as we were introduced to Umbria by the Wacks' waxing eloquently, so we were responsible for some medical friends coming. Professor David Marsh was with me at Hope Hospital, and we did a joint metabolic bone clinic together for a while. I also made three excellent *Medivision* orthopaedic films with him on examination of the limbs. So I approached him in 2005 to ask if he'd make one on examination of the spine. By then he was a busy London Professor, and he politely declined, but at least we had re-established contact. Hearing we had retired to Umbria triggered a letter from him a few months later. He and his wife Norma were coming to a conference in Florence in the summer and could they come to stay? 'Of course', I said, 'but it does come with a health warning, namely that you might end up buying a house here'. In the end they went overboard and bought a ruin with trees growing through it, and a nesting porcupine. They completely rebuilt it on the old footprint into a quite stunning old-looking modern property. And since David has the same University pension as I do, it was he recently who pointed us in the direction of an English *commercialista* who explained just how much our Italian one had got our tax situation wrong. Like completely! It seems we'll never get our overpaid tax back, but on the other hand we'll be able to offset every future tax bill against what the State owes us. So for the rest of our days we should at least have less negative money.

What happens in an expatriate community such as ours is very similar to what happens all over Italy, where there is the concept of the *cosca* or family group. And what my late friend Mario Spezi described as *mafiosità,* or mafiosity. Traditionally the group in this heavily-invaded land has had to look after itself in the face of all types of invader. The most obvious physical evidence of this is the heavily defended walled towns, which are also a great part of its artistic and cultural attraction. But one needs to understand that in winter Italians hibernate, so it is pointless trying to organise any public event like a concert, as I have done, outside a narrow summer season. In the summer it is quite astonishing how every small community goes to great lengths to organise the *sagra,* the street food festival, often with several in the same neighbourhood on at the same time. But this is not meant to be a promotional guide book. Suffice it to say that with our local expats, and our local Rotary Club, we have a very good social life, and in places like Perugia, Spoleto and sometimes Todi, one can get to some excellent summer cultural events.

CHAPTER 19

AN AFTERWORD OF CONCLUDING THOUGHTS

POLITICS AND MY LIFE

So how has politics influenced me? As a matter of fact, I never followed it too much until I saw a crisis coming, when I would start thinking and sometimes got stuck in. I recall around 1980, when junior doctors were getting very militant over conditions substantially better than those of a decade and a half before, I made and circulated a bumper sticker which said *Stop hospital strikes - Patients can't strike back.* I was impressed by the power of bumper stickers from our time in California where they had been *de rigeur.* One anti-Nixon one said simply *Sack the Coxsacker.* Of course my own bumper sticker had no effect, and was illegal anyway, but at least it made me feel better. Our sons remind me that the same year I actively canvassed for Margaret Thatcher against James Callaghan. I looked quite like the Liberal leader David Steele, and when I knocked on one door an elderly woman thought she had hit the political jackpot and almost kissed me. I did feel a bit mean as I disillusioned her on two counts. Maybe Maggie was a necessary evil; and then in 1982 at the height of her political depression, along came

David Coussmaker Anderson

South Georgia and the nicely-contrived Falklands War. Poor old Lord Carrington got the OTB, for that, but I see he is still alive at ninety-nine. What with Galtieri and the sinking of the *Belgrano,* Maggie was in clover for ten years. Like Churchill, I believe she was another constitutional negative empath (CNE). Her handbag-throwing tantrumic cerebral Waterloo may have lain in the fact that, building up for later Alzheimer's dementia, she cheated by being a workaholic who only slept for four hours a night. As well as Carrington, many of her more laid-back colleagues, some of whom like Nigella Lawson's dad still seem to me pretty odd, are still relatively *compus mentis,* while Maggie is now long post-compost.

I mentioned earlier that Myriam Spezi had seen me struck on the back by Michele Giutari on the way out of Court, and told me to watch out because that is a sign used by the *mafia*. So far I am still here, but I do confess that I may have been a little paranoid at times. But as the anti-hero Yossarian in Joseph Heller's classic novel *Catch 22* believed, just because you're paranoid it doesn't mean people aren't out to get you. One of the most depressing places we have visited in Italy is Monte Cassino, where its Polish War Cemetery, and its painstakingly-reconstructed Benedictine monastery stand as moving monuments to the senselessness of war, which are mostly driven by psychopathic leaders, their minions, and consequent mistakes. On February 15th 1944 the Monastery of Monte Casino was bombed to smithereens by the Allies in the mistaken belief that, in contravention to a bilateral agreement with the Pope to leave it neutral, it was being used as a German headquarters. An innocent intercepted German radio message recorded by a junior radio officer *'der sind noch zwei abt in der clöster'* ('there are still two monks in the abbey') was translated as *'der sind noch zwei abteilung in der clöster'* ('there are still two Divisions in the abbey'). The error was only realised by a senior intelligence officer when the bombers were already on their way. Confirmation bias is an extremely dangerous human behavioural trait, and in fact the destruction of the monastery provided the Germans with a much stronger defensive position, and added greatly to allied casualties.

IS THERE ANY PLACE LEFT FOR THE GENERALIST?

The famed Austrian physiologist and Nobel Prize winner Konrad Lorenz once said of modern experts, 'The specialist knows more and more about less and less and finally knows everything about nothing.' That has not been the path I have followed, and although I have been counted by some at times as being reasonably successful, I know that by many others I have not. There is one box I fully admit that I don't tick, and that is single-mindedness in pursuing one line to the exclusion of all others. Some see me as a maverick who has done many things badly and has too often dared to cross into other people's areas of expertise, even at the expense of neglecting my own. I am qualified as a physician, endocrinologist and medical academic researcher, and I should have stuck to that, they would say. As my former Research Fellow Stavros, who I launched into academic hyperspace, once told me pejoratively 'you could have been so good, David if you had just concentrated on one thing'. And it is certainly true that many people find success by doing just that. In fact, some can only achieve any sort of success and recognition that way, and their personality fits them perfectly for that approach. Such people see no continuing role for Leon Battista Alberti's concept of the Universal Renaissance Man, or polymath, who wanders off into other people's fields, making a nuisance of himself wherever he goes. They mistrust my approach on seeing something that doesn't make sense, namely to ask a question and hang around long enough to reassure myself that the question has been answered by someone who knows the subject better than I do, and whose job it is.

Rightly or wrongly, I have tried to do this probably more, and also more often, than most people. So in Medicine and Endocrinology I took a wander into studying and treating a bone disease (Paget's) that is certainly not endocrine in origin. Then my interest in medical education led me to question many other areas of medicine from the point of view of what the general student or doctor needs to know about it. It seemed self-evident that this was necessary in order to prevent patients from falling between two specialist stools, and the way I chose to do this was to film the specialist explaining and showing his approach. That in turn revealed a glaring hole in the World Health Organisation's approach to rabies prevention. Then by translocating to another country, and being interested in art and art history I came face to face with an ancient Chinese Culture and its carvings that were and still are being systematically ignored in an extremely dysfunctional modern China. This in turn revealed that this ancient Hongshan Culture had learnt how to carve a unique form of natural glass using impact microdiamonds, and how supposed-experts in that field were (and still are) ignoring something unique under their very noses, possibly for reasons of modern political expedience. And that brought me face to face with the strong possibility that our species *Homo sapiens*, seemingly hell bent on its own destruction, may have seen near-destruction in the past following a giant meteorite impact, something that is surely of relevance for the future.

In my ignorance I have questioned and still do, the current simplistic explanation for man-made climate change. I am especially concerned to see that people who should be addressing the physics of jet stream abuse by massive passenger jets, seem to prefer to hide behind the politically more convenient assertion that it is all due to greenhouse gases. Finally, the leisure provided by retirement in a foreign land has given me a role in studying and fighting injustice, including the release of one of the many people falsely imprisoned in the USA through the malicious exploitation of defects in the system by a murderous psychopathic serial killer. And all that leads me to question how our money is being mis-spent by politicians and other public servants the world over who seem to be well-paid not to do their jobs.

SO IS THAT A WASTED LIFE I SEE BEHIND ME?

I hope that in these pages I may have offered some support for the thesis that, although far from perfect, my wandering path through life was therefore not without interest, nor without entertainment, nor was it totally wasted. At the end of what has so far been a modestly satisfying and productive life, I have written this time-warped account with several things in mind. I have no idea if anyone else will find it interesting, but so far I have enjoyed plumbing the depths of my often distant memories, just for myself. Like that of everyone else, my life has been unique. But there are other reasons for making some sort of record, and mining the memories of an aging mind.

First, a good friend told me to do so, because she found some of my stories entertaining. Seven months ago, Carol Easton gave me the very kick-start up the retired backside of life, that I needed in order to put the computer equivalent of pen to paper. Secondly, I really feel I owe a debt of some kind, as one living long into retirement, to all those friends whose earlier demises made such a privilege actuarially possible. I know that in their heydays, the likes of Ian, Ray, John, Graham, Robin, Tony and many other friends who prematurely lost their physical, or worse their mental faculties before they could reap the rewards of retirement, would have reveled too in the pleasures of selective recapitulation. And some of this account is about events they participated in.

Third, I don't mind saying that I am worried about the future. As James Thurbur, quoting some pessimistic First World War General, wrote; 'Things look pretty bad right now'. I was quoting him sixty years ago, so what would he be saying now? Surely the human species has never before had to live under the exponential, now nearly vertical, pace of change, with no indication as to how or when it will stop; or if it doesn't, whether the planet will survive. Ever since *The Eagle*, Dan Dare, and the red planet, I have had considerable interest in extraterrestrial meteorite impacts and their denial, but what about an even more obvious intraterrestrial one? Has Society selected and is it still selecting for those with empathy-free psychopathic tendencies to run all aspects of this intragalactic ship of ours, about which by definition they couldn't give an intergalactic shit.

POWER, EMPATHY AND BALANCED POLYMORPHISM

There is a biological phenomenon called balanced polymorphism, best illustrated by sickle-cell anaemia seen in Africans. One gene makes the red blood cell infected by the *falciparum* malaria parasite become sickle-shaped as the cell's oxygen tension falls, so it stcks in capillaries and is eliminated by scavenger macrophages. The gene has been selected for because it protects against malignant malaria, which is otherwise often fatal. But two genes cause sickle-cell anaemia, which is also fatal. So in populations exposed to *falciparum* malaria, the sickle-cell gene frequency increased until malaria deaths become balanced by deaths from sickle-cell anaemia. Might something similar have happened with regard to the empathy-deficiency gene? Some empathy helps socialisation, but too much damages our competitive species' competitiveness. On the other hand lack of emotional empathy is socially destructive. Has modern civilisation selected for the negative-empathy gene as a kind of balanced polymorphism, whereby in the short term the world works better with one such gene, while two are a recipe for self-centred leadership and society's self-destruction through greed and aggression? If so what can the rest us do about it?

Anyone who has read this account will realise that I take no solace from the apparently comforting thought of a life after death and with neither body nor brain. I strongly doubt whether religious beliefs always help people who hold them to live this one, which I contend is the only one of which we can be certain, any better. At least my religious disbelief keeps it all very simple. In the strawberry patch of life that I have enjoyed, and recorded here in writing to the best of my wilting memory, that was it. A great privilege to have existed, and to live long enough to tell the tale. Of course, I apologise to anyone I have upset by what I have written, or worse by their involuntary omission. As my good friend Bill Lasley used to say by way of excuse many decades ago in California, 'I only said it because I meant it'. We are none of us perfect, but I crave forgiveness just the same.

ILLUSTRATIONS

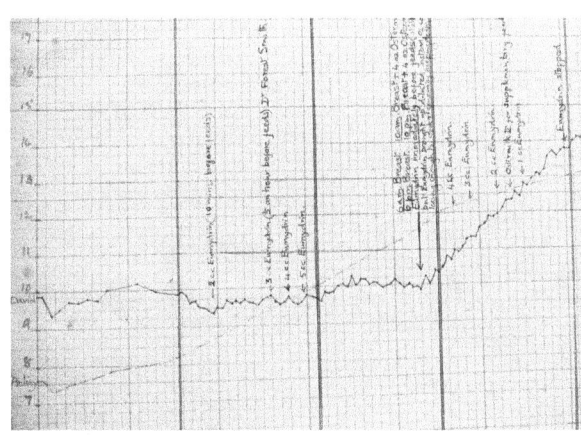

My mother Kathleen (née Hunt) kept a meticulous record of my weight, which was 10 lbs at birth, and remained unchanged at three months due to vomiting from infantile pyloric stenosis. The arrow at the inflexion point marks when she started immediately to preceed each feed with the antispasmidic Eumydrin; as vomiting stopped and I gained weight she progressively reduced the dose. The dashed line shows my brother's weight change superimposed.

Top left, W F Anderson, by L F Watton, in Oflag VIIC 1940, **right**, B&W of watercolour by DCA 1988. **Below**; Kongwa Hospital, B&W copy of watercolour by W F Anderson, 1949.

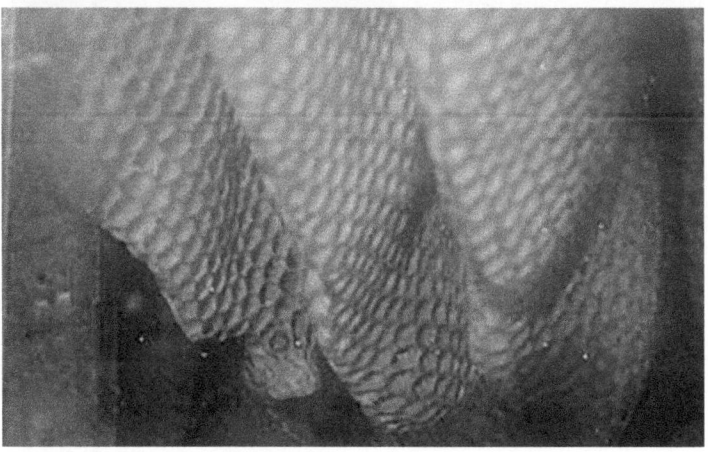

Natural beehive made by Arder in a hollow tree trunk, with (**below**) honey combs.

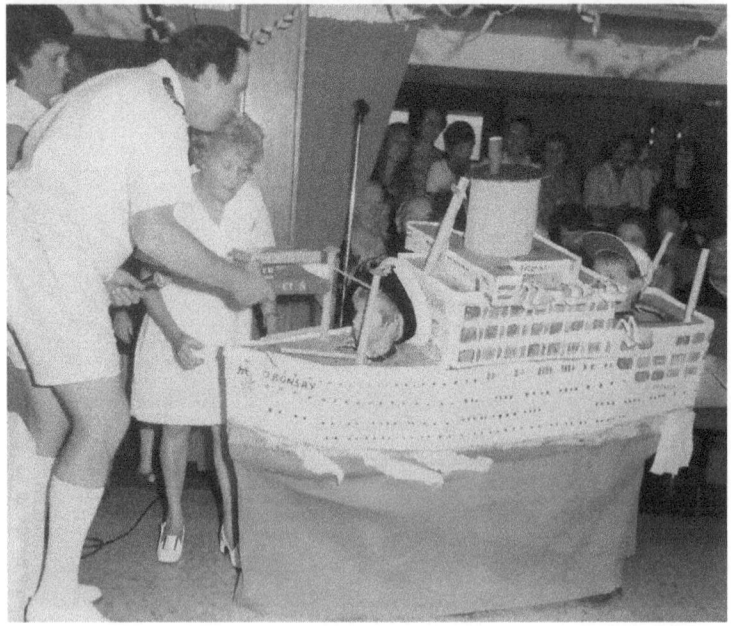

Top - the author (right) with Antony, and model car ferry made in metal by Dad.
Bottom – our three sons in cardboard SS *Oronsay*, which won first prize in the ship's fancy dress competition. Kenneth, our eldest, is hidden in the funnel!

'The Mount' (**top**), the house in Boundstone near Farnham that my parents bought in 1951. While all the time living there, Dad converted it single-handed and in his spare time over two years, into 'St Christoph', my parents pride and joy (**bottom**). This transformation was not without its dramatic moments (**middle**).

'The Hunting of the Ski', a family Ski poem from 1959, composed (with apologies to Lewis Carroll, and 'The Hunting of the Snark') in Gerlos, and illustrated by W F Anderson (Dad). See appendix for text of poem.

B & W version of Watercolour drawing of boats in St Andrews Harbour by DCA, 1959.

Wedding photograph of the author and Jennifer Calderwood, outside Burford Parish Church, July 18th 1964. It is hard to believe that two days before, the bride as Medical House Officer had been admitting patients on the Professorial Unit at Dundee Royal Infirmary.

B & W copy of watercolour portrait of fellow-patient Johann Mowinsky done by DCA in hospital, while recovering from acute anxiety and depression, summer 1965. Johann had an interesting war record.

B & W image of ink and colour drawing by DCA of Brigadier Sir Mark Henniker (Uncle Mark) who married Dad's sister Denys. He was one of our favourite, if somewhat eccentric, uncles, sketched here at the age of 81. He wrote four autobiographical books, including *Red Shadow over Malaya* and *An Image of War*.

Three generations at our silver wedding anniversary party in front of our house in Bramhall, July 18th 1989. Top, David and Jenny; middle, my parents, Will and Kathleen and Jenny's, William (Pard) and Elizabeth Calderwood; bottom, Neil (left) Bruce (centre) and Kenneth (right)

Ink and wash sketch of the artist and potter Albert du Mesnildot, by DCA, Aups, Le Var, France, November 1988.

Pictures in our collection by two of our favourite modern artists. *Three Riders*, ink drawing, 1988 by Geoffrey Key, (top, with permission of artist). And *Six Figures*, B & W image of colour drawing, by Albert du Mesnildot, d 1990, (bottom).

B & W image of colour woodblock print of *The Monkey Bridge in Moonlight*, by Ando Hiroshige (ca1840). Recognised as one of his finest woodblock prints, this *kakemono-e*, is printed in two separate halves. We bought our copy in Nikko, Japan, in 1983. The two halves match perfectly in colour and tone. When viewed from the right, the eye is drawn up the gorge, and when viewed from the left towards the mountain.

Top: B & W Image of watercolour by DCA of view of the Pat Sin range from our house in Nai Chung, Hong Kong, 1995
Bottom: B & W Image of watercolour by DCA, from Bruce's New Territories house, Hong Kong, 2016

Black and white copy of caricature of the author done from memory by Mario Spezi, given to us for our Golden Wedding 2015. Mario, journalist, author and talented caricarturist for *La Nazione*, became a good friend over the time of the appeal of Amanda Knox and Raffaele Sollecito. Reproduced with permission from Myriam Spezi.

B & W Image of watercolour sketch by
DCA, Qinghai Province 1993

B & W Image of watercolour sketch by
DCA, Borabadur, Indonesia, 1996

B & W Image of Ink and watercolour sketch by DCA, Irrawady river cruise, Burma, March 1994

B & W image of Ink and watercolour sketch by DCA, Inle Lake, Burma, March 1994

B & W Image of watercolour sketch, Buffaloes on beach, by DCA, Thailand, 1995

B & W image of watercolour sketch, Restaurant, by DCA, Trinidad da Cuba, 2010

This is the very first piece of Hongshan nephrite jade I bought in 2000, and is pale green in colour, and depicts the head of the baby being born through the oedematous vulva. The pixie-like figure is squatting in the delivery position. The shine on the head is due to skin oils which have prevented weathering after burial. I see this as the Goddess of Safe Delivery. (See *Hongshan Jade Treasures - the art, iconography and authentication of carvings from China's finest Neolithic Culture. by David C Anderson, Tau Editrice 2012, ISBN 9788862442152*)

The author photographed (by Josef Muller) beside one of the larger Hongshan *shui jing* horned cow gods, in a shop in Shi Li He market in Beijing, 2010. The glass is streaked through with red which maps to iron, aluminium, potassium and traces of sodium (mapping by Johnson Matthey Ltd UK).

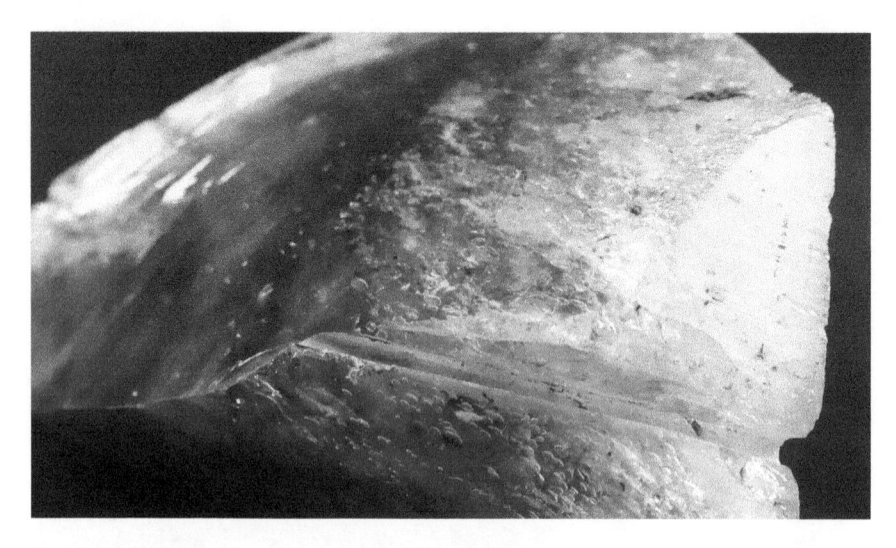

A 12 kg 'splat', in red-streaked *shui jing*, with circular saw marks

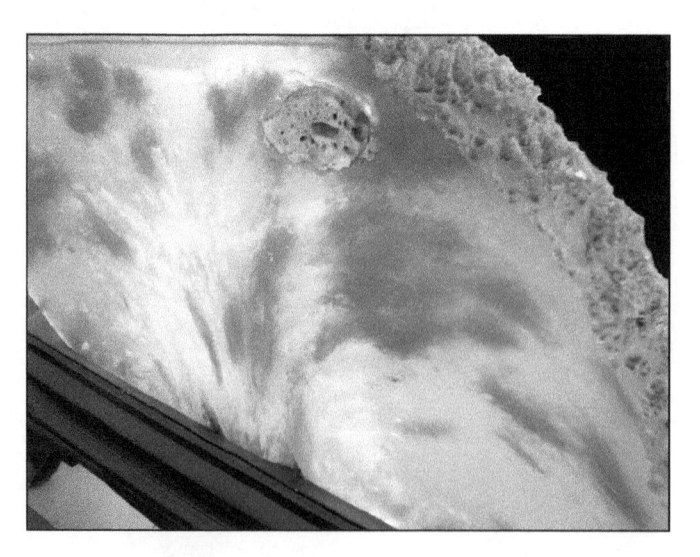

A 66 cm diameter red-streaked slice of *shui jing* silica glass, clearly carved from a sphere, photographed by the author in a shop in Beijing in 2010. Note soil 'melt' on the surface and incorporated into the body of the sphere; and also cut mark at top, where the circular saw wandered off line. Locating the glass mine is central to finding the impact site, which if as suspected is in *Tong Liao* province, may support the author's twin craters impact hypothesis.

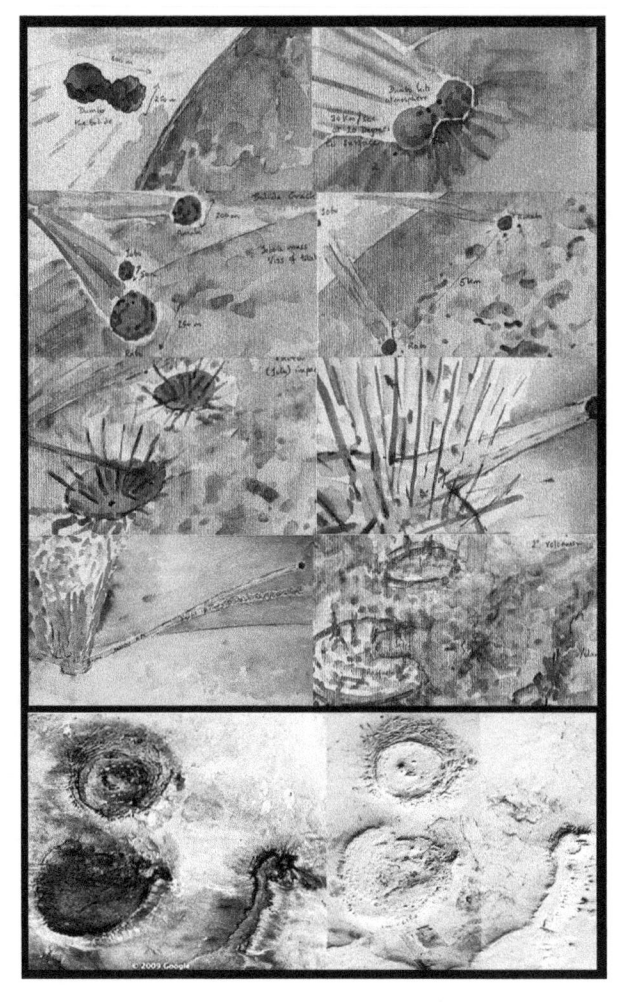

Possible model of twin craters impact. Bottom - two images of the twin craters at 114.24 44.24N, from Google Earth, summer and winter. Top, (going from left to right and top to bottom) - watercolour drawings by DCA of possible model for triple impact from a dumbell-shaped bolide measuring 250 X 600 metres, velocity 20 km/s, which broke in three on hitting the atmosphere. Smallest, 50 metre, (waist) fragment, retarded by the shock wave to maybe 10 km/s, bounces off exploding southern crater, aspirating liquid silica tail which cools and lands far away in part as spheres. Reactivation of rifting volcanism in Abag Qi field causes experts to conclude the craters are primarily volcanic.

Composite from Courtroom doodles by DCA, from the 2010 – 11 first Appeal of Amanda Knox and Raffaele Sollecito. The case is discussed in full in *Three False Convictions, Many Lessons – The Psychopathology of Unjust Prosecutions, by David C Anderson and Nigel P Scott, Waterside Press, 2016, (ISBN 9081909976351 - see back flyleaf)*. More than anything else, experience fighting this injustice illustrated to me the importance of sometimes minding other people's business as well as one's own. In Italy, the USA and many other jurisdictions those responsible aren't minding the business of administering justice, for which they are being very well paid from the public funds.

Appendix

RECITATIONS AND POEMS

1) British Sovereigns from 1066 (from Mr V T Paton's Pilgrim School date list)

*This is of course, not original, but I have never forgotten it; (note there is no reference to that cad Oliver Cromwell). By the way, the Duke of Marlborough's telephone number, (BROM 4689, on the same date list), relates to the battles of **B**lenheim (1704), **R**omilles (1706), **O**udenard (1708) and **M**alplaquet (1709). We had no idea what the war was about.*

Willy, Willy, Harry, Ste,
Harry, Dick, John, Harry Three,
One, Two, Three Neds, Richard Two,
Henry Four, Five, Six, then who?
Edward Four, Five, Dick the Bad,
Henry's Twain, then Ned the lad.
Mary, Bessie, James the Vain,
Charlie, Charlie, James again.
William and Mary, Anna Gloria,
Four Georges, William and Victoria.
Edward Seven, King George Five,
Edward, George, and who's alive?

2) Sam's Low Note, by Conrad Hartley

My late friend Conrad wrote this recitation when his wife Nancy was away giving a concert with the oboist Leon Goosens. I first heard it given by Conrad himself as an interlude in one of our concerts in Bramhall in around 1981. He died not long afterwards, and my later rendition of it had the approval of his wife Nancy

Tha's 'eard of Sam Locket the singer,
As sings i't ole chappil choir,
Tha's noticed 'es not bin there recent,
I'll tell thee 'ow't come ter transpire.

They was singin a thing up at chappil one neet,
As were full of ff's and pp's,
And no matter as 'ow they sung loud or sung soft,
They just could not sing it to please.

Conductor 'e said as they sung pretty good,
And they sung pretty loud, 'e'd grant that,
But 'e wanted much more at the top of page four,
Where't basses was down on E flat.

Conductor 'e said, and 'e said it again,
Tho' there's plenty of row from the lasses,
It sticks out a mile that to do it i' style,
Us must 'ave more noise there from't basses.

When basses 'eard this all their faces went red,
And they looked at each other all 'umble,
'Cos every man knew that down there on E flat,
'e could nobbut just grunt or p'raps mumble.

Poor Sam was fair worried - It upset the lad,
That the basses should be the weak part,
So 'e called for 'is cards an' give up 'is job,
To devote all 'is time to 'is art.

'E spent all 'is days just a-singin low notes,
From risin' ter goin' ter bed,
Till 'is mother said 'Dad, tha'd best look to yon lad',
Cos I don't think 'e's reet in 'is yead!

But Sam kept on singin till one Friday neet,
'E felt summat go in 'is throat,
'e uppened 'is gob, and believe it or not,
There emerged a tremendous **Low Note.**

Sam relit the fire, put picture back straight,
An' buried canary, poor bird,
Then 'e grabbed fer 'is 'at and run chappil-wards quick,
Fer 'is wonderful note ter be 'eard.

When Conductor saw Sam 'e said 'Sammy me lad,
Of the basses round 'ere tha'rt the best,
And sin' tha's come back, and it's basses we lack,
Go an' sing thy part there lad, wi't rest.

Well the choir started singin, but Sam, 'e kept mum,
Till they came to the top of page four,
When 'e gave all 'e'd got, 'is front teeth went red 'ot,
And conductor fell flat on the floor!

The organist fell off 'is seat in a fright,
So great was the dreadful vibrations,
Three winders was brokken, and out went the light,
And the lasses all 'ad palpitations.

They picked up Conductor, and dusted 'im down,
'e says Sam, as a note that's just fine,
But tha's brekkin too much lad, us can't afford thee,
I must ask thee ter kindly resign.

So Sam's back at 'ome and 'e's doin' 'is best,
Ter try for ter lose 'is low note,
'e gargles terrific and drinks a specific,
Designed ter play 'ell with yer throat.

And if 'e's successful and ruins 'is voice,
And 'e may do because 'e's a trier,
I think that some Sunday before very long,
Tha'lt see 'im back there i't choir!

3) Sam's Trip To Tibet, by the Author

I wrote this at the end of an excellent two-week holiday in Tibet, during which one of the high spots in Lhasa was an afternoon at the local Yak Races, where our group watched from the stands, among the cheering cadres. It's too long, but otherwise fits the genre.

When Sam won the pools 'is wife Alice
Said, 'You've worked all yer life, take a rest
We'll live off proceedings of money accrued'
So they asked bank, and bank said, 'Invest'!

T'investments they made steady income,
They was wisely advised on the gilts
And the market kept pace with inflation
In't new 'ouse they put carpets and quilts.

But in time Sam got bored with just sitting
And watching 'is winnings grow bigger,
So 'e'd wander i't bookshop and rummage through books,
Until one day 'e found one on Buddha.

Now until then Sam's views on religion
Were vestigial and ill-formed at most,
But this book it gave 'im a strange feeling,
Like 'e felt sort of 'arf like a ghost.

As 'e thumbed through the pages and pictures
In sepia, (book dated from yore),
Monks, temples and all kinds of Buddhis -
Well 'e felt like 'ed seen it before.

'E constructed a prayer wheel from paint tin,
Lived on Yoghurt and Yoga and dung,
And 'e started to mutter them sutras -
Summat like 'mani pemi o'hung'.

To meditate came to 'im natural,
E'd think about things in the book.
To go blank 'e just thought of the missus
And on came a transcendent look.

The GP just said 'e were crazy,
Psychiatrist said 'he's too rich'
On account of 'im muttering 'mani' -
Meditation were making 'im twitch.

So 'is wife worked on ways to lose savings.
She bought pearls and took cat to the vet,
Brought 'ome bumf on them culture safaris,
And Sam picked on Lhasa, Tibet.

'Tibet' said 'is wife 'are you barmy?
You get out of breath on the stair,
And you can't walk to't shop on the corner,
Never mind two miles up in the air!'

But Sam in 'is mind seemed more motive -
'E started to go to 'keep fit',
Chucked the fags and the beer and did press-ups,
And read about Yaks in Tibit.

They decided to travel all stylish,
Not economy as in the past -
First Class in a Seven-Four-Seven Boeing;
Hong Kong, Chengdu, then Lhasa at last.

T'arrangements were totally faultless,
Thanks to travel firm Grumble and Kent.
They sorted out passports and visas,
And took folks with a wide range of bent.

T'other trippers all thought Sam peculiar,
What with tantrums and tantras and that -
For twelve FEC a monk shaved 'is 'ead bare,
Then 'e covered it up with an 'at.

There were skilled chap in charge of it all,
A feller called Gerald by name -
'E knew all sorts of lingos and coped with the locals,
And when things went wrong 'e took the blame.

Sam tried 'ard t'enjoy monasteries,
Where't llamas and dogs would reside -
But 'is 'eart gave a flutter at the smell of Yak butter -
Just the thought of a Yak gave 'im pride.

While Alice was reading them guide books
She'd test 'im on Panchens and Llamas,
But 'is mind wasn't there, it were up in the air -
Calming yaks were more to 'is Karmas.

One day Gerald suggested the races,
Where there's yaks of all colours and sizes -
Sam leapt at idea and prevailed upon Alice -
Quite strangely 'e knew all the prizes.

Now a Yak's not a born racing animal,
It's shaggy and doesn't know much,
Preferring the grass to a chance to run past,
It'll race best if kicked in the crutch.

The yaks were all decked in their carpets,
With the riders on top all precarious -
Red flag went down fast and with whipping,
They ran off in directions various!

One lump of a bull were called Dorgin,
Who ran like a yak out of hell.
'E won the first 'eat by a lap and a half,
Then stopped dead - by gum did that crowd yell!

The poor rider Yormud shot out of the stadium,
And landed severely concussed.
On calls to the crowd there were no other takers,
It seemed that big Dorgin was bust!

At that very moment a funny thing 'appened -
Sam started to talk in Tibetan,
'E said that 'e'd once been a champion yak rider,
And 'e thort 'ed be well worth the bettin.

Now Tibetans are folk who enjoy a good larf
So they lifted old Sam up on't saddle.
Sam comforted Dorgin and Dorgin grunt back,
Sam said 'laddie, run fast and don't faddle'.

Sam's 'at flew off at the turn of first bend
So 'is bald 'ead shone out like a lantern.
The crowd gave a roar, like they'd seen it before,
What with altitude Sam weren't 'arf pantin!

This last race it were just once round the track -
Both Dorgin and Sam were fantastic.
Tibetan Sam rode like a yak-rider born,
Crowd felt they'd seen something monastic.

They won by a length against favourite beast,
Then old Dorgin di'n't slack for a lap,
While Sam stood on Yak's back throwing punches in't air,
The reincarnate Panchen Yak!

4) The Hunting of the Ski *(with apologies to Lewis Carroll)*

This was a combined family effort written at the end of a skiing holiday in 1959, in Gerlos, Tyrol, finished by Dad and beautifully illustrated by him. (see illustrations)

Just the day for a ski! the *MUMDAD* exclaimed
As they sat in the *Edelweis*
Just the day for a ski! they chortled with glee
We'll practice *HERR MOSER'S* adweiss.
They had Rücksachs and Skiwachs and Skisticks galore
And gay-coloured waterproof pants

And maxims and slogans and twenty Stembogens
All carefully polished by *HANS*.
They had Käse and Butter and allerlei Futter
All carefully prepared for the Wurst
And kickturns and quickturns
And all kinds of Slickturns
Precautions most carefully rehearsed
They had fifty-five skis and fifty-five skins
With their names clearly painted on each,
But alas! for they found
When they came to reach down
That their bindings were miles out of reach!

'We'll ski up by bus!' the *MUMDAD* proclaimed
It's a rule that I practice and preach
If your breakfast is shaken down nearer your boots
Then your boots shake up nearer your reach.
THE BUS is both beautiful, cosy and warm
Its driver both speedy and tried
Our skis are kept PARALLEL all out behind
Our knees are bent double inside
We will bus to the *PLATTE*
And when we've done that, a
Small schuss down a slope might be tried.

They fell in their hundreds
They fell in their thousands
They fell in the numbers between,
They fell on their Hosen
They fell on their Nosen
Their craters are still to be seen.

Just ski as I ski! cried the *MUMDAD* with glee
Just follow my tracks
With the slowest of wax

And try and imagine you're me.
With this he did hurtle
And promptly turned turtle
And vanished completely from view.
When he opened his eyes
He discerned with surprise
That his left ear was under his knee
Frozen stiff with a curse
His feet were reversed
FOR HIS SKI WAS A BOOJUM you see!

We'll ski down by bus! roared the *MUMDAD* with cuss
As he combed out his sticks from his hair
THE BUS is both beautiful, cosy and warm
Its driver both speedy and tried
You pay your fare twice
Which is pleasant and nice
Since you pay for the road <u>and</u> the ride.
We will stem all together
Come *feohn* or fine weather
We'll snowplough and slither and slide
And when we get down
We'll declaim to the town
The wünderbar BOGENS we tried.
We'll go to HERR STORKEL
and give hime a Talkel
And complain of the boojamish skis
And have it arranged to get them exchanged
For a pair that run backwards with ease
We will close up the gaps
In our breeches and caps
With a series of badges most droll
That cover our harms and speak of the charms of GERLOS in
SCHÖNEM TYROL

TWO MORE SERIOUS POEMS

It's All About Control... (1992) *written in anger)*

You'd be amazed if you could see
The pettiness that's in the lee
Of certain at the cutting edge
Astonished how one man could dredge
So shallow yet so deep

You'd be bemuzed by how much face
Might lie within one carpark space
Yet evil men may use the trivial
To needle yet still seem convivial
So others are deceived

You'd be astonished if you saw
The pictures that one man could draw
Paint images of foul abuse
In words no grown-up man should use
So others hold their peace

You won't believe until you've learned
No stones a man will leave unturned
To gain a handle on his friends
Control is where the matter ends
Then they turn silent

You would not credit till you'd heard
Despotic threats go undeterred
The psychopathic man in power
External smile concealing glower
It's all about control

To my Mother... (1995), *written with love)*

You were my first smell, sight and sound
Child's love and joy to be around.
The beauty of your smiling face
No other beauty could replace -
You were my mother.

First memories your tenderness,
And saying prayers where we'd confess
To sins of paediatric scale -
God bless and help us not to fail
O darling Mummy.

Through Cheniston, and Granny Hunt,
The wartime sirens, second front,
And Arder's pipe and honey bees,
Sandcastle flags, dear Dad's release
Our special mother.

Then through the pain, and through the joy
Of growing up rebellious boy -
Conflicting passions, peaks and troughs
Appendices and Whooping coughs -
Loved like no other.

Your cello's sound, sung nursery rhymes
Firm arbiter of nursery crimes!
At pilgrim schools of work and drudge
You wrote us letters, sent us fudge
That tasted like no other.

You taught me how to say my prayers,
Then later taught our children theirs -
The innocence of Kingdom-Come,

I never meant to hurt you, Mum,
And yet I did, dear Mother!

Then later, love was found elsewhere,
But in the background you're still there -
A haven in a Boundstone blest,
Where sometimes we'd come home and rest
With greatly-loved grandmother.

Throughout your life you would sustain
More than one lifetime's share of pain -
The nightmare crash, distorted face -
External splints kept jaws in place,
Dear proud, brave mother.

We can't believe that now you're gone
Immortal soul that soldiered on
Face crushed, colostomy and hip
Pace-maker with life-saving blip
You seemed bionic, Mother.

Yet through it all would break a smile,
And laughter you could hear a mile -
The wear and tear could not destroy
Your beauty and your inner joy
Our dearest Grandy, Mummy.

So now we grieve and give our thanks,
For sharing laughter, sharing pranks.
Yours was a long life, rich and full
Saint Christoph's made his final call -
God bless you Kathleen, Mum!

Three False Convictions, Many Lessons
The Psychopathology of Unjust Prosecutions

David C Anderson
and Nigel P Scott

A new perspective on the roles of psychopathology, confirmation bias, false confessions, the media and internet (amongst other causes) of unjust accusations. Putting lack of empathy at the fore in terms of police, prosecutors and others, it considers a wide range of other psychopathological aspects of miscarriages of justice.

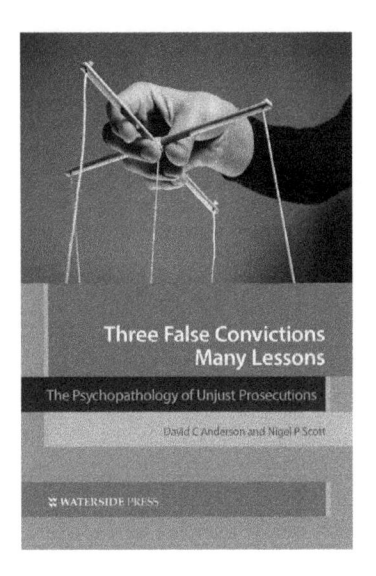

By looking at three high profile cases — those of **Amanda Knox and Raffaele Sollecito** (Italy), **Stefan Kiszko** (UK) and **Darlie Routier** (USA) — the authors show that motive forces are a mind-set in which psychopathy (what they term 'constitutional negative empathy') may be present and the need to reinforce existing supposition or lose face plays a large part.

Darlie Routier is still on Death Row in Texas despite overwhelming evidence that her conviction for killing her own child is false, whilst Knox, Sollecito and Kiszko have been vindicated by the highest judicial authorities and telling evidence. The authors show how and why unfounded rumours still persist in the Knox/Sollecito case and advance a new theory that the Routier killings were the work of a notorious serial killer.

Paperback & ebook | 2016 | 280 pages | ISBN 978-1-909976-35-1 | Waterside Press

Lightning Source UK Ltd.
Milton Keynes UK
UKHW012144180821
389073UK00001B/88